Mingulay

An Island and Its People

To Caroline

Mingulay

An Island and Its People

Ben Buxton

Birlinn

First published in 1995 by
Birlinn Ltd
13 Roseneath Street
Edinburgh EH9 1JH

ISBN: 1 874744 24 6

A CIP Catalogue record for this book is available from the British Library.

The publisher acknowledges subsidy from the Scottish Arts Council
towards the publication of this volume.

Cover design by Janet Watson
Designed and typeset in 11½/14pt Berkeley by Janet Watson

Made and printed in Finland by
Werner Söderström OY

Contents

Deserted Village on Mingulay

From a photograph by Margaret Fay Shaw Campbell

Not far had men's hands to raise from the stony ground
Blocks the ice and rain had hewn.
The dry-stone walls of the houses of Mingulay still stand
Long after the sheltering roof is gone.
Not far had the heather thatch to blow back to the moor.

Children were born here, women sang
Their songs in an ancient intricate mode
As they spun the wool of sheep on the hill
By a bog turf fire hot on the swept hearth-stone.
Earth's breast that nourished and warmed was near
As cow-byre and lazy-bed
Made fertile with sea-wrack carried up from the shore
In creels of withies cut in a little glen,
Near as shelter of hill-side, fragrance of clover-scented air.

Not far had the dead to go on their way of return,
Not far had the circle of the old burial-ground
Whose low wall sets its bound to encroaching wild
That never has put on pride of human form,
Worn face of maiden or fisherman, mother or son.
Never far the washer of shrouds, the hag with grey hair;
Yet those who here lived close to the mother of all
Found, it may be, in her averted face, little enough to fear.

Kathleen Raine.

Notes to readers
To minimise referencing, reference numbers are not generally given where the source, if in
published form, is quoted in the text; the reader can refer direct to the bibliography. If no source
is given for details of the islands' histories, the information has been obtained verbally from the
people of Barra and Vatersay listed in the Acknowledgements.

The forms of place names used, if found on the Ordnance Survey maps, are those given on
the maps.

Foreword and acknowledgements

My interest in Mingulay goes back to 1975 when, aged sixteen, I stayed there during one of many summers spent wandering in the Outer Hebrides. In 1980 I carried out an archaeological survey of the village area for a student dissertation, and some years later I embarked on what has become this book, focusing on the more recent history. Despite the remarkable amount of information which has emerged, I am aware that the book is still only a beginning, for research of this kind, using written sources, oral history and fieldwork, can never end. Being a non-Gael has been a handicap as regards my understanding of a distinct culture, and I have been unable to make full use of the potential of oral history.

This book is in fact about four islands: it includes, more briefly, the three other formerly-inhabited islands south of Barra – Berneray, Pabbay and Sandray. These islands were closely associated with Mingulay, but very much less is recorded of, or known about, their histories.

Over the years, I have received help from a huge number of people, too many for me to mention them all by name. They have helped in various ways, including providing information and advice about the islands, and places and people connected with them; suggesting sources; making material available; advising on, and translating, Gaelic; and commenting on drafts of text. I am particularly indebted to the following: Dr Alan Bruford and Ian Fraser, School of Scottish Studies; Dr John Lorne Campbell, Canna; Hugh Cheape, National Museums of Scotland; Patrick Foster, University of Sheffield; Andrew Kerr, Barra; and Ian MacDonald, Gaelic Books Council.

I am indebted also to the people of Barra and Vatersay for sharing their heritage with me, an outsider with no island connections. Without their marvellous support this book would be much the poorer, but I hope they will forgive what will be, for them, its inevitable shortcomings. Special mention must be made of Mary Kate MacKinnon, Glen, and I am also grateful to the following: Peggy Ann Campbell, Vatersay Village; Donald Ferguson, Borve; Morag MacAulay and the late Calum MacAulay, Castlebay; Ishabel MacDougall, Glen; Morag MacDougall, Caolis; the late Nan MacKinnon, Vatersay Village; Archie MacLean, Skallary; Donald MacLean, Eoligarry; the late Jonathan and Marion MacLean, Uidh, both formerly of Mingulay; Mary MacLean, Eoligarry; Calum MacNeil, Nask; Catriona MacNeil, Vatersay, formerly of Mingulay; Catriona MacNeil, formerly of Kentangaval; John MacNeil, Nask; John Alan MacNeil, Castlebay; Mary Ann MacNeil, Vatersay; Morag MacNeil, Garrygall; Neil MacNeil, Castlebay; Teresa MacNeil, Bruernish; Roderick MacNeil, Kinloch; Margaret Nixon, Uidh; the late Donald Sinclair, Garrygall; and Lisa Storey, formerly of Vatersay. I would also like to thank Mary Sinclair, Registrar, Father Donald MacKay, Roman Catholic priest, and Rev. Dr Donald Greer, Church of Scotland minister. I am grateful to Richard Langhorne of Museum nan Eilean, Stornoway, and Mary Kate MacKinnon for enabling me to work on an exhibition about Mingulay as part of a student project in 1991, when some of my work in Barra was undertaken.

I would also like to thank: Colin Archer, Lisbon; Eve Beadle, Bruton; Derek Cooper, Richmond; Trevor Cowie, National Museums of Scotland; Rev. Dr Mark Dilworth and Dr Christine Johnson, respectively former and present Keepers of the Scottish Catholic Archives; Professor Alexander Fenton, Dr Margaret MacKay, and Donald Archie

MacDonald, School of Scottish Studies; Lesley Ferguson, RCAHMS; Noel Fojut, Historic Scotland; Angie Foster, Barra; Fiona Gorman, Arran; Eleanor Hunter, Glasgow; Bill Lawson, Genealogy Research Service for the Western Isles; Rev. Alan Macarthur, Lochcarron; Dugald MacArthur, Connel; Dr Martin MacGregor, Museum Sgoil Lionacleit; Ian Maciver, National Library of Scotland; Fiona MacLeod and Robert Steward, Highland Regional Archives, and their predecessors at Inverness Public Library; Alasdair MacRae, Dunblane; Helen Murchison, Achintraid; Joan Murray, Scottish Natural Heritage; Rev. Douglas Nicol, Church of Scotland, Edinburgh; Robert Smart, St Andrews University; and Francis Thompson, Stornoway. To the staff of various other collections of material, and to other individuals who have helped, I extend my thanks.

For permission to reproduce material I am grateful to the following: Comunn Eachdraidh Bharraigh agus Bhatarsaigh (plate 4); HarperCollins Publishers Limited and Dr Kathleen Raine (the poem 'Deserted Village on Mingulay'); the Keeper of the Records of Scotland (material in the Scottish Record Office); Teresa MacNeil (Neil MacPhee's letters and song); the Trustees of the National Library of Scotland (plate 21, and Hector MacLean's letter); the Trustees of the National Museums of Scotland and Alasdair MacRae (letters of John Finlayson and Morag Campbell Finlayson); Roberton Publications ('Mingulay Boat Song'); St Andrews University (Robert M. Adam photographs); School of Scottish Studies, Edinburgh University (tape recordings of Mingulay people and quotations from *Tocher*); Scots' College, Rome (letters of Fr N MacDonald); the Stevenson family (writings of David and Robert Stevenson).

Finally, I must thank my parents, for always supporting my Hebridean ventures. Above all, I must thank my wife, Caroline, with whom I have shared many happy times in the islands, for her support, ideas on innumerable drafts of text, and for giving me time off from family responsibilities.

Photograph Credits:

Plates 8, 9, 10, 11, 12, 13, 14, 15, 16, 17, 18, 19 and 20 are by Robert M Adam; plate 4 is by RMR Milne; plate 1 is by William Norrie (published in Harvie-Brown and Buckley 1888); the remainder are by Ben Buxton.

List of Maps:

1

'The Nearer St Kilda'

"Away beyond Skye, and seen from it in misty outline on the edge of the ocean, stretches a series of islands from the Butt of the Lews to Barra Head. . . As seen on the map the group looks like a stranded icthyosaurus of geological times, the Lews forming its skull, the Uists its chest, and the Barra Isles the detached vertebrae of its lower spine.

At the very point of the saurian tail rises the rocky islet of Bernera, terminated by the grand cliff, where gleams the lighthouse of Barra Head. Immediately to the north of this island there hides a larger island called Minglay. It bears a population of interesting people having the least possible intercourse with the outer world, to which it is almost unknown even by name. The other islands between Barra Head and Barra are tenanted only by the lightkeeper and his family, and by sheep and cattle and their few attendants. Minglay thus forms an isolated colony in the Atlantic, in all respects a nearer St.Kilda, as remarkable for sea scenery, solitariness, self-containedness, and the peculiarities thence arising, as the more popular place of pilgrimage."

With these stirring words William Jolly introduced his article 'The Nearer St Kilda: Impressions of the Island of Minglay', published in 1883. It is fitting to quote this introduction to the first and only comprehensive description of the island when it was inhabited. Mingulay is indeed comparable to St Kilda, one of the best known and most written about of Scotland's islands, 64 kilometres (40 miles) west of the Outer Hebrides.

Mingulay is the last but one of the chain of small islands forming the southern end of the Outer Hebrides (also known as the Western Isles and, in the past, the Long Island) which form the northwesterly bastion of Scotland (map 1). In size 4 kilometres (2½ miles) long, north-south, and 3 kilometres (1¾ miles) wide, it is the second largest of the five principal islands south of Barra: Vatersay, Sandray, Pabbay, Mingulay and Berneray. From the sea, however, it appears to be the biggest, as Vatersay, though having a larger surface area, looks like two small islands, having a low and narrow middle; and Mingulay is much the highest of the five islands, rising

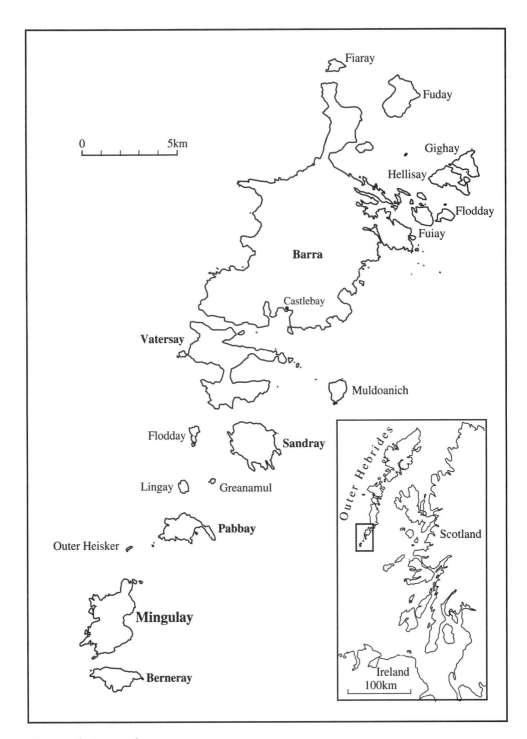

Map 1. The Barra Isles

to 273 metres (891 feet). This accounts for the probable origin of Mingulay's name – 'Big Isle' in Old Norse. Each island has its own distinctive character and feel; of the four formerly-inhabited islands covered by this book, Mingulay, Berneray and Pabbay have most in common with each other in terms of remoteness, physical features and recent human history, while Sandray is different in many ways and, being nearer to Vatersay and Barra, was more influenced by those islands historically.

The islands are part of Barra Parish, described in 1847 as "composed of a cluster of islands surrounded by a boisterous sea, making the passage from one island to another a matter of very considerable hazard"[1]. There is another group of small islands off the north east coast of Barra which, being close to Barra and sheltered by it from the Atlantic, have a different character from the southern isles. The whole group is known as the Barra Isles. All five of the southern islands were inhabited into this century, Mingulay latterly having by far the largest population; but since 1912, when Mingulay was finally abandoned, only Vatersay has had a permanent population. Several of the islands off the north east of Barra were also inhabited, though none continuously in the 18th and 19th centuries. The 'capital' of the parish, since around the middle of the last century, has been Castlebay, where the castle of the MacNeils of Barra commands an islet in one of the best natural harbours in the Hebrides.

Mingulay's shape was likened by Jolly to a "rude figure eight written with a shaky pen" (map 2). The broad eastern indentation is Mingulay Bay, called Church Bay by Jolly; at its head is a fine sandy beach, and above that, and now partially buried in it, the remains of the village. Lush green pasture, the former fields of the inhabitants, extends inland into a broad glen enclosed by an amphitheatre of barren hills. Starting at the south east of this arc, they are Hecla, a pleasing cone, rounded Carnan, the highest at 273 metres (891 feet), joined by a ridge to rugged MacPhee's Hill on the north. North of MacPhee's Hill a narrow bulge (the 'Ard') forms the northern point of the island, and a fourth, though much lower, hill, Tom a' Reithean. The southern and eastern slopes of the hills descend fairly gently to the sea, and a small valley, Skipisdale, opens onto the south coast. Most of the western and northern slopes, by contrast, are truncated abruptly by tremendous sea cliffs, eaten away by the incessant pounding of the Atlantic.

The cliffs are Mingulay's most notable feature, first described in awesome terms in 1840[2]. The highest of these, Biulacraig or Aoineig (also called Eagle Cliff[3]), reaches 229 metres (753 feet), and as late as 1878 was thought to be the highest sea cliff in Scotland[4]. It is exceeded in western Scotland only by those of St Kilda. Jolly described it thus:

11

"It rises from the Atlantic in an unbroken wall facing the north. . . It consists of layer upon layer of thick bedded gneiss, traversed by numerous veins of red felspar and by a broad basaltic dike which has thrust itself through the strata with volcanic power. In front of it and running parallel to it, a lower cape juts out

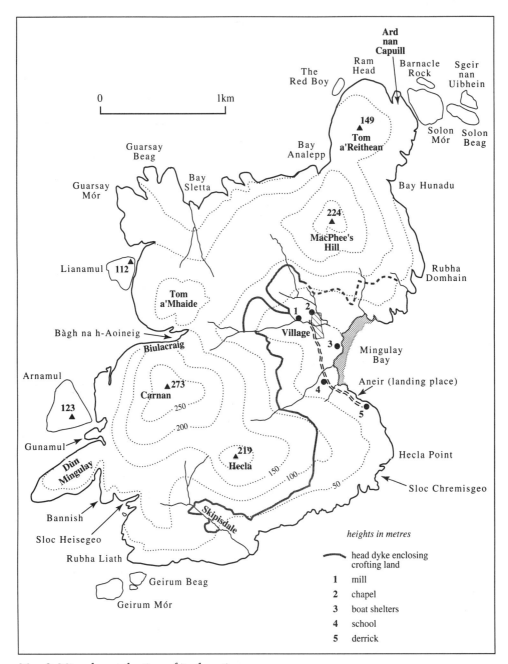

Map 2. Mingulay at the time of its desertion

into the ocean, separated from the Aonig by a narrow ravine, into which the sea rolls hundreds of feet below. This cape forms an admirable point for seeing the rock. . . There the mighty vertical precipice towers right in front of you, revealed from base to summit, ledge above ledge, in inexpressible grandeur."

The cliff was the crest of the MacNeils of Barra, and 'Biulacraig' formed the rallying cry of the clan[5]. The top of it can be seen from Barra, including parts of Castlebay.

While the cliffs may not be the highest in Scotland, the cliff scenery rivals any. "It is hardly possible to point out a scene more worthy of being visited for grandeur and variety than that of these rocks, particularly during the months of June and July", wrote Alexander Nicolson, minister of Barra, in 1840, referring to the "innumerable tribes of aquatic fowls" with which they are festooned in the summer. A feature of the cliff-bound coastline is the number of deep chasms with which it is riven, and the interplay of chasms, promontories, and precipitous sea stacks provides an endless variety of dramatic vistas. This is especially so at the south west end where the peninsula of Dun Mingulay and the stack of Arnamul enclose an inlet into which a precipitous peninsula, Gunamul, protrudes.

Through the neck of this headland, the sea had, wrote J. Wedderspoon after a visit early this century:

"cut a winding tunnel about 60 to 70 feet in height, and 50 yards in length. The mouth of the tunnel looked black and forbidding, strange noises issued from it magnified by countless echoes; sea-birds in myriads poured from the opening, their clamour barely heard in the babel of sounds. The sea chafed and churned with the strife of conflicting currents in the narrow channel, and as the boatmen half shipped their oars under the gloomy archway, the warning injunction on 'Dante's Inferno' occurred to my mind. Fending the boat off the opposing rock with the oars, we glided into the unknown. The black walls rose perpendicular from the depths below, and disappeared into the impenetrable darkness overhead. . . with a sigh of relief we emerged from that battlefield of titanic forces. . ."

According to Jolly, the caves and arches "are called by the natives *cailleach*, or 'old woman'. When the sea rushes into one of them, it causes a concussion of air and water which results in a kind of deep hollow snort and upward rush of spray, which is picturesquely described by the natives as 'the old woman taking snuff!'"

The cliffs of Mingulay and Berneray are among the most important breeding grounds for seabirds in the west of Scotland, ranking with the outliers of the main Outer Hebridean chain such as St Kilda, North Rona,

13

the Flannans, and others. The islands' importance contributed to their being created a Site of Special Scientific Interest in 1983 (see below), and in 1994 the islands received additional recognition and protection by being created a Special Protection Area. This designation, by the Scottish Office (acting on a European Community directive with the recommendation of Scottish Natural Heritage), applies to sites used by internationally important populations of breeding species of seabirds. These species, with numbers and percentages of British populations, are: razorbill, 16,890 pairs (12%); guillemot, 30,900 individuals (3%); fulmar, 10,450 pairs (2%); kittiwake, 8,600 pairs (2%); and shag, 720 pairs (2%). In addition to these five, ten other species of seabirds breed on the islands: storm petrel, common and arctic terns, great skua, black guillemot, puffin, and four species of gull: common, herring, greater and lesser black-backed[6]. Manx shearwaters, which the people had caught for food and used for paying the rent, inhabited the summit of the stack of Lianamul (123 metres, 368 feet, high, plate 5) until the late 18th century, when they were driven away by puffins. "The natives, in revenge," wrote the naturalist Harvie-Brown in 1887, "have extirpated them on the larger stack of Arnamul, in order to preserve the grazing for about a score of sheep"[7]. Birds are attracted not only by the cliffs and coastal rocks and caves for nesting sites, but by the rich fish supply in the area, where the currents of the Sea of the Hebrides and the Atlantic meet[8]. As in St Kilda, the birds and their eggs were an important source of food for the islanders, who also sold their feathers for cash.

The stacks attracted attention much earlier than the cliffs of the main island. One of them is presumed to be the "Scarpa Vervecum, i.e. of wethers" referred to by Buchanan in 1592; the name is Latin meaning 'green stack' or 'green scarp', the 'wethers' meaning the sheep which grazed their summits. Martin Martin, about 1695, described fowling operations on Lianamul, and in 1794 MacQueen wrote: "Close by the island of Mingalay is a high rock, with very luxuriant grass growing on the top of it. The inhabitants of this island climb to the top at the risk of their lives, and by means of a rope carry up their wedders to fatten."

Harvie-Brown considered Lianamul

"the most densely packed guillemot station he had ever seen, owing to the unsur-passed suitability, regularity, depth and number of the breeding ledges, along many of which two men could crawl abreast on hands and knees, with a roof of solid rock above. . . the top of the stack is tunnelled and honeycombed by puffins. . . and over their heads waves a dense crop of red-seeding sorrell in summer. Later in the year the whole surface is one sticky compound of mud and dung, feathers, bad eggs, and defunct young puffins ankle deep or deeper", a wonderful

fertiliser, if only it were accessible. *"Formerly"*, continued Harvie-Brown, *"the stack was reached by a suspended rope-bridge from the mainland across the great chasm, but for many years back it has been reached at a landing place, and by a severe climb, only in exceptionally fine weather, from the seaward side, near the southern extremity."*

This 'rope-bridge' may in fact have been a rope of horse hair tied to the mainland, by which, tradition has it, one could swing out over the abyss onto the stack. The rope was secured to the top of the cliff, and by climbing down to a lower level, one swung over to a place on the rock wall opposite.

The cliffs are not only striking visually: the roar of the sea, the cacophony of the birds, wheeling about or sitting on the ledges, and the smell of their guano, are all part of the experience. It was Alexander Carmichael's opinion that "There is probably no more interesting island in Britain than this Island of Miuley (an anglicised spelling of Mingulay's Gaelic name), with its wonderful precipices, long narrow sea galleries, several hundred feet high in the perpendicular sides, and marine arcades, winding their gloomy subterraneous ways under the precipitous island. To boat through these galleries and arcades needs a calm sea, a good crew, and a steady nerve." Writing in 1883, he claimed to be "the first to discover, and the first and last to go through much the longest, largest, and gloomiest of these wonderful sinuous sea arcades".

According to local tradition, French gold intended for Prince Charles's army in the Highland uprising of 1745 is supposed to have been hidden in a sea cave on the west coast. This provides the basis for Neil Munro's novel *Children of Tempest*, the climax of which involves an imaginary climb on the cliffs.

Mingulay's appeal was, and is, due not only to its intrinsic attractions, but also to its remoteness and inaccessibility. It was described in 1897 as "an island so remote that it is easier to reach America than to get there"[9]. To do so from Barra, 19 kilometres (12 miles) distant, one has to contend with the fierce tide races between the islands, as well as with the often unpredictable and rapidly changing state of the Atlantic and of the weather. In the days of the oar and the sail these were major considerations. But that is not all. There is no sheltered landing place on the island. Mingulay Bay, where the landing places are, is exposed to the wind and the swell from most directions except the west, and getting ashore was, and still is, a matter of jumping onto rocks; the inhabitants had to land their boats on the beach. They were often cut off for weeks on end, and even today, though motor boats make getting there easier, a landing is still dependent on the state of the swell.

15

The young naturalist Theodore Walker described his journey south from Barra (along the west side of the intervening islands, it being more usual to keep to their east) in the lighthouse mail boat, in June 1869:

"We have passed Pabba's precipices and are in the Sound of Mingalay, where the billows of the Atlantic, meeting the waves and tide of the Minch, the tide running like a mill-race, the huge waves are humbled, and in rage and despair are leaping, foaming, tumbling and whirling us close under a reef of rocks. . . Ram Head [Mingulay], hideous in the gloom, is blotted out by the fierce rage of the storm. A yell in Gaelic as Rory and his man spring to the sheet! I grasp the tiller as they tear down the sail; the wind rages and screams round us; the angry waves are white with foam, as the fierce gale strips off their tops, blending salt water and rain, and mist, and sea, and sky, all in gloom. The foam is dashed in our faces, as, encased in waterproofs from head to feet, I clench my teeth and grasp the tiller.

Rory says it is impossible to reach Barra Head today, as wind and tide are against us, and as we have manfully battled with wind and tide for six long cold hours, we are unwilling to turn back. Rory says he can land us on Mingalay; there are two men there who can speak English, and we can get shelter, and cross over the Sound of Bernera to Barra Head if the weather moderates. . . A quarter of an hour's cold wet sail, with the salt foam in our faces – an indistinct black mass rises, seemingly pressed down by the weight of clouds; it is the beetling cliffs of Mingalay. A white gleam of sand in a sheltered nook, on which the ground swell is heavily breaking, a few battered boats drawn up, a black amphitheatre of hills, and we catch a dim outline of a group of huts as we sail past. Into a sheltered cove Rory glides, and as the boat is lifted on the wave we spring out, catching and dragging out our gun-cases and impedimenta. A parting cheer to Rory, and here are we on a barren island, on which no strangers have landed for more than a year."

An idea of the violence of the sea and wind in the area is gained by the fact that the cliff tops of Mingulay and Berneray are drenched with salt spray in times of storm, and in about 1868, a huge wave washed right over the islet of Geirum Mor, 51 metres (167 feet) high, between Mingulay and Berneray, taking sheep with it. During a storm in 1836 a block of rock, estimated to be 504 cubic feet (142 cubic metres) in volume and 42 tons (42,672 kg) in weight, was moved by the sea five feet (1.5 metres) from where it lay on the coast of Berneray[10].

In terms of its size, cliffy bird-inhabited coastline, eastward facing glen, bay and village, formerly-inhabited secondary valley, and inaccessibility, Mingulay was and is a 'nearer St Kilda', or rather, a nearer Hirta, the principal island in the group. The rather austere and forbidding grandeur of Village Bay, Hirta, however, finds no parallel in Mingulay, which is altogether more welcoming if less impressive. There were similarities in some aspects of the way of life of the islanders too, which was part of the lure for visitors to both islands. Visitors often compared the two, as we have seen; Harvie-Brown found Mingulay "of fresher interest, and much more primitive than St Kilda, especially as regards the cottars' and crofters' houses."

Geologically, the Outer Hebrides are composed of Lewisian Gneiss, a hard, acidic, metamorphic rock which represents the roots of a mountain chain once extending through Greenland and North America before being split up by continental drift in more recent geological times. The rock is the oldest in Britain, and amongst the oldest in the world, around three thousand million years old. The banded and twisted gneiss bears witness to its tortuous history of deep burial in the earth's crust and metamorphosis by tremendous temperatures and pressures. In places the gneiss has developed into so-called 'flinty crush rock' associated with a major fault running east of the islands, and actually running through the east side of Sandray, giving that side its distinctive appearance. In Mingulay, Berneray and Pabbay the layered gneiss tilts from west to east, which partly accounts for the islands' distinctive profiles. Lines of weakness in the rock caused by joints are exploited by marine erosion to form deep chasms, promontories and, ultimately, stacks (precipitous islets) where the line of weaker rock has been eroded away completely. Vertical intrusions of softer igneous rocks (dykes) are likewise eroded out. The peninsulas of Gunamul and Dun Mingulay owe their existence partly to a dyke, forming their necks, and in time they too will become stacks.

During the Ice Age (the last phase of which ended about 10,000 years ago) the islands were scoured and smoothed by the ice sheet moving west from the Scottish Highlands, and this has also influenced their topography. Existing east-west valleys and other lines of weakness were gouged out and deepened, and when sea level rose after the Ice Age – a process continuing to this day - the deeper valleys were flooded to form the present-day sounds. The ice deposited boulder clay on the islands, and this survives in the area around Mingulay Bay, and southwards to Skipisdale, and on the north coast of Berneray. The boulder clay contains mainland rocks, and this accounts for the presence of 'alien' material, including large blocks, on the islands[11].

The rock and the wet climate together are responsible for the barren aspect of the islands, typical of the Outer Hebrides as a whole. The gneiss is impermeable and weathers to form a thin acidic infertile soil which accumulates in depressions leaving a good deal of rock bare. However, much of Mingulay is covered in peat. This has formed from decaying vegetation which, because of the impermeability of the rock and the heavy rainfall, does not decompose but gradually builds up to depths of up to two metres. The peat was cut as fuel by the islanders. The main features of the islands' climate are rain and wind. Rainfall, while not as high as on the mainland, is spread fairly evenly throughout the year; winds are predominantly south westerly and frequently blow as gales, especially in winter. Summer and winter temperature variations are not great, and snow and frosts are not common.

The peat supports the maritime grassland and heath characteristic of the Outer Hebrides – composed of heather, sphagnum moss, sedges and grasses. There are no trees, the only representative of that class on Mingulay being a species of poplar (aspen) growing to about half a metre (2 feet) in height on a cliff above the beach. This, and ivy, rose and wood horsetail also found there in 1938, were thought to be survivals of formerly more extensive woodland; none of them were recorded in 1985. Other notable plants are the sea holly, which is very rare in the Outer Hebrides, and was noted as early as 1883 by Jolly; and the sea milkwort, which is normally found at sea level, but grows on the high cliff-tops because of the spray and seagull manure. Since 1938 heather, which was formerly rare, and bracken, have increased, while weeds associated with cultivation have decreased or disappeared[12].

Around Mingulay Bay the heathland gives way to the vivid greenery of the former croftlands of the inhabitants. Here the soil is based on boulder clay and shell sand blown from the beach, and some of it was fertilised and cultivated for generations. The inland margins of the area, defined by the head dyke, are returning to a heathland state in places.

The varied summer flowers are a delight. The green pastures around the bay are spangled with buttercups, daisies, birdsfoot trefoil, ragged robin, silverweed and yellow flag (iris); while on the heathland are marsh orchids, scabious and sundew.

Mingulay and Berneray together were created a Site of Special Scientific Interest in 1983[13]. It is a grade 2 site (on a scale of two) of national importance on account of its maritime and paramaritime vegetation, rocky shore and cliff habitats, and the seabirds. The islands are the only ones in the main Outer Hebridean chain to be described as 'oceanic' in ecological terms, and to be designated in this way; they are thus comparable to the outliers of the main chain such as St Kilda and others mentioned above[14]. Their designation as a Special Protection Area tightens planning controls further, and restricts the kinds of activities permitted on the islands.

An interesting feature of the bay is the accumulation of sand and its penetration inland. Above the high water mark of the beach there is a large area of sand rarely, if ever, covered by the sea. The Ordnance Survey maps of 1878 and 1901 show the high water mark in the same position as it is now (map 3), yet the photograph of 1887 (plate 1) shows the sea lapping the edge of the village, while showing a ridge of sand where the map marks high water mark. Today the stream drifts over this dry part after heavy rain, and the sea occasionally forms small pools where the stream has lowered the surface. This part of the beach is bounded to its north by a system of dunes, and the sandy area continues inland to the west for some distance, up to a height of about 30 metres (100 feet). The high proportion of sand in the soils inland show that sand has been blown inland over a long period, and this is also shown by the fact that a midden of Iron Age date, approximately 2,000 years old, rests on sand. There has been appreciable change this century in two respects. The lower parts of the village have been over-whelmed by up to a metre and a half (5 feet) of sand; there is no sign of sand in the photographs of 1887 and 1905, but by 1922 the advance had begun.

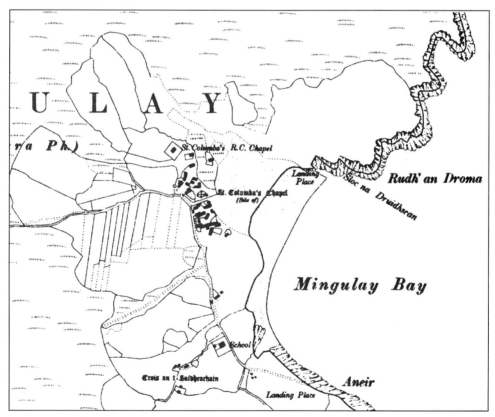

Map 3. Mingulay Village and its environs in 1901 (reproduced to scale from the 6 inch to 1 mile Ordnance Survey map. The name Crois an t-Suideachain refers to the three symbols 1cm to the east).

The movement of sand in the village had ceased by the 1970s, and vegetation has stabilised it. The other change has been the development of sand dunes on the north side of the beach, partly on areas of sloping land surface, partly on the dry part of the beach. These dunes developed dramatically in the 1950s and 60s, and have now been largely stabilised by marram grass. There has been similar accumulation of sand on the east coasts of Pabbay and Sandray, and there are beaches on the east coast of Vatersay. This contrasts with the main islands of the Outer Hebrides from Barra northward, where most of the sandy beaches are on the west coasts.

This is the scene on which the human story of the island is set, a story which began perhaps 5,000 years ago. What is the evidence for this story?

Until Mingulay appears in the historical record in the 16th century, much of the evidence is archaeological. Thereafter, there is a remarkable amount of documentation for such a small and relatively insignificant island, making Mingulay amongst the best documented of those islands in the Outer Hebrides which have been inhabited in recent times[15]. It is this, as much as the story of the island itself (which in many respects was representative of the Barra Isles as a whole), which makes Mingulay remarkable. In this respect, too, Mingulay is comparable to St Kilda; the amount of documentation, however, is very much smaller than for St Kilda, which was much better known and easier to get to by the later 19th century. St Kilda has many detailed contemporary accounts written both by visitors, some of whom stayed for long periods, and by resident incomers; and there is more information recorded by or from the islanders, who were evacuated in 1930[16].

From 1549, when it was first mentioned, until the mid-19th century, little is recorded for individual islands, and most of what there is is ecclesiastical. One well-known contemporary account is that of Martin Martin, about 1695. He was a native of Skye, and as such one of the few native writers about the Hebrides. He has a good deal to say about Berneray or Mingulay, perhaps both, clearly derived from hearsay and much of it of dubious reliability; there are enough indications to make it very likely that Mingulay was intended, but one can't be sure. It is a pity he did not visit the islands personally as his own descriptions of other islands are apparently much more reliable.

During the 19th century the fingers of state bureaucracy began to penetrate the remotest corners of the British Isles, and interest of a scientific nature was awakening. Communications were improving, breaking down the barriers of isolation, and the opening of the Barra Head Lighthouse on Berneray in 1833 drew attention to the area and made travel south of Barra easier. The result was an explosion of information relating to Mingulay; there are visitors' accounts of Berneray as well, but not for Pabbay or Sandray, and much less in the way of other records, folklore, and oral tradition. The bulk of this book, therefore, covers the last fifty or so years of the Mingulay community's life.

There are three main types of evidence: records of government and other organisations, visitors' and other contemporary accounts, and local sources. The first state-initiated records of the smaller islands are the detailed censuses which began nationally in 1841, and were taken every ten years subsequently; they record details of individuals as well as housing. National registration of births, marriages and deaths began in 1855, though there are church registers from 1805; and the first Ordnance Survey was conducted in 1878. By the end of the century there are records and accounts relating to education, the church, crofting, fishing, health; and, in this century, records of the desertion. Since Mingulay and its neighbours were deserted, their histories have received scant attention; their fauna and flora have attracted more interest[17].

The scenery, natural history, and archaeology of the Outer Hebrides, and the way of life of the inhabitants, which had remained backward in the material sense compared to the mainland, began to attract travellers during the 19th century. The Mingulay visitors we know about – those who wrote about their experiences – were a varied and sometimes colourful lot, all sharing a determination to get there against all odds.

The seabirds on the cliffs attracted natural historians from the 1860s. Captain Elwes visited in 1868, the young Walker brothers in about 1869, and J.A. Harvie-Brown landed from his own yacht in 1870 and 1887, gathering material for his book on the fauna of the Outer Hebrides. In the latter year he brought his own photographer, William Norrie of Fraserburgh, who took the earliest known photograph on the island (plate 1). Harvie-Brown made friends with Mingulay's schoolteacher, John Finlayson, with whom he later corresponded. Robert Adam, the botanist and celebrated photographer of the Scottish scene, spent a week in Mingulay in June 1905 with his brother James and a friend, Charlie Watt. At first they camped, but when the weather deteriorated they moved in with John MacLean (Barnaidh; Iain Chaluim Iain) and his family[18]. Adam's main interest was in the flora and fauna, but he also took the marvellous photographs of human interest illustrating this book, the only ones known of the island when it was inhabited, apart from Norrie's and one of village houses in 1909[19]. Adam's photographs are a great tribute to his skill and determination. He was only nineteen at the time, and the apparatus – heavy box camera, tripod, and hundreds of glass plates – was heavy and cumbersome. Getting photographs of people who were no doubt apprehensive and suspicious was a great achievement, as was the photographing of seabirds in perilous places on the cliffs, with no telephoto lens to help him. Adam paid a second visit in 1922 when only ruins remained.

T S Muir, the antiquary, visited in 1866, and was the first visitor to write about the contemporary inhabitants and to take an interest in Mingulay's human past. The folklore of the Outer Hebrideans was the subject of much interest from the 1850s, when it was realised that they had retained much more than people on the mainland, whose knowledge of traditional lore was fast dying out. A collector for John Francis Campbell of Islay visited Mingulay in 1860, and Alexander Carmichael, another collector and an authority on the islands, visited on numerous occasions in the 1860s and 70s. Father Allan McDonald of South Uist and later Eriskay was also interested in the folklore, and visited on a number of occasions between 1884 and his death in 1905.

Another visitor with an ostensible interest in folklore was Ada Goodrich-Freer. She visited in 1898 and wrote an account quoting a number of historical stories. She was in fact on a secret mission to seek evidence of second sight in the Hebrides, on behalf of the Society for Psychical Research. She also purported to be a medium and a clairvoyant, but she was eventually exposed as a fraud and had to flee from England in 1901. Many years later, it was discovered that she was a fraud in another sense – much of the material she published as her own had been pirated from other collectors[20]. Her Uist and Barra material was collected mainly by Father Allan McDonald, of whose assistance and good faith she took advantage. The Mingulay stories she quotes were almost certainly recorded by him, perhaps at the time of her visit; she had no Gaelic and did not reveal in her book that Father Allan accompanied her on her visit to Mingulay.

Several supporters of Mingulay's Free Church school visited it in the 1860s, and William Jolly visited in 1878 and 1879, and possibly later, in his capacity as school inspector. Mrs Frances Murray, her husband and daughters were early examples of tourists, landing from their schooner in 1888.

Most of the contemporary accounts of the way of life of the islanders, while being important sources of detail, suffer from their being based on only very brief visits, and being coloured by the romanticism, prejudices and ignorance of their authors. Most of the visitors were non-Gaels writing for geographically, and culturally, distant readers, or, in Murray's case, an actual audience – her account was written as a lecture. Hers and Jolly's accounts in particular are aimed at portraying the islanders in ways to suit their purposes. In some cases, details can be shown to be wrong, where there are other sources of evidence. It is not only the outsiders' accounts that cannot be relied on absolutely; all the sources of evidence need to be considered in the context in which they were produced.

Local sources should be the best in any study of local history. There are few contemporary native sources, but we are fortunate in that tape recordings of several Mingulay people talking about life there were made in 1960 in Vatersay. They were made by Lisa Sinclair of Vatersay whose father, Duncan Sinclair, was one of the first of the 'Vatersay raiders' from Mingulay. She was then working at the School of Scottish Studies in Edinburgh, and spent a holiday at home recording people who had left Mingulay in their youth fifty years before (see Appendix 4). She wanted information of a general nature about the way of life of the islanders, and in this she was in advance of her time, for in those days interest in oral tradition in Scotland still concentrated on folklore, stories, songs and music. It was only nine years since the School of Scottish Studies had been established to collect and study such material. Her interest in her people's heritage was also unusual for this period.

The tape recordings relate to the last decade or two of the community's life, and in some cases they refer back to the informants' grandparents' generation. Although details are sometimes contradictory, they are almost our only native source, without which our knowledge would be much poorer. They are, of course, in Gaelic, and many terms, some used in a way unique to Mingulay, have thus been preserved. The recordings were the first, and for many years the last, attempt to record something of a vanished community and way of life; they are especially valuable as there is nobody now living who knew Mingulay, except as a young child. There remains, however, a great deal of knowledge among the people of Barra and Vatersay, many of whom are of Mingulay descent. Other local sources include the letters of Neil MacPhee, and letters written by, or rather on behalf of, other islanders at the time of the desertion; and the petition for landing facilities. There are also the stories, songs, and other folklore recorded from Mingulay people; the letters of the schoolteacher John Finlayson, and various school records.

In the early 1980s a local history society, Comunn Eachdraidh Bharraigh, was formed in Barra, a result of the growing collective interest of the islanders in their heritage; the annual Gaelic festival, the *Fèis*, another expression of the revival of interest in the heritage, started at about the same time[21]. This was part of a movement in the Outer Hebrides in general, and further afield. The society mounted an exhibition on the history of Mingulay in 1992, and this created great interest among the people of Barra and Vatersay. Objects from Mingulay were located, many of them by the descendants of their former owners, and much information was unearthed.

From these various sources, and from what is known of the islands in general, we learn something of the Mingulay community in its last few centuries, and particularly in its last few decades. Until the 19th century it was basically self-sufficient, but dependence on the outside world steadily increased. The people lived by fishing, raising crops and animals, and fowling. They had a rich oral culture, and were devout Roman Catholics. A school was established by the Free Church in 1859, and this was succeeded by a state school. In the later 19th century fishing became an important industry, but the fishermen were handicapped by their isolation and the lack of an adequate landing place. Pressure on the land grew with the rising population, which reached a peak of over 160 in the 1880s, and the village became overcrowded and insanitary. Conditions deteriorated, and in 1907 desperate Mingulay men took the law into their own hands and followed Barra men in grabbing land on Vatersay. For this they were tried and imprisoned, but they won the land and settled there. By 1912 Mingulay was deserted. The story is in many respects unique, but it is also an example of life in the Barra Isles as a whole; and in a broader sense, it illustrates many themes of Highland and Island history and society.

2
Early Times

This chapter considers, briefly, the archaeology and history of the Barra Isles, with the evidence of settlement on Mingulay where such exists, from the earliest times until Mingulay appears in the historical record in the middle of the 16th century. In a brief survey of settlement history of the Outer Hebrides such as this, generalisations will be inevitable.

In any discussion of Hebridean archaeology, the limitations to our actual and potential knowledge must be pointed out. Firstly, the archaeology of the area is less well known than that of mainland areas, on account of the relatively small amount of fieldwork and excavation, at least until recent years. Interest in the past concentrated on the more obvious and visible monuments such as defensive or religious sites. In Mingulay the Ordnance Survey in 1878, and the Royal Commission on the Ancient and Historical Monuments of Scotland (RCAHMS) in 1915, noted three sites: Dun Mingulay, the site of St Columba's Chapel, and the enigmatic Crois an t-Suidheachain. In 1911 a visitor wrote about what appears to be prehistoric occupation of the village area. The Ordnance Survey carried out further brief surveys in the 1960s and 70s. The present writer surveyed the settlement evidence in the area around the bay in 1980. There has been no archaeological excavation, though a prehistoric stone object and pottery were found during a soil survey in 1975, and Iron Age pottery was found by a party of students digging into a midden in 1971. Recent work, such as that currently being undertaken in the Barra Isles by Sheffield University, has revealed that the islands are covered with sites, many of them of unknown antiquity and purpose, and some types of site are unique to particular islands[1]. The Sheffield work in 1993 and 1994 showed that Mingulay has a greater density of sites than any of the other southern Barra Isles. Hebridean archaeology in general has its own characteristics, and conventional dating and cultural terms such as 'Neolithic' and 'Iron Age' are not always relevant.

Secondly, there has been considerable change in the environment of the Outer Hebrides since prehistoric times. Many coastal sites have disappeared due to the rise in sea level since the last Ice Age; the rise is estimated to have been by four or five metres (13 - 16 feet) since 3,000 BC. Woodland has disappeared, and the widespread development of peat since later prehistoric times has obscured many inland sites and formerly cultivated areas. Local erosion of the peat is now revealing some of these sites on Mingulay.

Thirdly, some aspects of material culture, such as building techniques, continued essentially unchanged until recent times. From surface inspection alone, the remains of grass-grown structures could be as early as prehistoric burial cairns, or as late as 18th, 19th or even 20th century shelters, peat stack platforms or animal pens; often such sites and structures were re-used and rebuilt over time. Mingulay is dotted with such remains, some of which do appear to be very early, but some of these sites may have been re-used in later times, even after the desertion in some cases.

Despite these problems, however, it is possible, from evidence from the island and from what is known of the prehistory of the Hebrides as a whole, to hazard guesses about Mingulay's early inhabitants[2]. Mingulay must always have been attractive to settlement, with its variety of food resources – fish, shellfish, seabirds – land for grazing and cultivation, and a beach for landing on. Although it is now regarded as relatively remote and inaccessible this was not so in the past, when the sea was a highway rather than the barrier it was to become in more recent times.

Somebody was the first person ever to set foot on the island. Who was it? The earliest trace of human activity in the Outer Hebrides dates to about 5,000 BC, the later Mesolithic period, in Lewis. There is botanical evidence of clearance of the scrubby woodland covering the islands at that time, which is presumed to have been by human agency. These islanders were not necessarily the first, for there is evidence of occupation of the Inner Hebrides more than 1,000 years earlier. They were hunter-gatherers who probably moved seasonally according to the availability of food, such as shellfish, or the resources of the woodland inland. In the Inner Hebrides many shell middens (rubbish dumps composed mostly of shells, the live parts of which had been eaten) of Mesolithic culture survive on coastal sites, but in the outer islands any coastal sites would have disappeared.

These Mesolithic people used flint tools, and some fragments of worked flint have been found on Mingulay, on the surface of the sandy area north of the beach[3]. Flint occurs naturally in the Outer Hebrides where deposited by ice from the east, so the flint was probably local or from a nearby island. One fragment, a scraper 3 centimetres (1¼ inches) long, is worked in a tradition characteristic of the Mesolithic period, but is not necessarily very early, for sites in the Inner Hebrides used by people of Mesolithic culture were occupied as late as the third millennium BC, long after the earliest sites of Neolithic culture appear in the fourth millennium BC. Furthermore, the flint occurs in small pebbles, the techniques for the working of which were limited, and remained static in the Neolithic and Bronze Age at the site of Allt Chrysal in Barra[4]. The use of flint stops altogether in about 500 BC in the Outer Hebrides. So the find indicates human presence on Mingulay at some time between perhaps 3,000 BC and 500 BC.

Agriculture, animal domestication and the more settled lifestyle characteristic of the Neolithic period reached the outer islands in the fourth millennium BC. The earliest evidence of human occupation of Barra is early Neolithic pottery dating from the late fourth millennium BC at Allt Chrysal. The best known legacy of the Neolithic, the megalithic tomb, is well represented in Barra, and the remains of probable megalithic tombs have been identified on Mingulay and the adjacent islands[5]. They originally consisted of a chamber or passage of upright blocks of stone, roofed with transverse blocks, and the whole covered with a mound of earth or stone. They were communal burial chambers serving families or groups of families.

Possible evidence of early cultivators on Mingulay was found during a soil survey of the area around the bay in 1975[6]. In many of the survey pits, charcoal was found, all well below the present surface. The charcoal was of heather, rank grasses and dwarf willow – similar, with the exception of the dwarf willow, to the present-day vegetation higher up the valley sides. The low level above bedrock of these charcoal layers, and the presence of layers of large stones above them, may suggest that the charcoal resulted from heath fires – on those sites or higher up – perhaps started by human agency to improve grazing, or to clear vegetation in advance of cultivation. The stony layers may result from the breaking up of the soil by early cultivators, and its movement downhill over time; or they may be the natural results of erosion of soil exposed by the removal of the vegetation.

Deep down in one of these pits, in the flat floor of the main valley, an exciting find was made: a fragment of worked stone. The stone is a portion of an originally lozenge-shaped, flattened beach pebble of local stone, 11 centimetres (4 inches) wide. A conical depression was sunk into the opposing flat sides, such that they almost meet in the middle. The stone appears to have broken during the making of these depressions.

The stone belongs to an enigmatic class of object known as pebble hammers (also known as mace heads and axe hammers). They are not closely datable, and examples found over northern Britain date from as early as the Mesolithic down to the Bronze Age and perhaps later in the Scottish islands. Some complete specimens were clearly hafted and shaped to be used as axes, but it is hard to imagine the intended function of the Mingulay stone.

Its dating is not helped by its location in the pit. It was found at a depth of 60 centimetres (2 feet), 20 centimetres above bedrock. Immediately above bedrock was a layer of coarse stones and some charcoal. Above this was a finer layer in which the stone was found; above this was another coarse stony layer, and then the main depth of sandy soil. The interpretation of the upper coarse layer is crucial, but is only guesswork. The land where the stone was found is slightly elevated within the valley floor, so that downward movement of material from the valley sides would not affect it. Possibly the stone and its context are associated with the introduction of agriculture[7].

The introduction of new religious and social practices, as well as new material culture, marks the beginning of the Bronze Age in the third millennium BC. Stone circles and standing stones are characteristic of the period. Examples of both are known in Barra, and a possible stone circle has been identified on the south coast of Mingulay[8]. Communal burial in chambered tombs was replaced by single burials in stone cists, often under cairns. About the middle of the second millennium BC, there was a deterioration in the climate all over northern Europe. Conditions became wetter and colder, the area of cultivable ground shrank, and in the islands peat, which remains such a feature today, began to develop on a larger scale than before. Much of the pre-existing landscape, including man-made features, was buried. Structures which could be burial cairns of this period have been identified on Mingulay, in some cases where the peat which covered them is being eroded away[9].

After the uncertainties of the earlier prehistoric occupation of Mingulay, it is a relief to be on the firmer and more certain ground of the Iron Age, the period from about 500 BC to about AD 500 in the islands. At least two sites belong to this period: a midden north of the village, and Dun Mingulay.

The sandy area north of the dry part of the beach appears to have been occupied over a long period in prehistoric and perhaps later times. The flint was found here, and burnt stone, animal bone, shells, and sherds of crude pottery abound; stone structures, including field walls, are being exposed by shifting sand. Erosion has exposed a midden which is the source of some of this material. The midden, which rests on sand, is composed of a dark lower layer and a lighter upper layer. The few sherds of pottery found in the upper layer in 1971 are different from those of the lower; one sherd, together with others found eroded out of the midden, is decorated, of a known Iron Age type: Clettraval Ware, dating from the last few centuries BC and the first few AD. A sample of midden material revealed bones of cattle, sheep, seal, cormorant and cod; and mussels, scallops and limpets. Many of the cattle and sheep bones were burnt and a few bore traces of chopping with a sharp tool. A fragment of saddle quern – a stone with a depression worn in it by the action of grinding grain with a smaller stone – indicates that the creators of the midden were growing grain [10].

No habitation associated with the midden has been identified, but there are various cairns, enclosures and other stone settings in the vicinity. The area has clearly changed considerably over time, for the field walls must have been built before the area was as sandy as it is now, and there are the foundations of a wall on top of the midden itself [11].

Further ancient finds were described in 1911 by a Mr. Wedderspoon, a sanitary inspector. He described a shell midden adjoining, or perhaps forming part of, the knoll occupied by the graveyard; it contained shells, split bones, teeth, "hammerstones split by fire", and two "basin stones", presumably saddle querns or trough querns, which are similar. No sign of this midden remains. He also records the discovery of a small stone bowl and what appear to have been querns, when digging the foundations of the modern chapel, which, he said, was "on the site of an older building, of which nothing remained but a shapeless heap of stones." Saddle and trough querns are normally thought to be prehistoric, but the presence of a trough quern in a village house, and of another outside a house on Berneray, may indicate otherwise. Goodrich-Freer also mentions the finding of "stones and ashes" on the site of the chapel, and pottery was found in soil survey pits in 1975. This site was clearly occupied sometime in the past, perhaps in prehistoric times, perhaps in medieval times prior to the legendary 'plague', which will be discussed in the next chapter.

The other site ascribed to the Iron Age is Dun Mingulay, the cliff-bound peninsula at the south west end of the island. *Dùn* means fortification, (in Gaelic it can also mean 'fortified place'), and duns are the most common and most visible type of ancient monument in the Hebrides. They are massively built, often with double walls with a gallery between, in easily defendable positions. They are usually roughly circular, and in some cases, known as brochs, the walls were carried up to a considerable height. They are believed to have been built during the Iron Age, and reflect a period of political instability and insecurity which affected the whole of Britain. Some seem to have been temporary refuges, while others were, or could have been, permanently inhabited; some evidence suggests that the inhabitants were of high social status. In the larger islands duns are spaced out in their own 'territories', but the smaller islands have only one or two. Mingulay is exceptional among the main islands south of Barra in that no dun has been identified. The name 'Dun Mingulay' refers to the peninsula and not to a structure. There is merely a short stretch of walling reinforcing a natural rock face across the narrow neck of the peninsula; in places it is a couple of metres (6 feet) thick and now less than one metre in height[12]. It is only an assumption that this is Iron Age in date. Dun Mingulay could have served as a refuge in an emergency, for a population perhaps living in Skipisdale as well as in the bay area, but why Iron Age society on Mingulay was apparently different from that on the other islands remains a puzzle.

Before leaving the prehistoric period we should consider other sites which may be early. Some of the structures dotted about the lower slopes, or on streams, which resemble shielings, appear to occupy platforms which could be prehistoric house sites in origin. A type of monument recently identified on Mingulay, but not found on the other islands, may be a prehistoric burial monument[13]. They are rectangular or sub-rectangular structures defined by single lines of upright stones, and there is no evidence that these were formerly more substantial. They always overlook the sea, and are aligned towards it, and often occur in groups resembling cemeteries. They are found mainly in the north and north west of the island, a long way from the settlement area, which might be evidence against their interpretation as burial monuments. An alternative interpretation for some of these structures is as platforms for peat stacks of relatively recent date. There are also a number of cairns, hut circles and other stone settings. A sheep pen built in the 1920s or 30s in Skipisdale occupies the remains of an earlier structure, which has features of a wheelhouse of Iron Age type[14]. The islet of Geirum Mor, off the south west coast, is alleged to have the remains of a building on it, variously identified as a dun or a chapel[15].

The middle centuries of the first millennium AD are as much a 'dark age' in the islands as in the rest of Britain. The period is referred to as 'Early Christian' or 'early medieval', and in eastern Scotland, 'Pictish', the Picts being the inhabitants of Scotland north of the Lowlands. In the Outer Hebrides Pictish finds are rare, and Mingulay's neighbour Pabbay boasts one of only two incised slabs, or symbol stones, found in the islands; the majority of these stones have been found in eastern Scotland. This stone can be dated to the seventh or eighth century and a bronze pin dating to the seventh century has also been found on Pabbay. These finds suggest that the islands were inhabited by people of 'Pictish' culture. Possible finds of this period on Mingulay are mentioned by Wedderspoon: "several ancient coins and bronze pins were found in the graveyard some years ago, and sent to Castlebay to be disposed of." Their location on the site of what may already have been a chapel and graveyard suggests this period, and coins were in existence then. In succeeding centuries the Pictish culture and language were submerged by the Gaelic-speaking *Scotti*, or Scots, Celtic people from northern Ireland who had begun to settle the western seaboard in the early centuries AD. They founded the kingdom of Dalriada, which united with the Pictish kingdom in the ninth century.

Celtic Christianity of the type introduced from Ireland by St Columba in 563 was based on the monastic ideal. The early monasteries consisted of chapels and cells within a 'cashel' or boundary. Very few such sites are known, but it is possible that Cille Bharra ('Barr's Church'), in Barra was such a monastery. (The name Barra is thought to derive from St Finbarr or Barr, traditionally believed to be the sixth-century Finbarr of Cork, but more likely to be the early seventh-century St Finbarr of Caithness, a Gaelic Scot.) Some early monasteries had hermitages or retreats on nearby islands, and Pabbay may have served such a purpose. The name Pabbay (Gaelic *Pabaigh*) is derived from the Norse for 'Hermits' Isle', indicating the inhabitants at the time of the Norse raiding and later settlement of the Hebrides which began in the late eighth century. An Irish monk, Dicuil, said of the Hebrides in about 825: "Some of these islands are small; nearly all alike are separated by narrow channels; and in them for nearly a hundred years hermits have dwelt, sailing from our Scotia. Now, because of these robbers the Northmen, they are empty of anchorites." Pabbay's Pictish symbol stone bears a simple cross, added at a later date, and two other slabs bear crosses which could date from this or a later period; a cross-incised slab has also been found on Berneray. If Pabbay was used as a retreat it is possible that other islands were too; they all had chapels in later times, and it is possible that these were early in origin or replaced early ones in the more settled times after the early Norse period[16].

Whatever its date, there is no doubt that Mingulay had a chapel; it was mentioned by Monro in 1549, and the memory of its site was retained. The officers of the Ordnance Survey were informed in 1878 of the traditional site of a chapel, dedicated to St Columba, with graveyard attached[17]. This was the knoll, occupied by the graveyard, next to the stream in the village, and the corner of a building is now visible on the knoll[18]. The dedication to St Columba does not imply an early date, nor does it indicate any particular connection with the saint, who is not recorded as having visited the Outer Hebrides. Graveyards on all four of the other main islands south of Barra are similarly the traditional sites of chapels, though only on Mingulay are there visible remains.

There is another site with religious associations but about which even less can be said with certainty than the chapel. This is Crois an t-Suidheachain, meaning 'cross of the seat (sitting place)'. The structures comprising the Cross, as Muir said the islanders called it, have entirely disappeared since 1915, but its site is known – a level area in the hillside above the road approaching the landing place at Aneir. Muir described it as "a curious though greatly reduced antiquity. . . What is left of it are the ground stones of three diminutive cells or chests, and a central heap, surrounded by a circle of loose stones about 42 feet [13 metres] in diameter." Unfortunately, his sketch-plan is inconsistent with this description in some details, and also differs from the RCAHMS sketch-plan of 1915; and the platform is hardly big enough to have accommodated Muir's 'circle'[19]. The largest structure on the 1915 sketch, 3 metres (9 feet 9 inches) long internally, is large enough to be what the Ordnance Survey described as "traces of a building" on the site, "which is traditionally believed to have been a place of worship erected by a disciple of St Columba"[20]. The structure is aligned east-west and could perhaps have been a small chapel or oratory. Jolly refers to "a cairn above the the south landing place, called St Columba's Cross, being looked upon as sacred", while the RCAHMS recorded that "open air mass is said to have been celebrated" there[21]. A 'mass stone' is remembered as having been built into the gable ends of a house built in modern style near the school in the early years of this century; it is not far from the Cross, which may have provided a suitable quarry, and may account for the tradition.

So while the religious associations of the site are beyond doubt, we can only hazard guesses as to its origin. If the central structure was a chapel, two others could, at a pinch, have been cells, though tiny ones. The site would then resemble a miniature cashel of Early Christian times, or, without the cells, some early chapels in Argyll which are similarly small and within enclosures. An alternative suggestion is that some of the structures – at least one of which seems to have consisted of large blocks of stone – may have originated as the chambers of a megalithic tomb of Neolithic type; or as the cists for single burials associated with cairns of Bronze Age type.

Another possible reference to the Cross is found in Martin Martin's account of 1695. He says: "there is in this island an Altar dedicated to St Christopher, at which the Natives perform their Devotion. There is a Stone set up here, about seven foot high, and when the Inhabitants come near it they take a religious Turn round it." Was this 'altar' the Cross? Or a standing stone? No other site in Mingulay or Berneray seems to match this.

With the advent of the Norse, or Viking, period in the Hebrides we are once again on firmer ground. The period began at the end of the eighth century with violence and plunder, and monastic establishments were favourite targets. Being on the sea route from Norway to Ireland and the Isle of Man, the Hebrides were used as bases for raids further south. According to one of the Norse sagas, which cannot be regarded as historically accurate, the first Viking to come to Barra was Onund Wooden-leg. He came in 871 with five ships, drove out a local ruler, Kiarval, and stayed for some years, plundering in Scotland and Ireland. According to the saga, "they went on warfare in the summers, but were in the Barra Isles in the winters." Some time later Onund arranged a marriage between a relative and a Barra woman from a family which had been established in the Hebrides for two or three generations. Graves of these early settlers have been found in Barra, dating from the ninth century, before the Norse were converted to Christianity. A gravestone found at Cille Bharra bears a cross on one side and a runic inscription to the deceased on the other, a clear indication that Christianity survived in Barra and had been adopted by the incomers by the 11th century[22].

As time went on the raiders from Norway became settlers, for it was land they lacked at home and which they wanted in the similar environment of the Scottish islands. The settlement was on such a scale – especially in Lewis, and Orkney and Shetland – that their language became the predominant one, certainly for topographical names. Although Gaelic reasserted itself after the Norse lost political control of the Hebrides in the 13th century, the place names survive (since Gaelicised, the Gaelic forms then being Anglicised) and remain the principal legacy of the period. Apart from the graves, the only other physical remains are possible boat graves on Vatersay and Berneray[23]. Other evidence is in the form of folklore in which the Norse feature, and the system of land ownership in the islands before the 19th century which was based on the Norse pattern.

A large number of the place names in the Barra Isles are of Norse origin (or are compound Norse-Gaelic), as are the names of the islands themselves[24]. The name Mingulay is thought to derive from the Old Norse *mikil*, meaning big, and *ay*, meaning island. In Gaelic it is *Miughalaigh*, pronounced something like 'mew-ul-eye', or *Miùghlaigh*, which accounts for the form *Mewla* given in a 17th century source[25]. Monro's version of 1549 – *Megaly* – is the earliest known; Martin Martin, 1695, gives *Micklay*. The current spelling and pronunciation in English has drifted further from the Gaelic than in other cases, possibly because of the various forms used by early writers and map makers.

The majority of Mingulay's known place names (of which those recorded by the Ordnance Survey are only some[26]) are coastal. They are descriptive or refer to an association, such as fishing. The commonest Norse element is the suffix *-geo* from Old Norse *gja*, chasm or cleft in a cliff. This is found in names such as *Sloc Heisegeo, sloc* being Gaelic for inlet or chasm, perhaps a later addition, the *heise* element being obscure. The suffix *-mul* is Old Norse for headland or island, and is found in the precipitous sea stacks off the west coast; in Lianamul the first element is Old Norse for flax (significance unclear), in Arnamul it is Old Norse for sea eagle or Arni (personal name).

33

The suffix *-nish* derives from Gaelic *nis*, itself derived from Old Norse *nes*, 'point', as in Bannish, 'white point', on the south west coast. Sletta as in Bay Sletta could be derived from Old Norse *slettur*, meaning sticks, perhaps indicating a place where driftwood gathered. Inland, the hill Hecla is Old Norse for 'hooded shroud'; there is another cone-shaped Hecla in South Uist. In Biulacraig, the great cliff, the final element *craig* is derived from *creag*, the Gaelic for 'cliff'; the origin of the other element(s) is obscure, but the word order is Norse. In *Skipisdale*, the southern valley, the suffix *-dale* is derived from Old Norse *dalr*, valley, the first element being derived from Old Norse for ship, a reference perhaps to the landing place at its outlet[27].

A very interesting name recorded by Father Allan McDonald (with no indication of location) is *Suinsibost*[28]. The suffix *-bost* is common in some former Norse areas, and is derived from Old Norse *bolstadr*, farm. If this applies to Suinsibost (the derivation of the rest of the name is uncertain), it is very significant, as no other derivatives of *bolstadr* are known in the Barra Isles. It is also firm evidence of Norse settlement; but even without it, the number and variety of the names, and the intimate knowledge of the island they indicate, make it almost certain that Mingulay was inhabited by Norse speakers. The nearest certain Norse settlement name, *Sheader*, is in Sandray. The Gaelic names probably date from a later period, and many also indicate their economic association. For example, at the northern end of Mingulay is *Ard nan Capuill*, 'headland of the horses'; off the north coast is *Sgeir nan Uibhein*, 'skerry of the eggs' (of sea birds); and in Bay Sletta is *Sloc na Muice*, 'inlet of the pig', meaning sea-pig or whale. A few names are English, and relatively recent in origin. MacPhee's Hill, for example, originates from the MacPhee of the legend of the plague discussed in the next chapter.

The Hebrides and the Isle of Man formed the Kingdom of the Isles from the ninth century. The Norse grip weakened in the 12th century with the emergence of a chieftain in Argyll, Somerled, who expanded his territories to the islands, including Barra. The Hebrides remained under nominal Norse control until 1266, when they reverted to the Scottish crown, and were ruled by Somerled's descendants, the Lords of the Isles.

The Scottish clans originated in the period between the twelfth and fourteenth centuries. The Gaelic word *clann* means 'children', and in medieval Highland society the term referred to a grouping who claimed kinship with, and owed allegiance to, the hereditary chief. The clan owned a particular territory within which all property was held by the chief on behalf of the clan; the clan members or tenants paid rent for land in kind and in military service. Sometimes the chief leased portions of land known as 'tacks' to his close kinsmen, known as 'tacksmen', to whom tenants paid their rents;

Mingulay is not known to have been a tack, but Vatersay and Sandray were in later centuries.

By 1427 the MacNeils had emerged as the 'chiefs' of Barra, for in that year they were granted the Barra Isles by the Lords of the Isles. They had probably been the chiefs for some time, however, though their history is obscure. They themselves claimed descent from Niall Naoigiallach, 'Neil of the Nine Hostages', King of Ireland in the fourth century AD, and they believed that the 21st chief, Neil, came to Barra in the 11th century.

As for ecclesiastical history, the Roman diocesan system of church organisation was introduced in the 12th century. The chapel at Cille Bharra became the parish church and the parish was within the Diocese of the Isles, the bishops being based successively in the Isle of Man, Skye, and Iona. Many of the chapels in the Hebrides, including the present one at Cille Bharra, were built at around this time, which could be when the chapels in the islands south of Barra were built. This is a more likely date than an early medieval one, but without basic information such as original dimensions, it is impossible to be sure.

In recent times the village at Mingulay Bay was the only centre of population. There are three other sites, however, which could have been settlements in the not-too-distant past, perhaps in medieval times. Two of these are close together in Skipisdale, which, tradition has it, was inhabited at one time. They consist of chaotic clusters of small, much-ruined buildings, cairns and enclosures. From surface examination, the earliest buildings seem to be circular, interconnected and substantially built; they resemble pre-Norse structures known in the Western and Northern Isles. There are remains of later, sub-rectangular buildings, perhaps shielings or permanent dwellings[29], and the most recent structures are small sheep pens, for a ewe and lamb, built in the 1920s or 30s. The sites are near the stream, and one of them is surrounded by a large enclosure wall.

Skipisdale was croft land in recent times, and lazy-beds (cultivation ridges), probably dating from the 19th century, show that crops were grown here. Above the lazy-beds on the eastern side of the valley, on the slopes of Hecla, a field system can be seen which is much older than the lazy-beds. It consists of roughly rectangular fields defined by stone dykes, much overgrown, and the vegetation they enclose now is that of the heathland. These fields may have been associated with a population living in the nearby houses, in which case what we see in Skipisdale today could be a medieval or prehistoric landscape. There was a landing place on the coast, further evidence that Skipisdale could have supported a self-contained population.

The third settlement site is on the eastern slopes of Hecla. Here there is a more coherent cluster of perhaps ten small buildings, sub-square or sub-rectangular, some of them carefully built with squared internal walls. These features suggest a later date than the Skipisdale buildings. Isolated buildings, possibly dwellings, have been identified, one south of the group just mentioned, and one on the eastern slopes of MacPhee's Hill[30].

Other possible remains of the medieval period are small buildings on grassy patches near streams. In larger islands these could be interpreted as shielings, inhabited during the summer while the cattle were taken to the grazings some distance from the villages, but in a small island like Mingulay it is hard to believe that there would be a need to stay overnight when the village was never far away. Possibly the distant ones such as those in Skipisdale did serve this purpose, while others may have been daytime shelters. The remains of what appear to have been stone-built 'shelters' have been found dotted along the coastline all over the island, perhaps used by people fishing or fowling, or as huts for drying fish or birds[31]. They would thus be comparable to the 'cleits' of St Kilda.

So there is ample evidence of human occupation of Mingulay going back perhaps five thousand years. Occupation was not necessarily continuous, but, given the attractions of Mingulay, it is very likely to have been so.

3

The People and their Culture

"The people exhibit the usual double type of race characteristic of the Islands and Highlands – the dark-skinned, dark-haired, dark-eyed, firm, and bilious Celt; and the light-haired, fair-skinned, blue-eyed Teut, descended from the invading Norsemen – but the races are now much mingled. The men are, in general, short and well-knit, with the broad shoulders and stout arms of all fishermen. They are generally pleasant in countenance, with healthy, bronzed complexions, but shy in eye and manner, the effect of their seclusion. They are frank and outspoken when addressed, but mostly wait to be spoken to; and mild and respectful in tone. They have an intelligent expression, greater than might have been expected in the circumstances. The women, so far as I saw them, were remarkable for neither good nor bad looks, but the girls were amiable looking, and some were bright and comely. . . The people are singularly retiring, and distrustful if not suspicious of strangers, even more than the St Kildans."

Such were William Jolly's impressions, based on brief visits as a school inspector. Ada Goodrich-Freer and a female companion stayed for at least one night in 1898, and, being women and being dependant on the islanders' hospitality (and being accompanied by someone the islanders knew, Father Allan McDonald, though Goodrich-Freer did not reveal that in her account), had rather different experiences:

"They welcomed us with the utmost cordiality, and their kindness and cheerful readiness to take any trouble for our pleasure or convenience, we can never forget. So far are they from exploiting the stranger, as is the custom in St Kilda, that we had the greatest difficulty in persuading them to take payment even for labourious services, and to prevent them from robbing themselves to give us such necessaries as added greatly to our comfort."

TS Muir, who visited Mingulay very briefly in 1866, was less flattering:

"The people, like their houses, look, in great part, exceedingly poor; and that their minds are in no way better conditioned may be readily guessed, since the only instruction they have, religious or secular, is what is laboriously driven

into them at a school that was instituted. . . by some benevolent ladies connected with the Free Church".

The Mingulay people – *na Miughalaich*, as they were known – were of traditional Barra Isles stock in terms of their culture, religion (Roman Catholic), and language (Gaelic). The surnames were those common in the islands, first recorded in 1805 when the registers of the church at Craigstone, Barra, begin: MacNeil, MacPhee, Campbell, MacLean and MacDonald. MacNeil was the most common and a John MacNeil was recorded as early as 1745, as a witness in the enquiry into the Jacobite uprising in the Highlands of that year[1]. Two more names, MacKinnon and Gillies, appear in the 1830s, and another, Sinclair, in the 1860s. A number of others had only a brief presence. The written records only give names in English, and because the number of surnames and christian names was limited amongst the islanders, it is not always possible to identify individuals. There were, for example, at least six Donald MacNeils in 1896[2]. In everyday life, surnames are relatively insignificant and little used in Gaelic. People (of both sexes) are identified by their own, their father's and their grandfather's christian names or nicknames, giving a patronymic such as Iagan Dhòmhnaill Nèill, 'John of Donald of Neil', as John MacKinnon, the joiner, was known. This gives people an acute sense of genealogy, history, and community. The first-born child would be named by the father, the second by the mother, and so on.

Some of these families were known for certain characteristics. The various families of MacPhees, who claimed ultimate descent from the legendary Kenneth whom we shall meet in the next chapter, were descended from Donald (Domhnall Iain), known as Dòmhnall Mòr ('Big Donald'; many of his descendants were also big!). He married Anne MacNeil in the 1820s and they had three sons who all had large families. The MacPhees were regarded as scholarly, and two of Donald's grandsons, Neil (Niall Chaluim, whose father appears in plate 8) and Donald (Dòmhnall Dhòmhnaill or Dòmhnall Bàn, fair-haired Donald), were exceptional. Neil MacPhee (1874-1927) acted as scribe for the Vatersay raiders in 1908-9, and his eloquence, command of English, and grasp of the wider political dimensions of the affair were quite remarkable for someone whose opportunities in life had been so limited. He was equally at home writing in English, a foreign language, as he was in Gaelic, the writing of which was taught as a school subject only towards the end of his school career. He was known as 'The Scholar' in Vatersay where he lived from 1908, and where he was clerk of the grazings committee of Eorisdale and Vatersay townships. He kept a copy (or perhaps a draft) of every letter he wrote, in letterbooks, and these show that he was not afraid to challenge any politician who did not support the raiders. He also composed songs, and one of these is given in Appendix 2.

Neil's cousin, Donald MacPhee (born 1870), was interested in the traditions of the island, which he wrote down in Gaelic and English. He led prayer meetings and services in the absence of the priest, but was reprimanded by the priest for going too far for a lay person. Another cousin, Mary MacPhee (Màiri Iain Dhòmhnaill, born 1866) was a great storehouse of Mingulay traditions, folklore and songs. She passed these on to her daughter, Nan MacKinnon of Vatersay (Nan Eachainn Fhionnlaigh, 1902-82), who became famous for them and was recorded extensively by the School of Scottish Studies. Nan was born in Kentangaval, Barra, and moved to Vatersay in 1908; she never visited the island she knew so much about.

The MacKinnons came to Mingulay in the 1830s, when two, both Donald, married Mingulay women. The Donalds were first cousins from Tangusdale in Barra, where the family was known as *na Greusaichean*, the shoemakers. The men were craftsmen in wood too, and Dòmhnall Nèill Nèill (1811-88) and his son John, born 1858 (plate 4), continued this tradition in Mingulay. John's name crops up again and again in the tape recordings as the builder of a modern house and a water mill, a maker of spinning wheels, furniture, church fittings, a plough and a boat, and even as a tailor. He must have been one of the better off of the islanders. Donald was the 'constable', or landlord's representative in the community, a post which in Mingulay seems to have been informal.

Sinclair was not a local name, and originates from Duncan Sinclair (Dunnchadh Dhòmhnaill, 1805-74), a Protestant from Appin in Argyll, although his forebears were from Caithness. He was employed by MacNeil of Barra as a shepherd in Vatersay and perhaps elsewhere, an example of a Protestant outsider being employed in preference to a local Catholic. He married Mary MacNeil of Mingulay in 1833 and they had seven children. Each parent seems to have wanted the children to follow their religion, with the result that some of them were baptised by both Protestant and Catholic clergy; the children all grew up as Catholics, however. At some time between 1841 and 1845 the family moved to Berneray, where Duncan remained as a crofter. He must have had an education himself, for he was concerned about his children being educated, and seems to have taught them himself[3]. He was also interested in the antiquities of the islands; in 1866 he pointed out the 'Cross' to Muir, who said that Duncan "regarded the object as something very astounding". Three of his sons were used as authorities – almost the only native ones – on the place names of the southern islands by the Ordnance Survey in 1878. Duncan's son John moved to Mingulay with his Barra wife in about 1868, attracted, perhaps, by the school which his children could attend, as well as by the croft he took on. Another son, Andrew, also moved to Mingulay on his marriage to Catherine Campbell (Catrìona Nèill Eachainn) of Mingulay; another, Donald, lived in Pabbay for a time, and another, Peter, remained in Berneray. The story is told that one of Duncan's brothers wanted to leave money to his Berneray nephews, but when he discovered they were all Catholic, he decided instead to leave it to the town of Oban, where Sinclair Drive is named after him.

These few examples show that intermarriage among the people of the various islands was common. In the fifty-six marriages of Mingulay people which took place in Barra parish between 1855 and 1907, twenty-six of the partners were from Barra (many from Tangusdale in particular), twenty-one from Mingulay, four from Berneray, four from Pabbay and only one from outside the parish – John Finlayson, the schoolteacher. There must have been many more marriages to outsiders, held in the spouse's parish, but it was rare for such couples to settle in Mingulay, not surprisingly! In one case, the wife, Margaret Milne, was from Peterhead, where she probably met her Mingulay husband, Neil MacDonald, when he was there during the herring fishing season. Before the people of Sandray and Vatersay were evicted in 1835 and 1850 respectively, there were marriages between them and the Mingulay people too. Marriages between Catholics and Protestants were permitted, though not approved of, and the ceremony had to be a Catholic one for the Catholic to remain in the Church. Of the marriages between Mingulay people, many were inevitably between cousins, second cousins being the closest permitted if the bishop granted a dispensation. It may be noted that not one person was recorded in the censuses between 1861 and 1891 as 'blind, deaf and dumb, imbecile, idiot, lunatic.' A number of illegitimate births were recorded. In one case, around 1850, the name of the father, from Mingulay, was given, which was most unusual. He and the mother, from Barra, had two children. Such cases occasionally occurred when one party was Protestant, and social pressure made it difficult for the couple to marry. In this case, however, both were MacNeils, and so this explanation is unlikely. Marriage between people from different islands partly accounts for the movement of people between the islands, which was common right up until the desertion, other factors being eviction or moving for reasons of work or education.

Nearly all of these marriages took place in Barra, and this was normal before 1855 as well. They were performed at the Church of St Brendan at Craigstone until 1889, when the Church of Our Lady, Star of the Sea, Castlebay, opened and became the favoured place. Of the six exceptions, four took place in Mingulay (in the 1870s and 80s), the others in Pabbay and Berneray. Two marriages were held on the same day in November 1871, one in Mingulay and one in Pabbay, and this must have been arranged with the priest. It was risky for the priest to commit himself to going to the southern islands for a particular time, because of the unpredictable conditions of the sea and weather. Father Allan McDonald *"once went to Mingulay to hold service, meaning to return in the evening and to marry a young couple in Barra the next day. Over seven weeks passed before he could get back. He spent the time in religious exercises among the people, and in collecting old lore; and the marriage party spent it in dancing, singing and composing songs on the anxious bride and groom."*[4]

Families were often large, with up to ten or even more children, though not all children survived. The census returns between 1841 and 1891 show that three generations sometimes shared a house; one house had eleven inhabitants in 1861. By contrast, some households consisted of only one or two people, usually unmarried or widowed. Some families had young adults, mostly female, living with them, described as domestic servants. These may have been relatives, but it is curious, as there is no tradition of servants among the ordinary people in the islands; the Barra returns are similar in this respect. Unmarried daughters are also often described as servants, while teenage boys above school age are usually described as fishermen. Men's occupations are almost invariably given as crofter or fisherman, but there are a few exceptions such as boat carpenter, shoemaker, and sailor.

In reality the men were all crofter-fishermen, and were fowlers, builders, joiners and many other things too. Women's occupations are described simply in terms of their husbands' or fathers' occupations, even though some worked in their own right as gutters in the herring industry in later years. Women did as much of the croft work as the men, if not more, and not only when the men were away fishing. They also had their own work to do – food preparation, making cloth and clothing, and child rearing.

In terms of numbers, the earliest population figure is fifty-two in 1764,[5] and in 1794 eight families were recorded[6] (see Appendix 1). By 1841 the population had doubled to 113 in eighteen families, the highest of the smaller Barra Isles. The peak was reached in the 1880s: 150 people in thirty-four families were recorded in the 1881 census, but many men were away fishing at the time, as in previous years, so that the censuses are likely to be under-estimates. There are three higher figures: 164 people in 1883, 160 in 1888 and in 1896[7]. The population declined to 135 in thirty families in 1901, and the evacuation began in 1907.

Society was patriarchal: men held the titles to crofts, although there were cases of widows or single women being the tenants. Only men signed the petition for landing facilities and the deed of agreement for the derrick provided[8]. The men made the day-to-day decisions, and from the middle of the 19th century at least there was a nominal 'leader' in Donald MacKinnon, the constable. In the last decade or so Michael Campbell, nicknamed "Teac" (Mìcheal Nèill Eachainn, born 1867) emerges as a prominent person, and was the leader of the Mingulay contingent of the Vatersay raiders in 1907. He was a former teacher and could speak English[9]. Because of Mingulay's remoteness, the factor (estate manager) from 1840 onwards rarely visited and was not the ogre he was to the people of Barra. The most important single figure in the people's lives, however, was the priest of Barra, whose role was not only pastoral. He was involved in the provision of the landing derrick in 1901, and in the final desertion.

The community was close-knit and self-contained, and island life was communal and co-operative, as it had to be. Families would help each other with tasks such as digging the arable land in spring, peatcutting, building, and families or individuals in need would be taken care of. Fishing and waulking (fulling cloth) were communal activities done by men and women respectively. The whole community helped in the landing of the boats. In the absence of regular visits from the parish priest, the people held their own services and prayer meetings. In the long winter evenings people gathered in someone's house for the *cèilidh* – storytelling.

Being close-knit did not mean that the community had "the least possible intercourse with the outer world", as Jolly maintained. In the later 19th century, fishermen sold fish in Glasgow and in Ireland, and both men and women worked in the herring industry on the east coasts of Scotland and England. Many men worked in Glasgow in the winter, and earlier in the century had worked at the harvest in the Lowlands. And even Jolly admitted that "the food supply is supplemented from Glasgow".

The whole community would take part in special occasions such as weddings and funerals and in annual festivities. The wedding was preceded, some weeks earlier, by the *rèiteach* or betrothal ceremony. The custom in Barra early this century was for the prospective groom to go to the house of his bride-to-be to seek the approval of her father. He was accompanied by a friend or relative who might become the best man at the wedding, who would extol the virtues of his friend to the father. The father's approval was a mere formality, for preparations for the celebrations, which followed immediately, were well under way[10].

The wedding ceremony and celebrations would last at least two days, for the couple had to go to Barra for the wedding itself, and the celebrations followed their return to Mingulay. Mary Campbell attended the wedding celebrations of John Sinclair (Iagan Iain Dhunnchaidh) and Anne Campbell (Anna Dhòmhnaill Chaluim) in April 1902[11]. The party began in the afternoon of one day and continued into the next day. It was held in the bride's house, and everyone who could, attended it (at a time when the population was about 135!). Two or three tables were set end to end, and the couple were welcomed to the first table, with their closest relatives next to them. Children sat at their own table or on the floor, young ones with their mothers. The best man and another man gave out the drams of whisky, and two girls waited on the tables with food: soup, meat, kail, followed by tea. The brother of the groom made a speech praising him. They then adjourned to the house next door for those who had come from a distance to change their clothes, and in the other end of the house the dance started. They danced to the bagpipes, played by two or three pipers in turn; there was no fiddler. There would be another meal later, with tea, wine and drams.

Most weddings occurred in autumn and winter, presumably because people were busy with fishing and croft work in spring and summer. This would have made it harder to arrange a date and to invite people from other islands, because of the weather being even more unpredictable than usual at those times of year.

Catherine MacNeil described funerals in Mingulay[12]. There would be a wake the first night after the death, when people would gather in the house of the deceased, and stay up all night saying prayers and telling stories, and food was served. In Barra, the body, wrapped in a shroud, was placed in the coffin which was brought to the house in the morning, and a requiem mass was held in the church. In Mingulay, the people had to take the funeral service themselves; one of the elders would perform this function, probably in the deceased's house. The coffin, which was blackened instead of being covered with a cloth, was then taken for burial in the graveyard, and the men who carried it were given tobacco.

There were various annual festivities and associated customs. At New Year children went round the houses reciting poems, and were given barley bannocks in return[13]. At Hallowe'en children stole cabbages. The story is told of three girls who were raiding a vegetable garden one Hallowe'en night when they saw a youth they thought they knew; he ran off, and they followed. However, they thought there was something evil about the youth, for he could walk up the sides of rock with ease. The girls crossed themselves and returned home. They found the youth they thought they had seen at home, where he had been all the time. They later told the priest, who said they had done the right thing[14]. This must have happened in the 1820s or 30s. There were numerous religious holidays throughout the year, some associated with the cycle of the seasons and crops. On St Michael's Day, at the end of harvest (29 September), the people made a special dish, a chicken and barley soup[15]. No agricultural work was done on St Patrick's Day, 17 March[16]. All saints' days seem to have been school holidays.

The Gaelic culture of the Mingulay people was of the Barra tradition, a tradition expressed in stories, songs, beliefs and superstitions and customs. Some examples of these have been recorded, first from about 1860 when folklorists, finding that knowledge of cultural traditions was fast dying out on the Scottish mainland, scoured the islands. They found that the inhabitants of Barra and Mingulay had retained more of their culture than almost any others. This was due partly to remoteness, and partly to their being Catholic, as explained by Samuel Johnson who regretted that he had not got to any Catholic islands, where the old ways survived, on his tour of the Inner Hebrides in 1773. "Popery [Catholicism] is favourable to ceremony; and among ignorant nations, ceremony is the only preservative of tradition. Since protestantism was extended to the savage parts of Scotland, it has perhaps been one of the chief labours of the Ministers to abolish stated observances, because they continued the remembrance of the former religion."[17] But while some rejoiced in this survival, others condemned it as evidence of cultural 'backwardness', and their Catholicism also as 'backward'. For instance, the report on education in the Hebrides of 1865 said of Barra: "The natives are far behind, as might be supposed, in knowledge and culture."[18]

The storytelling tradition of Gaelic society is remarkably rich and varied. The clan chiefs had bards and *seanchaidhean* or *shennachies* (oral historians) who maintained clan traditions, and there was also popular lore. These stories are of various types: heroic, historical, supernatural; many of the heroic stories, such as those of Ossian, a legendary Irish warrior-poet, are variants of stories known throughout the Highlands and Islands and in continental Europe. Storytelling was the main occupation during the long winter evenings, when people would gather at someone's house for a *cèilidh*. The cèilidh was an informal and impromptu gathering, quite different from the formal occasion the term is applied to today. Its participants were mainly men, and men were the reciters; the listeners would mend the fishing nets of the householder, while the women of the house got on with carding and spinning wool. Stories often took hours, even days, to recite; Catherine MacNeil remembered her grandfather Malcolm MacLean (Cadaidh) telling a story lasting three days[19]. Hector MacLean of Islay, who took down stories for the collector John Francis Campbell, wrote of storytelling in the islands in 1860:

"In the islands of Barra, the recitation of tales during the long winter nights is still very common. The people gather in crowds to the houses of those whom they consider good reciters to listen to their stories. They appear to be fondest of those tales which describe exceedingly rapid changes of place in very short portions of time, and have evidently no respect for the unities. During the recitation of these tales, the emotions of the reciters are occasionally very strongly excited, and so also are those of the listeners, almost shedding tears at one time, and giving way to loud laughter at another. A good many of them firmly believe in all the extravagance of these stories.

They speak of the Ossianic heroes with as much feeling, sympathy, and belief in their existence and reality as the readers of the newspapers do of the exploits of the British army in the Crimea or in India; and whatever be the extravagance of the legends they recite respecting them, it is exceedingly remarkable that the same character is always ascribed to the same hero in almost every story and by almost every reciter."[20]

MacLean wrote to Campbell from Barra in 1860:

"I was over at Minglay last week and saw Roderick MacNeill who is so celebrated among the people here as a story teller. I have written several of his tales which appear to me to be remarkable for vivid and painted dialogue. He is an animated and spirited old man and though crippled to a certain extent by rheumatism his vivacity is not the least damped and the vigorous activity of his mind is not the least impaired; 74 and not a trace of dotage. He hobbles about bareheaded and barefooted and is said not to have worn shoes for the last fifty years. He tells his tales with extraordinary effect being a capital natural elocutionist using pause emphasis gesture and inflection of the voice to express passion sentiment and character fully as well as though he had been trained by some of the best actors of the day. . . He has many stories borrowed from other sources than Highland but he gives them all a Highland form."[21]

Campbell himself met and painted MacNeill (Ruairidh Dhomhnaill, died 1875) (plate 21), whom he called 'Ruairidh Reum', or 'Rory Rum the Story Man', while storm-bound in Mingulay with Alexander Carmichael in 1871[22]. Carmichael later wrote:

"MacNeill was then ninety-two years of age. He had never been ill, never had shoes on, and never had tasted tea. His chest was as round as a barrel, and measured forty-eight inches in circumference. He had been an extraordinary

'rocker' after birds, moving about on precipices of eight hundred feet sheer down to the sea, where a goat or cat might hesitate to go. So powerful was the man that wherever his fingers could get insertion in the crevices of the rock he could move his body along the face of the precipice without any other support."[23]

Carmichael said of MacNeill and two South Uist storytellers that they "expressed regret that they had not a better place in which to receive their visitors, and all thanked them for coming to see them and for taking an interest in their decried and derided old lore. And all were courteous as the courtier."[24] Campbell described him as "the best climber [i.e. fowler] in Minglay till he got past work."[25] By the time of their visit, MacNeill was living with his daughter Anne MacNeil, the midwife, whom we will meet in chapter 9[26]. As will be seen in the next chapter, he was not native to Mingulay, but had come from Greian, Barra, and before that, from Sandray, where he was living at the time of his marriage to Flora MacNash (Floraidh Iain) in 1815. The accounts of MacNeill are very valuable, as they are the only ones of a native islander.

Superstition and belief in the supernatural was as much part of life as the islanders' Christian faith. Stories of the supernatural, such as those of the *each-uisge* ('water horse'), were common in the islands. A water horse was believed to have lived in a bottomless well in a hollow near the summit of MacPhee's Hill. It had been foretold that a beautiful maiden would be strangled in a contest between man and beast at this spot. A certain Finlay, son of Iain, son of the Black Fairy was searching for sheep on MacPhee's Hill when he heard fairy music, and a beautiful fairy appeared. He fell in love with her, although he had his own sweetheart, and he would meet her in the hollow on the hill. One day the water horse came out of the well and overpowered Finlay, shouting, "Death upon thy head, O Finlay, son of man!" His former sweetheart, hearing his cries, rushed to the place, to find the water horse about to drag him into the well. She cried, "Oh God, dear Finlay, sorry I am for your plight this night!" On hearing the name of the deity, the fairy vanished, the water horse strangled the maiden, and dragged Finlay into the depths[27].

There were stories of 'second sight', or the foreseeing of future events, though Mary Campbell knew of no one with these powers in her day[28]. It was to seek evidence of this that took Goodrich-Freer to Mingulay, though she doesn't say what she found there. In one of the stories, a girl was lifting a creel of peats on her back when she saw a strange man standing before her. As they talked, she saw a boat some miles away capsize, and all its occupants were thrown into the sea. The girl cried out, but the stranger assured her that what she had seen bore no relation to the present; the grandparents of those thrown overboard were not yet born. The girl returned home and told her story, and the people named the area where the boat capsized Cuan a' Bhòcain, 'Sea of the Ghost'[29]. It was in this area that a boat from Pabbay was lost with all hands in 1897, but the story, of course, originated long before that.

Fairies and ghosts were very real to the islanders. The fairies could be good; for instance, Michael MacPhee and some others gathered the harvest of a man in difficulty, who, when he discovered this, thought the fairies must have done it[30]. But more often the fairies were to be avoided, and measures were taken to avoid them; mothers used the threat of the fairies to keep their children in order[31]. The fairies lived in knolls, and their music was often heard.

The singing of song was part of everyday life. There were love songs, songs in praise of people, songs of historical events, and songs of the supernatural. There were work songs to accompany all sorts of rhythmical and repetitive activities – spinning, weaving, waulking (fulling cloth), preparing food, milking, ploughing, rowing. Waulking songs, described in chapter 8, are thought to have originated in the 16th and 17th centuries, and have features which are unique in Western Europe. Once widespread in western Scotland, they survived in South Uist and the islands of Barra into this century. The subjects of the songs touched on every aspect of the old way of life, and served to keep memories of it alive[32]. The source of some of the songs in the 19th century was the collection of Father Angus MacDonald, priest of Barra from 1805 to 1825. When he left to become Rector of the Scots College at Rome he gave his collection to the young John Campbell (mac Nèill) of Mingulay. Angus MacDonald's successor wrote to him in 1830 saying that Campbell was "all the winter nights amusing the Mingalay people with your library of songs."[33] He could be the same person as the "Eoin, an old man on Mingulay" used as a source of Angus MacDonald's poems by Father Allan McDonald of South Uist and Eriskay[34]. As well as singing the traditional songs, people would compose songs about particular events. The song about the adventure of the Mingulay man in Appendix 3 was composed by Allan MacLean, priest at Craigstone, Barra, between 1837 and 1840[35]. Singing was not accompanied by musical instruments; the bagpipes, the only instrument mentioned, accompanied dancing.

Mingulay's most famous song – outside Barra and Vatersay that is – is *The Mingulay Boat Song*. But neither the words nor the melody originate any-where near Mingulay; it is a romantic invention of the 20th century. It was devised in 1938 by Glasgow-born Sir Hugh Roberton, who was very fond of the melody of *Creag Ghuanach*, a song from Lochaber, which celebrates a crag near Loch Treig. He needed a sea shanty, and so he adapted the music, chose the romantic name Mingulay, and composed the words. It was to be sung in F, slowly and rhythmically[36].

> Hill you ho, boys; let her go boys;
> Bring her head round, now all together.
> Hill you ho boys; let her go boys;
> Sailing home, home to Mingulay.

It is ironic that this song should be the only well-known song associated with the island, and, for many, the only reason they have heard the name Mingulay at all.

4
Chiefs, Landlords, Tenants

A ccess to land for growing food and pasturing animals was a basic
necessity in the Highlands and Islands, and land tenure and the people's
relationship with those who owned the land is a fundamental element in the
history of the area.

As we have seen, Barra and its islands were held by the MacNeils from at
least as early as 1427. One of the best known of Mingulay's legends concerns
the origin of the people and their holdings, and the role of the chief. Every
version of the story, written or oral, differs in details but the basic elements
remain the same. This is Nan MacKinnon's version, just as she herself
wrote it:

*"This happened in the fourteenth century. MacNeil of Barra, who was in
Eoligarry House at the time, was wondering why the Mingulay people weren't
coming over to visit Barra as usual. So he sent a boat over to Mingulay to
investigate, but when the boat arrived at Mingulay, there was no sign of life on
the island, so the older men who were on the boat ordered a young lad of 17 to go
ashore and find out what was wrong. The young lad was no other than the eldest
son of Kenneth MacPhee, who was only a baby in arms when his father fled from
the island of Eigg, at the time when St Francis's cave was set on fire by the
MacLeods of Skye. The boy did as he was told. He entered all the houses in the
village, but they were all dead. He was in such a state after finding them dead
that he called out at the pitch of his voice, before he got near the boat, "Oh God,
they're all dead."*

*'In that case,' one of the older men called out to him, 'if it's a plague that killed
them all you've got a stomach full of it already, so you'd better stay where you are.'*

*The boy cried and begged them to come back, but they wouldn't and he was
left on the island alone for six weeks on end. His father, Kenneth MacPhee, was
wondering what happened to his son, and walked all the way to Eoligarry to ask
the Chief what happened. But after getting there, the Chief wouldn't answer. So
MacPhee got very angry and told the Chief if he wasn't willing to tell him the
truth about his son, he would suffer for it, and threatened to pull his house down.
So the Chief had to be honest about it all, and told Kenneth MacPhee that his son
was left on the island of Mingulay in case he would carry with him any of the
plague or whatever disease that killed the Mingulay people. And the Chief told*

him to pick his own men and go to Mingulay and that the island would be theirs free of rent as long as any of his generation lived.

And Mingulay was rent free till such time as the Gordons bought Barra. So there were no survivors of the Plague, as it was called. The boy that was left there alone is said to have lived on the sheep that he killed with his pocket knife, and shellfish. And the hill that he used to climb to see if there was any sign of a boat coming is called 'MacPhee's Hill' to this day."[1]

While a number of details are at variance with known facts – the MacNeils didn't move to Eoligarry until the 18th century, and Mingulay was not rent-free before 1840! – and it is easy to dismiss the legend as no more than that, it is quite possible that elements are true. The entire population could have been wiped out by an epidemic, for epidemics were common right up until the last years; the population of St Kilda was greatly reduced in 1724 by a smallpox epidemic. According to another version related by Nan MacKinnon, the village was burnt down and rebuilt on a new site, astride the stream, where it is now; again, this is plausible, for houses visited by 'plague' have been abandoned within living memory in Barra. In 1898 an islander said the old village could have been on the site of the new chapel, for 'stones and ashes' were found while digging the foundations[2]. The link with the Eigg massacre – in which the MacLeods of Skye suffocated the MacDonalds of Eigg by lighting a fire at the mouth of the cave they were hiding in, in a revenge attack – provides an indication of date; its supposed date was about 1577. This would make the plague near enough Martin's time, about 1695, for him to have mentioned it, but he didn't, and there are no other contemporary references to it.

An early record of the story dates to 1868, when a visitor noted:

"Tradition relates that the island was colonised 314 years ago, but the whole colony was swept off by some epidemic. The next colony, acting on the advice of a medical man, paid more attention to the necessary sanitary conditions, and built their houses on the side of a small stream which flows through the township."[3]

The MacNeils were not the only overlords of the islands south of Barra. In the earliest account of Mingulay, about 1549, Sir Donald Monro, High Dean of the Isles, describes it as "Inhabit and veill manurit [cultivated], guid for fishing and corne, perteining to the Bishope of the Iyles."

There are various references to the connection of the southern islands with the Bishops, giving rise to the term 'Bishop's Isles'. The 'five isles of Barray' are listed in a rental of the bishopric of 1561[4]; Martin Martin, writing about 1695, says they were "held of the Bishop", but elsewhere he says that Barra "and the adjacent lesser islands belong in property to MacNeil. . . He holds his lands in vassalage of Sir Donald MacDonald of Slate" (Sleat, Skye). This refers to MacDonald holding the 'superiority' of MacNeil's lands, which confuses the picture still further. J L Campbell has found that, earlier in the 17th century, "the lease of the teinds of the Bishop's Isles were held by Sir Dugald Campbell of Auchinbreck. In 1617 the Bishop of the Isles complained to the Privy Council that the tack duty had not been paid by Sir Dugald since 1611. In 1623 Ruairi Mor MacLeod of Dunvegan gave a lease of these teinds to Neil Og MacNeil [of Barra]; they had been assigned to Ruairi Mor by Sir Duncan (? Dugald) Campbell of Auchinbreck."[5] This complicated and confused picture suggests that the islands were not of great importance to anybody, and exactly what their attraction was is not clear.

According to an account of 1620, the MacNeil, the 'Master or Superior' of the southern islands, received as duty "half of ther cornes, butter, cheese and all other comodities which does Incres or grow to them in the yeare. And hath ane officer or serjeant in everie Illand to uptake the samen."[6] Martin Martin says much the same, adding, "the Steward of the Lesser and Southern Islands is reckoned a great Man here, in regard to the Perquisites due to him. . . the Measure of barley paid him by each Family yearly is an Omer, as they call it, containing about two Pecks." (A peck is a variable unit of volume.)

Martin has a lot to say about the islanders' relationship with MacNeil, which, while it is not always entirely credible, is worth quoting here. "The Natives never go a fishing while Mackneil or his Steward is in the Island," he maintains, "lest seeing their plenty of Fish, he might take occasion to raise their Rents." To suggest that MacNeil would have been so deluded is absurd, especially if, as Carmichael says, he stayed for a month in Mingulay, on either side of Lammas Day (August 1st)[7].

MacNeil is portrayed as a paternalistic clan chief in the best tradition, fulfilling his obligations to his tenants and ensuring their support:

> *When a Tenant's Wife in this or the adjacent Islands dies, he then addresses himself to Mackneil of Barray representing his Loss, and at the same time desires that he would be pleas'd to recommend a Wife to him, without which he cannot manage his Affairs, nor beget Followers to Mackneil, which would prove a publick Loss to him. Upon this Representation, Mackneil finds out a suitable Match for him; and the Woman's Name being told him, immediately he goes to her, carrying with him a Bottle of strong Waters for their Entertainment at marriage, which is then consummated.*

If a tenant died, the widow likewise applied to MacNeil for a new husband, and if a cow was lost, MacNeil replaced it. MacNeil also took in elderly tenants and maintained them until their death. Of the islanders, Martin Martin says:

> *"The inhabitants are very Hospitable, and have a Custom, that when any Strangers from the Northern Islands [of Barra] resort thither, the Natives, immediately after their Landing, oblige them to eat. . . this Meal they call Bieyta'v, i.e. Ocean meat, for they presume that the sharp Air of the Ocean, which indeed surrounds them, must needs give them a good Appetite. And whatever Number of Strangers come there, or of whatsoever Quality or Sex, they are regularly lodg'd according to ancient Custom, that is, one only in a Family; by which Custom a Man cannot lodg with his own Wife, while in this Island. Mr. John Campbel, the present Minister of Harries, told me, that his Father then being Parson of Harries, and Minister of Barray. . . carry'd his Wife along with him, and resided in this Island for some time, and they dispos'd of him, his Wife and Servants in manner above mention'd: and suppose Mackneil of Barray and his Lady should go thither, he would be obliged to comply with this ancient Custom."*

Another source for these early times is Alexander Carmichael, writing in 1883. "Of old," he says, "the crofters of Miuley paid their rents in birds to MacNeil of Barra. These birds were principally the young of the shearwater, and called by the people, Fachaich, 'fatlings'. The land was divided into crofts called Clitig, Feoirlig, Leth-Pheighinn, and Pheighinn." The Pheighinn or Penny Croft paid two barrels of 'fachaich' rent, the Leth-Pheighinn or Halfpenny Croft paid one barrel, and so on. Carmichael said that the people were not allowed to collect the birds until MacNeil's arrival in mid-July. His assertion that "probably not less than twenty barrels of these birds went to MacNeil yearly" is hard to believe, as there can never have been enough holdings to pay such an amount. The system of land tenure described by Carmichael, based on 'pennylands', was Norse in origin and was common in the Hebrides. As we will see in the next chapter, the way the land was worked in these pre-crofting times was known as 'runrig'; the arable land was held in common by the tenants, and shared out at intervals according to their rental.

How long the payment of rent in kind went on in the Barra Isles is hard to say. By 1764 the Mingulay rent was £12[8], which, if there were eight holdings as there may have been thirty years later, meant an average of £1 10s per holding per year. The islanders could have paid this from the sale of feathers, cattle and fish.

In addition to rent, MacNeil could expect military service from his tenants, and it seems that Mingulay men served their chief in this way in the Jacobite uprising of 1745, which he supported. Goodrich-Freer told a story heard from an islander relating to this time:

> *"There was about this time a soldier, who had been in the '45, who belonged to Mingulay. He was great uncle's son to Ian yonder, the son of Hamish, and he had some money, and the soldiers were coming after him. His brother advised him to put away the money in case of what might happen, but he said 'they've not done with me yet'. However, he was surrounded by soldiers, and Captain Scott (whose name is execrated in these islands) ordered him to be shot, and he was robbed and murdered at the back of the house where the stackyard is.*
>
> *Captain Scott, with some more of his kind, went off in a ship to Tiree. He was only just in time, for his superior officer, on coming to Mingulay, was shocked to hear of his brutality, and said that if he had been there, it was Scott himself would have been shot."*

Another possible indicator of the violence of the time is the name of the hill above the southern edge of the village: Cnoc na Croicheadh, 'Hill of the Gallows', ie where a hanging, or perhaps more than one, took place.

There were dramatic changes in the Highlands and Islands in the 18th and 19th centuries. The old clan system crumbled during the 18th century, the death blow being the repressive measures following the defeat of the Jacobite uprising of 1745. The clan chiefs, deprived of their traditional status and role, and, increasingly, leading expensive lifestyles in London and Edinburgh, needed regular cash income. In the islands and parts of the mainland they achieved this by establishing commercial ventures such as kelping – extracting an alkaline ash from seaweed to use in the soap and glass industries – fishing and sheep farming. In order to accommodate the huge number of kelpers needed by the industry, chiefs divided up the former commonly-held arable land into individual parcels of land called crofts, their tenants being called crofters. Because the tenants had a cash income – indeed the conditions of their tenancy forced them to work for the proprietor – the crofts were deliberately kept small, insufficient to support them alone. Eventually, the clan chiefs were forced to sell up altogether, and by the end of the 18th century few were left in possession of their ancestral lands[9].

In Barra the MacNeils survived until well into the 19th century, although their traditional role was reduced to that of mere landlord. The last chief, General Roderick, who ruled from 1822 until 1836, felt no sense of compassion or responsibility to his tenants; his tyranny has been largely forgotten only because it was overshadowed by that of his successor[10]. Kelping was introduced in the 1760s [11], and the crofting system between about 1815 and 1820[12]. When the market for kelp collapsed in the 1820s due to the lifting of the duty on cheap Spanish imports, imposed during the Napoleonic wars – the population was no longer of any economic value to MacNeil, and, deprived of an income, unable to support itself. The most fertile land was cleared of its human population to make way for sheep farming, which was more profitable. Such 'clearances', as they became known, were a feature of Highland and Island history for over a century. They explain why, for example, settlement in South Harris became concentrated on the rocky and inhospitable east coast, while the green and fertile west coast is enjoyed largely by sheep and cattle. The island of Sandray was cleared of its people about 1835, and stocked with sheep. There was much hardship and emigration – much of it voluntary, as conditions were so bad, – largely to Nova Scotia, Canada. MacNeil went bankrupt in 1836[13], and the ancestral estate was sold in 1839, to a speculator who re-sold it in 1840[14].

And what of Mingulay all this time? Although isolated, and having no kelp, it was not unaffected: the population, rent and number of crofts all increased in the early decades of the century. In 1794 Mingulay had eight families (possibly eight holdings)[15] which could have meant a population approximating to the fifty-two recorded in 1764[16]; by 1841 the population had risen to 113. While there was a similar doubling in population over the same period in Barra, the increase in Mingulay was due at least in part to immigration. A number of families moved there from nearby islands in the 1820s and 30s; they had young children, and the date of their arrival can be found from the places and dates of birth of the children[17].

Roderick MacNeill, 'Rory Rum the story man' and his wife Flora (MacNash) arrived in about 1825 from Greian in Barra, from where it seems that they were violently evicted. MacNeill was recorded in 1871 as saying that "my fresh new house was burned over my head, and I burned my hands in rescuing my dear little children. Oh the suffering of the poor folk! The terrible time that was! The land was taken from us, though we were not a penny in debt, and all the lands of the townland were given to the lowland farmer beside us. . . my people were scattered, some of them in Australia, some of them in Canada."[18] Three other families came around 1835. Neil Gillies (Niall Eòghainn) from Glen, Barra, and his wife Flora (MacNeil), came from Glen. Donald MacKinnon (Dòmhnall Nèill Nèill) and his wife Flora (MacNeil) from Mingulay came from Allasdale in Barra. His cousin Donald MacKinnon from Tangusdale, Barra, and his wife Marion (MacDonald) from Mingulay, moved to Berneray from Tangusdale before settling in Mingulay. John MacNeil and his wife Mary (MacNeil) came from

Sandray in 1835-6, victims of the clearance of that island. John MacLean and his wife Anne (MacNeil) came from Berneray sometime in the 1830s. The arrival of these people within a short period perhaps indicates that the crofts were being created then, a good deal later than in Barra; certainly, the incomers were crofters by 1856[19].

Of these six families (and no doubt there were more), therefore, two were evicted from their former homes, and another victim of eviction (from somewhere in Barra) was reported in 1831. Father Neil MacDonald of Barra wrote to his predecessor, Angus MacDonald: "poor Neil Bane (ie Bàn, 'fair') is evicted to Mingulay with 18 or 20 head of cattle, he is not pleased." The next sentence reads: "It is reported that the poor creatures will at Whitsunday be sent elsewhere, except Neil Campbell, who will have no more allowed him than one cow."[20] It is reasonably clear that this refers to Mingulay, and there was a Neil Campbell there at the time, whom Angus MacDonald had known; but the threat does not seem to have been carried out. Neil Bàn was apparently settled in Mingulay officially, but whether the others were is not known. Nor is it known whether the other incomers left their old homes and arrived in their new ones by choice. In some cases, the wives were from Mingulay anyway, but whether people in general could move about the islands as they pleased at this time is not clear; as it was very common, it is probable that they could. So it is uncertain whether there was a particular reason why people moved there, or whether it was coincidence that several families settled there at the same time; as suggested above, perhaps it was at the time of the creation of crofts there. There was no immigration on any scale to Pabbay and Berneray, which presumably were not regarded as being capable of supporting more people.

While some people were attracted to Mingulay, others decided to emigrate. One of these was a Malcolm MacNeil in 1828[21]. Another was Jane Campbell, who had already left the island to marry Roderick MacNeil of Cuithir, Barra. They emigrated in 1821, and their first child, Alastair, died on the voyage to Cape Breton, Canada. In the same year Malcolm MacPhee (Calum Iain Ruairidh) also emigrated to Cape Breton[22]. No doubt others emigrated, though not in large numbers. When the first schoolteacher arrived in Mingulay in 1859 he was asked to read letters people received, and some were from Canada[23].

The increase in population was not matched by the increase in the number of holdings, now crofts; there were eleven in 1840[24], only three more than in 1794 (if there really were eight then), and it is not known whether new land was made available. This must have caused hardship, and this period can, perhaps, be identified as that during which the well-documented hardships later in the century originated. These conditions must have been made even harder to bear by the draconian increase in rent for the island, from £12 in 1764 to £82 in 1840[25], an average of nearly £7 10s per croft. Most of this increase must have been in the later years, for in 1816 few Barra rents were over £3[26].

The Barra estate, together with South Uist and Benbecula, was bought in 1840 by Colonel John Gordon of Cluny, Aberdeenshire, who, like all the new owners of former clan lands, had a purely commercial interest in his lands and tenants. He was, however, one of the worst, and when, in the years between 1846 and 1851, the failure of the potato crop due to blight caused famine in the Highlands and Islands, he became notorious for his meanness in providing relief in the form of grain (to sell, not to give away), and 'food for work' schemes. These schemes resulted in public works such as the building of roads[27]. Gordon continued, on a larger scale, his predecessors' policy of evicting destitute tenants to create sheep farms. Many of these emigrated voluntarily, but others were literally forced onto emigration vessels, creating scenes similar, as one observer reported, to slave catching on the West African coast. Most of these emigrants went to Quebec and Montreal[28].

How the Mingulay community fared during the famine years can only be imagined; in Barra, the winter of 1846-7 saw the people reduced to near-starvation, eating their seed corn, and there were outbreaks of cholera[29]. The Mingulay people may have been better off; perhaps, having a variety of food resources, such as seabirds, they were less dependent on the potato. A possible candidate for a 'food for work' scheme is the road which connects the village with the landing place, built by 1861-3[30]. A track which runs along the western slopes of MacPhee's Hill may also have been built at this time, to ease access for ponies fetching peat. One thing is certain: there were no evictions. There is no tradition of this, and the records of the families confirm it. The population, in fact, continued to rise, to 114 in 1851, and 145 in 1861. There may have been some immigration in the 1850s of people evicted from elsewhere, such as Vatersay, as there had been earlier; John MacLean and his family came from Pabbay. Mingulay was probably too inaccessible, or otherwise unsuitable, to be viable as a commercial farm, unlike Vatersay, from which all crofters were evicted at this time (1850)[31].

Despite Gordon's well known and well remembered outrages, some of his initiatives deserve credit: he reduced the small tenants' rents considerably, and increased the number of crofts (though not necessarily the total area of land for crofting). The rent for Mingulay was reduced from £82 among eleven tenants to £48.16.8 among nineteen tenants by 1845, averaging just

over £2.10s[32]. The former rents were fixed when the kelping industry in
Barra was at its height, but had never been reduced when it collapsed. This
was bad enough for tenants who had done well out of kelping, but far worse
for tenants like those in Mingulay who had no access to kelp, and could
never have paid such rents in the first place. So the reductions seem to have
been a belated recognition of a gross injustice, for which Gordon himself
was not responsible. The last Gordon proprietor, Lady Gordon Cathcart,
inherited the estate in 1878, about the time of her last visit in her fifty-four-
year 'rule' from her Berkshire home[33]. She was accused of indifference to the
plight of cottars (landless squatters) in Barra, but in reality it was her factor
(estate manager) who ran the estate.

At one time the Mingulay people had their own "benefactress of the
island", a Mrs Knight, mentioned by John Finlayson in 1888, but nothing
more is known about her[34].

Compared to the upheavals of the first half of the nineteenth century in
the Barra Isles, the second half was relatively peaceful. But in other parts of
the Hebrides evictions and other injustices continued, and it was a result
of continuing pressure by and on behalf of crofters and cottars that the
government was forced to act. A Royal Commission – the Napier
Commission as it became known – was established in 1883 to "inquire into
the condition of the crofters and cottars in the Highlands and Islands of
Scotland". The Commission took evidence at various locations, including
Barra, from crofters and cottars themselves as well as estate officials and
others; it also surveyed each croft. It was the first attempt to address
grievances which had been ignored by the establishment – because its own
members, the land-owning classes, had been largely responsible for them –
since the collapse of the old order.

The estate factor, Ranald MacDonald, gave evidence as to conditions in
Mingulay:

*"The island of Mingalay, which was said to be a pretty good island, is found to
be most unsuited to the people, if we judge by their circumstances and the amount
of their arrears. . . They are upwards of ten years' rent in arrears, and in
consequence of the difficulty of getting to the island, they have enjoyed for some
considerable period a certain amount of Home Rule, and the result in Mingalay
has certainly been most prejudicial. The man who was a sort of constable there
met me when I was last in Barra, and told me of the state of the people, and I was
really sorry that they should be left in such an island; but, in consequence of their
attachment to the locality, and the difficulty of even recommending crofters to
leave one place and go to another, they must just be left there. Latterly, however,
they found the place so unsuitable for them that I had several applications from*

57

Mingalay people to come over to prosecute the fishing here [Barra]. *I told them that those who were good fishermen would certainly get a share of what was proposed to be a sort of club farm for Castlebay. . . [if they would]. . . disencumber themselves of what really interferes with the continuous prosecution of the fishing"*[35], by which MacDonald meant having more land than would suffice to grow potatoes and graze a cow. In other words, to give up crofting and fish full-time, which the people did not want to do, and anyway, fishing was impossible in winter because of the sea conditions. In these respects the islands could not be compared to the Scottish east coast, the model with which MacDonald was comparing Barra unfavourably.

A small number of Mingulay people did, in fact, move to Glen, Barra, in or before 1883, but as cottars; and a few others took part in a scheme of the type referred to by MacDonald, in Garrygall. When asked why the people had left Mingulay, a Barra crofter said: "The island is so stormy that they could not live there; and there are too many there already."[36]

William Jolly said at this time that "When overtures were lately mooted in regard to their possible removal to superior holdings and better soil, they would not listen for a moment to such treasonable suggestions." This could be his version of MacDonald's story, adjusted somewhat to fit his romantic portrayal of the islanders as firmly rooted to their ancestral home; but perhaps he did know about some plan which is otherwise unrecorded.

At this time (1883) there were twenty crofts, paying between £1.10s and £5 rent annually; the total rent was £57.7s [37]. The population was at its peak - over 160 - as was the number of cottar families; there were fourteen more families than crofts in 1881. These cottars were usually relatives of crofters who had missed out when a croft passed to another family member. They paid no rent and, being landless, often depended more on fishing; in Mingulay, however, it is likely that there was little distinction in practice, and that they shared the work and produce of relatives' crofts.

The result of the Napier Commission was official recognition, for the first time, of the grievances and needs of the crofting population, and led to the passing of the Crofters Holdings Act of 1886. This gave crofters security of tenure of land and dwellings, and was a landmark in crofting history. A Crofters Commission was set up to assess rents and compensate tenants for improvements carried out on crofts; the lack of such reward had always been a disincentive to making improvements. The Mingulay tenants applied in 1887 to have their rents assessed, which involved detailing such work[38]. When the commissioners visited the island four years later, "they found", wrote John Finlayson, "that the people, though on oath, concealed a large part of their live stock. This criminal action might have biased the decisions, so that the reduction [in rent] on this island was only 10% whereas in all the Hebrides it reached 37%."[39] (The average reduction in Barra was 35%.) Most of the rent arrears, totalling £1064 in 1891, were cancelled; almost nothing had been paid in the previous ten years, and one tenant owed about forty years' worth. Arrears soon built up again. In 1897 Finlayson wrote: "The few who used to pay regularly don't pay now because they find that those others who don't pay are not punished or evicted. Want of discipline is a great fault in this instance."[40]

In 1906 a government investigator singled out Mingulay for condemnation for non-payment of rents and rates in the Uists and Barra, finding that neither had been paid for some years. He blamed this on the islanders' unwillingness, rather than inability, to pay, but he also said that "no attempt has been made to make a collection. . . the previous factor, by personal visits and threats of legal diligence, succeeded in recovering a fair proportion of the rents in arrear." He went on, "Mingulay has never paid a penny in rates, yet it gets the benefits from the rates of school buildings, education, poor relief and vaccination. It seems to me that an example, even at considerable cost, of a recalcitrant ratepayer in Mingulay might probably be beneficial."[41]

It is doubtful whether the Crofters Holdings Act or the rent reductions made much difference to the Mingulay people, having had security because of their isolation, and having paid rent only irregularly. But they must have made a psychological difference, and this may have led Finlayson to declare in 1889 that "the crofters are getting very assertive now. They don't scruple to argue a point with the factor. 30 years ago a wink or wince from that bugbear was enough to kill or settle a crofter."[42] The Act did nothing for the cottar population of the Highlands and Islands, as it did not allow for the creation of new crofts. This omission was addressed by the establishment in 1897 of the Congested Districts Board, which was to fund, in addition, projects such as improvements to roads and harbours. It was this agency which funded the Mingulay derrick and bought Vatersay for crofting use, as we will see.

5

A living from the Land

"Mingula is a rough hilly island, but everywhere there is good pasture, and the little cultivated patches beside the village appear to thrive better than could be supposed in a place of the kind."

So wrote Muir in 1866, capturing the two elements of the land-based economy. The traditional Hebridean economy was a largely subsistence one, based on a combination of agriculture, stockraising, and exploiting the natural resources of the sea and seashore. This was the case in Mingulay from early times until the 19th century, when the population became too high for the island to support, and the people had to supplement their income from other sources. Most of the information we have on crofting – which is how the land-based economy was organised from the early 19th century – relates to the last few decades of the community's life.

Although only a small fraction of the land area of Mingulay was suitable for cultivation, it was fertile. The best land was at the head of the bay and on the lower slopes of the main valley, as can be seen by the lush green pasture there today. The soils in these areas are based either on boulder clay or on sand blown from the beach, and would have been fertilised with seaweed and manure. There are traces of cultivation on the poor peaty soils around the south east coast as far as Skipisdale, where there is more good land.

Until the early years of the 19th century, agriculture would have been practised under a system found all over Europe and known in the Highlands and Islands as 'runrig', whereby the arable land was held in common by the tenants, who shared it out at yearly or longer intervals. The advantages of this system were that each tenant would, over a period of time, get a share of the best land, and that working and maintaining the land was a communal responsibility. But there were many disadvantages. The land, though fertilised, was over-used and crop rotation was unknown. There was little incentive for tenants to improve land which they knew they would soon lose. There were fewer field walls, so straying animals were a problem.

As described in the previous chapter, crofting was introduced to Barra by 1816, though perhaps not to Mingulay until some years later, and the arable land was enclosed with stone dykes into plots, or crofts, rented by individual crofters. Elements of the old system seem to have survived in Mingulay, however, as will be seen. The complex field system which was surveyed for the first Ordnance Survey map in 1878 and which survives to this day probably dates to this period of enclosure, or perhaps to the early 1840s when more crofts were created. Traces of earlier boundaries can be seen in places – for example, a stone dyke running in a south westerly direction from the village, through the later strips and along the northern slopes of Carnan. Each croft consisted of some arable land and some pasture for animals, distinct from the common grazing which was the whole of the rest of the island. Arable and pasture land were located in different places according to suitability of the soil, and proportions of each varied according to croft.

Detailed records of the crofts in 1891[1] show that the tenancy of the crofts had become very complicated by then, and was not a simple matter of one tenant renting one croft. Many crofts were divided into fractions – quarters, halves, even thirds – each one rented by a different tenant who might have several fractions as well as, in some cases, one or more whole crofts. This was the case in Barra too; the division of crofts originated when a crofter divided up his croft for a son or daughter, but there came a point when no more subdivision occurred, and there was presumably none after the Crofters Act of 1886. In Mingulay, the rents paid by each tenant remained the same from the middle of the 19th century (with reductions in 1891), and the number of tenants remained at nineteen or twenty[2]. Eleven crofts were recorded in 1840, nineteen in 1845[3], sixteen and a half in 1856[4], twenty in 1883[5], and twenty-three in 1891. The increase after 1883 may have been a result of the Crofters Act, but the Ordnance Survey maps show that there was no significant change in the stone dyke boundaries (though some boundaries may have been of walls of turf, as was the case in Berneray; if so these were not marked on the maps) or in the total crofting area after 1878. There was great variation in total areas of crofts: from a little over one acre (0.4 hectares) to over sixteen acres (6.5 hectares), this croft being shared by three tenants. There was equally wide variation in the amount of land rented by each tenant. Donald MacKinnon, the constable, had the largest amount of land, about fourteen acres.

The total area of the crofting land was 137 acres (55.5 hectares), almost 10% of the area of the island, of which forty-two acres were arable and sixty-five pasture. The remaining thirty acres were described as 'common machair', for arable use, in which eight tenants had shares; machair is light sandy soil such as that in the main valley, but where this common machair was is not clear. This appears to be a survival of the old runrig system, and there were similar survivals in Barra at this time. Once laid out, the croft boundaries – the stone dykes anyway – would have remained largely unchanged. On the death of a crofter, the croft normally passed to a relative. The croft land was divided from the common grazing by the head dyke, made of stone and turf, and stout enough to keep animals out. From the details of improvements to crofts submitted with applications for rent reductions in 1887[6], it seems that crofters were responsible for maintaining their own sections of head dyke. Other improvements included land drainage by means of subsoil drains, and clearance of stones.

The best arable land, on the south side of the main valley, was divided by low dykes into narrow strips, perhaps originally one per croft (see map 3 and plate 10). The soil here is sandy, and although the eastern part inland from the beach was naturally so, towards the peaty hills some sand may have been brought in, and the land cleared of stones, all at great cost of labour and time. This area only accounts for about one third of the total described as arable; the rest was scattered about the area shown on the maps as being enclosed, such as the area north of the village and beach, and around the south east coast as far as Skipisdale. Most of the latter is peaty ground, but some of it was cultivated in strips called lazy-beds (*Fiannagan*), an unfortunate term, for the labour involved in making them was immense.

The strips were made by digging parallel ditches down a slope every couple of metres (6 feet), laying the peaty material on the intervening strips, then adding manure, perhaps shell sand, and seaweed, though Mingulay never had much of that. The result, common throughout the islands where damp ground was cultivated, was best suited to potatoes; indeed, lazy-beds became widespread only after potatoes were adopted on a large scale in the Hebrides from the middle of the 18th century. The potato's tolerance of poor soil and its high yields made it the most important food crop at a time of rising population in the late 18th and early 19th centuries. It could be said that the potato was partly responsible for this rise, and the poorer people became so dependent on it that, when the crop was struck by blight in the 1840s, famine ensued (the blight, a fungus spread by the wind, rotted the tubers in the ground)[7]. The Mingulay lazy-beds almost certainly date from the 19th century when the population was at its highest.

The arable land was fertilised in spring with seaweed, carried from the shore in sacks and fish baskets[8], manure from the byres, and peat ash from the fireplaces and hearths; in later years fish guts brought from Castlebay were used as an unsatisfactory substitute for seaweed, which was not plentiful[9]. Martin Martin said, in 1695, that "the Natives. . . fasten a Cow to a Stake, and spread a quantity of Sand on the Ground, upon which the Cow's

62

Dung falls, and this they mingle together, and lay it on the arable Land." The land would have been ploughed with spades of two types found in crofting areas. The *cas-chrom*, bent spade or foot plough, had a long iron-tipped blade fitted at an angle to the shaft for extra leverage, and it was particularly suitable for stony ground and lazy-beds. The *cas-dhìreach* or straight spade was used for the lighter sandy soil, the operators working in teams. Michael MacPhee remembered seeing both types in Mingulay[10], though by the time of the desertion they were being made obsolete by spades of modern mass-produced type. According to Father Allan McDonald, the *cas-chrom* was used by men on lazy-beds, the *cas-dhìreach* used by women on the lighter soils in South Uist and Barra[11]. The women would have been obliged to do work which may have been traditionally men's, when the men were away fishing in spring and summer. Only John MacKinnon (Iagan Dhòmhnaill Nèill) used a horse-drawn plough, which he made himself, as his croft was less stony than others. He also ploughed for Michael MacNeil (an Rìgh, 'the King')[12] (plate 4).

The first seed to be planted was sprinkled with holy water, and a blessing was recited: *Dia a chur buil is buaidh is toradh is cinneachdainn air* – 'May God send result, success and fruit and growth.'[13] Crops grown in the last years were barley, rye, small- or black-oats, potatoes, cabbages, carrots, and turnips (the last for winter fodder; hay was also cut for fodder)[14]. Some of the vegetables were grown in enclosures in the village. Barley was traditionally the main crop grown, but was overtaken by the potato, as we have seen. Mingulay potatoes were said to have been the best in the Hebrides[15]. The other vegetables were probably also introduced relatively late, though Martin Martin mentions the parsnip in Mingulay, which he describes as 'lately discovered'. Crop rotation was practised in crofting times, and it is not clear whether particular crops were grown on particular soil types. Planting, generally done by women, was finished in May or June, and the crops needed only weeding, by the women, until harvest in August or September. The cereals were cut with sickles and, in later years, scythes (larger than sickles, operated with both hands). There was always a rush not to be the last with the harvest as that person was said to 'have the *cailleach*' (old woman), a belief common in the Hebrides. The cereals then had to be processed to separate the grain from the ears and husks, and ground.

In the 18th century it was common practice in the Hebrides to pull up the crop by the roots and set fire to the ears, a handful at a time, dashing them on the ground at the critical time to shake off the grain before it too burnt. This was known as *gradanadh*, 'graddaning', and was condemned by contemporary observers as being wasteful of the straw which could have been used as winter fodder or as thatch. In later years the Mingulay method was to dry the ears in a corn-drying kiln. Most of the crofters had a kiln, housed in a barn[16], of a type common throughout the Highlands and Islands. The kiln consisted of a raised platform with a large stone-lined bowl sunk into it, to the bottom of which heat was brought from a fire, via a flue. The ears, detached from their stalks, were placed on a piece of sacking suspended from a plank straddling the bowl (in other areas more commonly placed on straw or sacking *over* sticks placed across the bowl), and dried for a couple of hours. The ears were then winnowed – thrown up into the wind so that the chaff (husks) was blown away and the grain fell to the ground or floor of the barn[17]. The barns were provided with an opening in the wall opposite the door, so creating a through draught suitable for this purpose.

Apart from some barley which was eaten in grain form, the grain was ground into meal. In early times, and perhaps even into recent times, grain was ground in saddle querns as described in chapter 2. In later times the rotary quern or hand-mill was used. This consisted of a pair of flat circular stones: a fixed lower stone, and an upper stone which was rotated on an axle set in the lower stone, by means of a handle on its edge. The grain was fed into the quern through a hole in the centre of the upper stone and the resultant meal was scattered around the edge. This was women's work, often done in pairs: one feeding in grain, the other grinding. These querns were made of local stone as late as the last decades, as John MacKinnon is believed to have made one. A third method of processing barley was to pound it in a stone 'mortar', with a wooden mallet, to remove the inner husk. One of these stones survives against the outside front wall of one of the newer houses. It is a rough cube, with a conical hollow 15 centimetres (6 inches) deep, of a type found more widely[18]. The pounded grain was called *cnotag*, and was used to make a chicken dish eaten on St Michael's Day (Michaelmas, 29 September).

Around the end of the 19th century, John MacKinnon built a mill on the stream a short distance above the village. He ground grain for the whole community, presumably for a fee, or a share of the meal, as poorer people continued to use the hand mills. Mary Campbell remembered sending four sacks of barley at a time to the mill. The building of a mill at this time, so soon before the desertion, is puzzling. Towards the end of the century most of the meal consumed in Barra was imported[19] and meal prices generally were falling. But landing imported meal on Mingulay was difficult, and, although this may have been eased with the construction of the derrick promised in 1899, this could explain the building of the mill. On the other hand, Mary Campbell said that meal was imported only when the locally produced meal ran out; also that a little white (wheat) flour was imported[20]. As in so many cases, the evidence is confusing. The mill may have been built in the 1890s, as Murray said there was no mill at the time of her visit in 1888, but it is odd that it is not marked on the 1901 map. Its life was short, for it had apparently been abandoned by 1905, when a photograph (plate 9) shows its roof to be in disrepair.

An unusual feature of the mill was its design. The surviving ruins show that it was built on the vertical, rather than on the simpler horizontal principle, which was more common in the Hebrides. This is explained by its origin – it was a copy of a mill built on Berneray by a lighthouse keeper from Fife[21]. MacKinnon may even have used some of the Berneray mill's parts, for this went out of use in the same period that MacKinnon built his. The wheel revolved vertically, powered by water brought in a channel from a point on the stream above the mill. The horizontal axle of the wheel powered, through gearing, the millstones in the mill itself. Another possible use of the mill was as a kind of lathe. There is a tradition that the mill was used for wood turning, which would make sense, as MacKinnon made spinning wheels and furniture; however, water-powered lathes are not known to have existed in western Scotland.

It was common throughout the Highlands and Islands for the use of both querns and mills to be forbidden by proprietors, forcing tenants to use the proprietors' own mills, for a fee. This was the case in Barra, where the sites where querns which had been seized were dumped in the sea or in lochs are remembered. It is hard to imagine that this rule could have applied to the outlying islands; querns were in common use in Mingulay and Berneray, and Berneray had a mill, as noted – the only one, apart from the proprietor's mill at Loch an Duin in Barra, shown on maps of the Barra Isles on the maps of 1861-3 and 1878.

Agriculture was always precarious in the Highlands and Islands, because of soil conditions, long winters, and crops being vulnerable to bad weather and disease; and its products often ran out long before the next harvest. Stockraising was of equal, and in earlier times probably of greater, importance. As I F Grant has said:

> *"The nature of the physical conditions of the Highlands of Scotland make them . . . more suitable for the raising of livestock than for the cultivation of crops, or perhaps one should say. . . the Highlands are less unsuitable for the raising of animals than for the growing of grain."*[22]

The Mingulay people kept cattle, sheep, ponies, poultry, and, before the end of the 19th century, pigs. The amount of grazing stock each crofter was allowed was theoretically fixed according to the number of shares in the common grazing each had, which varied according to their rental; this entitlement was known as the 'souming', but it was exceeded in many cases[23]. There were two points of access to the common grazing from the village which would have been used by cattle and ponies in winter: a northern one between the village and the chapel, and a southern one branching from the road south of the village. The crofters also had their own plots of pasture, and some of this was on the northern, steeper, side of the main valley, where plate 9 shows cattle, and barbed wire reinforcing a stone dyke.

Cattle were the most important animals, providing food – milk, butter, cheese and other products – throughout the year (although depleted in winter when fodder was short). This was particularly important during the spring and early summer when there was the danger of the produce of the land running out. The account of 1620 notes that butter and cheese were paid as rent[24], and in 1820 butter and tallow were being sold[25], though to whom is not recorded. Tallow is animal fat; it was sold for 6d per pound (2½p per 0.45kg), and quantities of seven and eleven pounds were recorded. It was formerly used in making, for instance, candles, soap, and lubricants; Berneray, Pabbay and Sandray also produced it, and it is known to have been exported from Skye in the 17th century[26]. It was among the commodities together with fish and, in Mingulay's case, birds and feathers, which were taken to Glasgow and elsewhere and bartered for commodities such as cloth, salt, and paraffin. Cattle were also one of the few commodities that could be sold for cash, with which to pay rent and buy necessities. In 1794 the average price paid for a cow in Barra was £2.5s[27], more than enough for the year's rent; but the difficulty of shipping so large a beast as a cow from Mingulay probably meant that only calves were sold off the island. Until the 19th century the cattle in Barra were black (ie 'unimproved'); they were later bred with mainland types to produce the Highland cattle such as those seen in the 1905 photographs.

Most of the crofters had at least one cow, some many more, plus calves; eighty cattle were recorded in 1856[28] and seventy in 1883[29], but these figures exclude cottars' stock. Most of the calves were sold when a year old at the cattle fair at Eoligarry in Barra, and buyers also came to the island. The cattle spent the summers outside on the common grazing or on the croft, and were milked and tended by the women. Catherine MacNeil said that in winter, from October to April, the cattle were housed at night (in the houses until the late 19th century, later in byres); the women still milked them but, since they were busy with spinning and other domestic work, the men tended them. Cattle were not eaten in later years, but Catherine MacNeil said they were in her grandfather's time, the beef being salted for winter use and shared out among the community[30]. Autumn slaughtering of cattle was common in the Highlands and Islands before the introduction of turnips in the 18th century made it possible to feed cattle in the winter.

Sheep were kept for their wool and for winter food, and in earlier times would have been milked. They needed the least attention of all the animals: they had the run of the common grazing all the year round, only needing to be rounded up for shearing in early summer and for dipping in late summer. Dipping, introduced in the late nineteenth century, involved everyone, including the children, who sometimes missed school because of it[31]. Most crofters had sheep, latterly of the Hebridean Blackface variety; there were 144 in 1856[32], 140 in 1883[33] (crofters' stock only). They provided all the islanders' wool needs, and some were killed and salted for winter use, five at a time, Mary Campbell remembered (but not shared out as the beef was)[34]. They were not sold off the island.

Sheep were regarded as sufficiently valuable for the people to go to extraordinary trouble and risk to land them on the precipitous sea stacks of Lianamul and Arnamul to graze their summits. MacQueen mentioned this in 1794, and as late as 1887 Harvie-Brown recorded that there were about five sheep on Lianamul, and twenty on Arnamul, which the people had cleared of puffins to preserve the grazing.

Ponies of the Barra breed were kept to carry the peat down from the hills in creels, in the summer and autumn. This was their sole function: they didn't carry seaweed from the shore, or goods landed at Aneir, as Mary Campbell said that the road was too rough for them to use[35]. Most of the crofters had at least one pony, and these totalled thirty-two in 1856[36] and thirty-five in 1883[37]. The ponies were hardy enough to be out all year round, but two crofters had stables in 1887[38], so their ponies must have been stabled in winter. These would have needed feeding, and bearing in mind the scarcity of fodder (hay and turnips) in winter, and the limited amount of work they did, it is surprising that so many were kept. The St Kildans had ponies for a time, but didn't consider them worth the amount of grass they ate[39]. So it is probable that they were bred for sale, as was the case in Barra, where foals were sold at six months or a year old. Barra ponies were in demand, and mainland dealers would attend the horse fairs at Castlebay[40].

Pigs were uncommon in the Barra Isles, but two visitors encountered young ones in houses in Mingulay: Walker in about 1869 and Murray in 1888. Poultry were kept in the houses and outside: John Finlayson kept hens 'on the hill' and complained of crows getting at the eggs[41].

The land also provided peat, which had been used as fuel from prehistoric times in the Hebrides. Mingulay was fortunate in having plenty of peat, and there was no restriction on its use, though there was a north-south division of the island corresponding to the north-south division of the village. The peat on the northern promontory (the Ard) was the best. A track which runs along the steep west side of MacPhee's Hill, as already mentioned, is believed to have been made to ease access for ponies. The Mingulay peat was also cut by the Berneray crofters, who had none on their own island.

Getting peat was a family activity that went on throughout the summer. Cutting began in May[42]. The peat was cut from vertical sections into brick-shaped pieces. The turf was first cut off with a spade, and the peats may have been cut with a special spade which had a blade at right angles to the main one; this was known as a *treisgeir* in Barra, where it was in common use. The waterlogged peats were laid out on the ground for a few weeks for the water to drain off, then laid upright against each other to continue drying. When hard and dry, they were carried down to the village directly; alternatively, they were built into stacks (see plate 8), possibly on the stone 'platforms' which can be seen dotted about in boggy places. The peats could thus be collected at leisure. Those who had ponies used them to carry the peats down to the village in creels, made from rods of black willow known to the islanders as *caol dubh*; it grew on the shores of Loch Sunart on the mainland, and was collected by the fishermen when fishing there. The rods used for the creels carried by ponies and people were thinner and more pliable than those used for lobster creels. The creels had one flat side for ease of carrying on the back, and were held, when carried by people, with one hand over the shoulder, and the bottoms were flat to ease loading on the ground.

The peats were built into big stacks in the stackyards of the houses, thatched with turf. A family might get through eight or nine stacks during the year, for the domestic fire was always kept burning.

Agriculture and stockraising, the elements of crofting, were therefore an important part of the island economy, but could not have supported life on their own; fishing, which we will look at next, and fowling together complete the picture. Crofting declined in relative importance in later years as fishing developed, and the sale of produce is not mentioned after 1820.

6
Fishing and the Sea

"The male portion of the population follow the calling of fishermen, and have the reputation of being industrious, skilful, and persevering."

This was one of the statements in a petition the islanders sent to the Secretary of State for Scotland, as will be seen.

In historic times, fishing was fundamental to the economy of the Barra Isles. The abundance of fish in the surrounding seas – amongst the richest of the Scottish west coast – made fish an important food item, and, in later years, cash earner. The earliest writers mention fishing, but a detailed picture is available only for the last twenty years or so of the community's life.

Until the 17th or 18th centuries, fishing from the Barra Isles was for home consumption, but by the end of the 19th century it had become an important industry based in Castlebay, Barra. Fishing from Mingulay was always handicapped by stormy seas and the lack of a landing place or anchorage for boats, but it was profitable, and the island's last inhabitants were engaged in fishing.

By the end of the 19th century there were three types of fishing from Mingulay: line fishing, herring fishing and lobster fishing. Fishing by line, for white fish – mainly ling, also cod, skate, halibut and monkfish – in the seas around Barra Head was the longest established. The lines were fitted with hooks so many fathoms apart, and baited with fish and shellfish. They were taken to sea coiled in baskets, set on floats and buoys, and then left, to be hauled in later in the day or the next day. There were great lines, for catching ling in deep water, and small lines and hand lines for catching flatfish in shallower water. In 1900 four boats carried between them thirty great lines, each averaging 600 yards (546 metres) long; twenty-four small lines, 240 yards (218 metres) long, and twenty-four hand lines, 60 yards long. Each boat had four or five crew[1].

The white fishing season lasted from March or April until August; the Barra men started in February but the conditions for launching and landing boats made this impossible from Mingulay. This was one of the complaints set out in a petition from the islanders to the Secretary of State for Scotland, appealing for improved landing facilities, in 1896[2]. It was sent via their MP,

James Baillie, who may have written it; there were a few errors of fact in it, suggesting that the writer was not local. It was signed by sixty-five of the island's men and boys, the teacher, John Finlayson, and the Barra priest, James Chisholm; the first signatory was Michael Campbell (Teac), who may have organised it. The petition pointed out that "many of the fishermen migrate for the season to the small island of Boreray [i.e. Berneray] where the access is much easier, and there they erect temporary huts and cure their fish." There was a curer in Berneray who bought the catches, but Ealasaid Sinclair said some curing was done in Mingulay, probably for home consumption.

The method of curing in Barra was described by Walker in 1764:

"When they bring the Fish ashore, they split and wash them and cleanse off the Blood and Slime with Heather Brushes. They then lay them in small Heaps, upon the rocks with a Layer of Salt between each two Layers of Fish. They are allowed to ly in this manner for two or three Days, when they are again washed in Sea Water, and laid out on the Rocks to dry: and in good Weather, they will be sufficiently cured in eight or ten Days."

In 1870 curers from the Scottish east coast developed Castlebay as a fishing port[3], mainly for herring, the only such port in the Outer Isles south of Stornoway, Lewis. Before this, and to a lesser extent afterwards, the fishermen of the Barra Isles took their catches to Glasgow, Tobermory (Mull), and Northern Ireland for sale or barter, returning with goods unavailable in the islands. The fishermen sometimes got stranded by bad weather along the route; on one occasion a crew spent nine days on the island of Coll helping a farmer with the harvest. The trade from Barra was described by Walker in 1764, and may have begun the previous century when trade between the Hebrides and the mainland first became significant[4]. The last MacNeil of Barra, General Roderick, attempted to get a cut of the profits of this trade from Barra, which may have been written into the terms of the tenancies of the crofts. His successor, Gordon of Cluny, complained in 1846:

"My fishermen persuaded me to supply them with tackle, that they might prosecute their calling, and be thereby enabled to pay their rents, but. . . they sent off their fish clandestinely to Glasgow, from where no money was brought back, but boat loads of raw-grained whisky, to be retailed in the islands. When I could get no rent, and saw my authority so completely disregarded, I made the best bargain I could with a fishing company from Lerwick, and instructed my factor to see that they got all the fish at the agreed price, the company giving the fishers oatmeal and tobacco for their own use, and a tally for what more they might have earned. . . as credit for their rental"[5].

From 1870 onwards, the fishermen sold most of their catches to the curers at Castlebay. The curers were merchants, or employed by merchants, and the fishermen contracted to sell to a particular merchant who paid them in credit at his shop. This so-called 'truck' system was controlled by the merchants; it "keeps them in a kind of slavery with the dealers with whom they have to do", said Mrs. Murray in 1888. The fishermen continued to sell some of their catches on the mainland and in Ireland, where they presumably got better prices.

Fishing from the shore on the island's east coast with bamboo rod and line was also popular, using seagull feathers rolled up as a fly, known as *maghar*. Flounder and saithe could be caught in the bay, which John Finlayson reckoned to be the best place for flounder in Scotland[6]. Saithe (cuddies) were also caught in shallow water using a method described by Michael MacPhee:

> *"They had a thing they called* tàbh: *that was made with a big hoop of osier and two ribs in the middle crossing over each other. And on top of these ribs was a net, fixed round the rim of it. A great long handle, roughly ten feet. And they would go to the craigs with the* tàbh. *The first thing they had to do was to go and gather* soll. *They would crush the* soll. *Well, soll is what they called limpets, whelks, winkles and little things like that pounded up together. When they had pounded that up they would call it ground-bait. They would let down the* tàbh *into the sea: they would scatter the ground-bait over it, and the cuddies would come to the bait. When they saw there was enough round the bait, they would raise the* tàbh *and the poor little cuddies were in the middle of it."*[7]

This method was used in other islands. Saithe liver oil was used as fuel for the lamps in the houses; the oil of the dogfish was used for curing sick cattle[8].

The rich herring stocks around Barra were hardly exploited until Castlebay's development as a port in 1870, due to the lack of adequate boats and nets; nets were needed because of the small size of the fish, in contrast to white fish. At first the fishing was monopolised by east coast fishermen who had the larger boats and nets needed, and local men were hired as crew. By 1880 the Barra men were able to buy boats of their own, worth £400 fully equipped, with loans from merchants and the landlord, Lady Gordon Cathcart[9]. In 1894 two of these larger boats appear in the records for Mingulay (which start in 1888), and their purchase, if they were the first, suggests growing prosperity. They were between 30 and 45 feet (9 - 13.5 metres) long, half-decked and single-masted, and had a crew of five or six. They would carry up to thirty-five drift nets each, twice as many as the smaller boats previously used. The crews slept in the boats at Castlebay at night, and at weekends left them there and rowed home in smaller boats, as they were too big to beach on Mingulay. Donald MacPhee (Dòmhnall Iain Dhòmhnaill) had one of these boats in the early years of this century, called the *Snowbird*, 40 feet long[10].

As in the case of the white fish, the herring were sold to the curers at Castlebay. During the herring season, from May to July, the village became a bustling metropolis, with hundreds of boats, and dozens of curers, based there. The industry provided work for thousands of people, on shore as well as in the boats. Thus Mingulay men were employed as carters and labourers, and in making and mending the nets, as well as on the boats themselves. The women worked in teams of three gutting the herring and packing them in barrels with salt for export to Glasgow and thence to the Continent and Russia. The work was hard and the conditions unhealthy from the stinking offal; and the sleeping accommodation in wooden huts was primitive and insanitary[11]. There were eighteen gutters from Mingulay in 1904, the highest number recorded, but none after 1908.

The herring migrate in July round the north coast of Scotland and into the North Sea. The east coast boats followed them, again with hired crews: twenty Mingulay men were so employed in 1892. Roderick MacNeil and one other man from Mingulay went right down the English coast, into the winter. The women also travelled to the east coast ports and as far into England as Lowestoft, gutting and packing. Mingulay boats pursued the herring as far as the sea lochs of the mainland and Skye, and the men spent the autumn fishing there.

Fishing for lobsters around the Barra Isles also developed late in the 19th century when it became possible to transport them live to southern cities by steamer and rail. It was carried on from Mingulay in relatively shallow water, from March to October, by the older men who didn't want to follow the herring. Boys were taken out in the boats to get their sea legs before embarking on more arduous work. The lobsters were caught in creels made from black willow (*caol dubh*), which grew round the edges of the sea lochs of Skye and the mainland, and were brought back by the fishermen when fishing there. The creels were made with a solid wooden base, with the rods bent over from one side to the other. This frame was then covered with netting, and an opening was left for the lobster to climb in. 210 creels were recorded in 1895, sixty in the last season, 1912. The creels were set, baited, on the sea bottom and marked with buoys. They were checked daily and the lobsters were taken to Castlebay for sale once a week, and the men were paid in credit at the merchant's shop.

72

There were various superstitions associated with fishing. It was believed to be unlucky to go out on a Monday on the first day of the season. It was also believed to be unlucky to meet a woman on the way to the fishing. The skipper of a boat once saw a mermaid; he ordered the crew to turn back, but never told them why.

The boats used for line and lobster fishing were latterly of the type used on the Scottish east coast, as seen in plate 19. Boats between 18 and 30 feet (5.5 - 9 metres) in length were used for line fishing up to about 8 miles (13 kilometres) west of Barra Head, with a crew of five or six; the smaller ones, under 18 feet, were used closer inshore. The recorded number of boats varies; in the 1890s there were six or seven, thereafter four or five (including the two herring boats). In 1903 one of the smaller boats was called the *Provider*, owned by Donald MacPhee (Dòmhnall Bàn), another was the *St Peter*, owned by A (?Angus) MacNeil[12]. John MacLean (Barnaidh) also had a boat. These boats were presumably purchased, but John MacKinnon is said to have made a small boat, and his father also made boats; the cradle used for boat building was still visible in the village in 1949[13].

The east coast boats were a big improvement on the locally-made Barra boats which they superseded. Walker, visiting Barra in 1764, was critical of the "smallness and insufficiency of their Boats, by which they are kept idle during a great part of the fishing Season, as they dare not venture abroad in them but when the Weather is very moderate; and they are likewise extremely defective in Lines and fishing Tackle."

MacCulloch described the boats in 1816 as

"very peculiar... the boatmen are their own builders, purchasing the timber from the northern traders. They are extremely sharp, both fore and aft. They have no floor, but rise with an almost flat straight side .. . from their lightness, they are almost as buoyant in a bad sea as a Norway skiff."

In 1819 a list was made of boats in the islands which were to be treated with 'carbon oil' or pitch. One of these was the *Kelly*, owned (?) by Hector Campbell of Mingulay[14].

Shellfish were not eaten in recent times, according to Catherine MacNeil, but sand-eels were eaten, and used as bait for lythe. Michael MacPhee described how he caught sand-eels:

"It was by night you caught them, at night time at low water with a spring tide . . . we had a sickle called a corran shìolag. . . *we would go to the beach and start making furrows with these sickles, sinking them about six inches into the sand, until we found a sand-eel. When you found one, you set your foot against the sickle and pulled it up very gradually to your foot and held it there. Then you*

put down your hand into the sand and caught it and put it in the bucket. . . some of them were about thirteen inches long. . . They were good to eat. . ."[15]

Fishing was always a hazardous occupation in seas with treacherous currents between the islands, and with unpredictable weather. In 1858 a boat and its crew of five (not, apparently, from Mingulay) was lost off Mingulay[16], and in 1897 a boat from Pabbay with five crew – most of the island's men – was lost in a storm south of Barra Head. This disaster is said to have led to a loss of confidence among the Mingulay people, and to have been a reason for the decision to evacuate. It was suggested in about 1866 that a breakwater be thrown across the west end of the sound between Mingulay and Berneray to create a harbour of refuge for fishermen[17]. This might have seemed a good idea on the map, but is quite absurd to anyone familiar with the islands and the raging seas. (It is a fascinating idea, though: had it been possible, Mingulay's southern valley, Skipisdale, where there is a landing place, might have been resettled and could have developed into a curing station.) Mingulay's biggest drawback was the lack of a landing place and anchorage, as will be seen. These difficulties were behind the applications by some of the fishermen for crofts in Barra in 1883.

Despite these drawbacks, fishing was profitable, and Mingulay was used as a base even after the last inhabitants had left. Although the majority of the people had left in 1907-8, and most of the rest in 1910, the records show that twelve fishermen and boys were working from Mingulay in 1911 (as in the previous two years), and ten in 1912[18]. They must have lived there only during the fishing season, for only six of the eleven people living in Mingulay in April 1911 were men. 1912 was the last year that fishermen were based there.

The economic and social impact of the fishing industry, particularly the herring industry, on Mingulay must have been considerable. For the first time many islanders – between thirty and fifty in the twenty years up to 1907 – were earning cash. Hired crewmen were paid a proportion of the boat's earnings: in a good year they could make £20-£30; in a bad year – which could mean glut as well as scarcity – almost nothing. The women could earn £4-£8[19]. The cash was used to buy foodstuffs, cloth, kitchen ware, tobacco and other commodities which in earlier times would have been regarded as luxuries. Many people were now absent from the island for long periods; those men who spent the winters working in Glasgow can hardly have been home at all. Inevitably, extra cash and less time meant that crofting and fowling, which coincided with the fishing season, declined. Travelling to other parts of Britain would have opened the islanders' eyes to how other people lived, and led to dissatisfaction with their own lot. It was ironic that while fishing brought prosperity to the community, it contributed to its decline and death.

With the increasing dependence on fishing, and on the outside world in general, the lack of a landing place or anchorage became more serious. The fishermen were, said the 1896 petition, "very much handicapped by having at the end of the day's fishing to drag up their boats high and dry on the rock [beach was meant] without any mechanical appliances, and in launching them again the crews are compelled to wade breast high, the launching being repeated on their return." Mingulay Bay is too broad an indentation to provide much shelter from the swell and wind, especially if from the south or east. There are two points in the bay where people and goods could be landed on the rocks: one on the south, Aneir (probably meaning 'landing place' in Gaelic; it was not one particular spot but comprised an outer one, Aneir a Muigh, and an inner one, Aneir a Stigh); and one on the north. The state of the sea and wind determine which can be used, but a calm sea is needed for both. Boats themselves had to be landed on, and launched from, the sandy beach, which, being exposed and steeply shelving, was often difficult, dangerous, or impossible. This, and the need to haul them up the beach, limited the size of boat that could be kept at Mingulay, hence the herring boats were left at Castlebay. To land a sailing boat, the men had to furl the sail, collapse the mast, move the ballast (beach boulders) to the stern or jettison it, and ride the boat up the beach with a wave[20]. The whole community helped haul it up the beach, on planks. During Robert Adam's stay in 1905 a sudden storm blew up and the islanders – mainly women and old men, the younger men being away fishing – rushed to haul a boat out of reach of the sea. Adam realised that the people could not go on much longer like this[21].

When the boats were in regular use they were left on the beach beyond the high water mark, but during the winter the smaller ones were dragged up a grassy slope above the rocks in the middle of the bay and secured in shelters from the gales[22]. These shelters (known in Barra as *bara*, 'barrow'), are boat-shaped enclosures of stone slabs embedded upright in the turf, and ropes were passed between opposing stones over the upturned boats. The three surviving shelters could accommodate boats up to about 6 metres (18 feet) long. They were used in recent times although they could be much older; such structures are well known in the former Norse areas of Scotland such as Orkney and Shetland, where they are known as 'noosts', but that does not imply a Norse origin.

In adverse conditions, which could last for weeks or even months at a time in winter, it was impossible to launch a boat or land an incoming one, leaving the islanders completely cut off. It was common for visitors to be marooned there, and, conversely, for islanders to be stranded in Barra waiting to come home. As related in chapter 3, Father Allan McDonald was once stranded on the island for seven weeks. The story is told of two men who went to Barra together, one to return after a short stay, the other to go to New York (!). The latter returned after three months to find his friend still waiting to get home to Mingulay. On another occasion conditions in the bay forced the islanders to resort to the desperate measure of carrying a boat over the island to Bay Sletta on the west coast, where it is possible to launch a boat, to get a doctor from Barra. The sea, once a highway, had become a barrier.

It is not surprising that there was not much of a postal service to Mingulay. It was said in 1904 that the post went monthly[23], and a James Stewart who lived in Mingulay in the last years was a postman[24]. The relief boat for Barra Head Lighthouse, which sailed down once a week in summer, once a fortnight in winter, must have been made use of by the islanders, although in bad conditions it would have been impossible for the boat to land anyone or take anyone off. In the later 19th century the fishermen would have gone to Castlebay regularly in spring and summer with white fish and lobsters, and would have brought supplies, but otherwise a boat would go over only every six to eight weeks[25].

In 1897 Dr. Ogilvie Grant, Medical Officer for Inverness-shire, said it was easier to get to America than to Mingulay. He went on to say of the inhabitants of Mingulay (and Eriskay):

"They are all hardy fishermen, well known for their skill. They have not been clamouring claimants for doles, and they badly require landing places to carry on their occupation. I am not likely to forget the difficulties I experienced when landing at Mingalay, or, when leaving it, I found that I could not get back to Castlebay, and had to take refuge from the storm in the Island of Bernera, and be for days the guest of the kindly lighthouse keepers; but my difficulties were trifling compared with the difficulties experienced by the people in landing their provisions. I was informed that it was no unusual occurrence for them to have to throw their bags of meal into the sea and drag them ashore by means of a rope. This, no doubt, is a state of matters that will soon come to an end owing to the institution of the Congested Districts Board."[26]

This prophecy was to be fulfilled little more than a decade later, though in a manner not, perhaps, anticipated by the doctor – the desertion of Mingulay and the Board's purchase of Vatersay. In the immediate term, however, an attempt was made to alleviate the problem. Although a government commission had been informed of the situation in 1890[27], nothing had been done, hence the islanders' petition, six years later. It called for the government's assistance in making a "boatslip with a boat-hauling convenience," for the building of which they offered free labour, and it concluded with the hope that "your lordship will lend a favourable ear to the cry of a sorely-distressed community". Again nothing happened, but the following year, 1897, the Congested Districts Board was created, with a remit which included the provision of piers, roads, etc, and an appeal by Barra Parish Council got things going[28].

The Board's engineer established that building a boatslip as requested, or a pier, was not feasible, the bay being too exposed and its floor too sandy. He supported an islander's suggestion of a crane or derrick which would hoist boats right out of the water, of a type which the Board had installed elsewhere. But, somehow, this ambitious concept was downgraded to one of merely hoisting loads, cattle and passengers into and out of boats. This rendered the whole project much less useful, but – and this must explain the change – it would be considerably easier and cheaper.

Arguments over the upkeep of the derrick once completed delayed the project still further, and it was not until March 1901 that the go-ahead for its construction was given. It was eventually agreed that the islanders would be given the derrick as a gift, and that they, with Michael Campbell (Teac) in charge, would be responsible for its upkeep. The men were to provide free labour, although, as Father James Chisholm of Castlebay, who had agreed to act as mediator between the Board and the islanders, pointed out, they were "not accustomed to such work".

The derrick was erected on a platform, blasted out of the rock and completed with concrete, a short distance east of the landing place at Aneir (see plate 20). Concrete steps linked the platform to the road, which was extended from Aneir, and to a small corrugated iron store. The derrick, made of wood and iron, was supplied with boxes for goods, canvas slings for cattle (though how cattle were meant to get to the platform is not clear), and a basket for people. On one occasion, it is said, some boys gave an old man who was being plucked from a boat more swings than he had bargained for. An iron ladder was supplied, presumably to fix to the platform edge for people to climb up from arriving boats in order to operate the derrick, and to climb down into departing boats, but it was never fixed. The engineer reported that the sea had been too rough to do it, but he had arranged that John MacKinnon would fix it, under the supervision of John Finlayson. The ladder can be seen on the road on the right of the photograph, and today reposes further along the road.

The derrick was completed in September 1901. The engineer reported that "the principal part of the inhabitants were present and expressed in loud terms their appreciation of the crane and surroundings as a great convenience to the island and its inhabitants." But within a few months there were problems: Father Chisholm informed the Board that the concrete surface of the platform was disintegrating, exposing the shingle packing underneath. The Board claimed this was due to the local sand being unsuitable, but an islander blamed poor workmanship. The Board were irritated, and nothing was done, as the photograph seems to show.

Shoddy workmanship was not the only defect of the derrick. In 1903 a Board official reported an islander as saying that "the crane is in the wrong place and is very little used and, generally, he was rather strong in his language about the way things had been done". A glance at plate 20 shows what the islander meant about the derrick's positioning: it was too far from the sea for a boat to approach safely, except in very calm conditions. None of the tape recordings mentions the derrick. Robert Adam was not landed by it; and the fact that the ladder was never fixed is further evidence of its lack of use. An official of the Board wrote in 1908 that "great difficulty is experienced in shipping stock, and a like difficulty in landing supplies"[29], an admission, probably inadvertent, of the failure of his own agency's project.

So while the derrick may have had its uses, the biggest problem – what to do with boats – remain unresolved. With better planning and more resources, it may be that a more substantial and useful structure could have been installed, but it is doubtful whether the winching of boats would really have worked in such an exposed situation. A winch for hauling boats up the beach, as originally requested, might have been more useful; the Board installed these in various places for only £25[30]. Ideal solutions, such as excavating a harbour and building a breakwater or pier, would have been very costly for such a small community. Lady Gordon Cathcart would not anyway have invested in a community which did not pay rent, and she, and the Congested Districts Board, may in any case have foreseen its eventual demise.

7

Catching the 'Feathered Tribes'

"Immense flocks of sea fowl frequent these rocks in spring, and, like the inhabitants of St Kilda, the people here add considerably to their means of living by their annual attacks upon the feathered tribes."

So wrote Mr Ross, a visitor to the school in 1868[1].

Seabirds and their eggs must have made Mingulay attractive to settlement from early times. Unlike fish, birds and their eggs could be taken without any special equipment, although latterly instruments were used. The birds were taken not only for food, but were used to pay rent, and their feathers were sold for cash. Fowling declined in the late 19th century, but continued until the desertion on a big enough scale for birds to remain an important item in the diet.

Martin Martin, writing about 1695, said that the people "take great Numbers of Sea-Fowls from the Rocks, and salt them with the Ashes of burnt Sea-ware in Cows Hides, which preserves them from Putrefaction." He went on to describe fowling on the stack of Lianamul:

"The Rock Linmull. . . is almost inaccessible, except in one Place, and that is by climbing, which is very difficult. This rock abounds with Sea-Fowls that build and hatch here in Summer; such as the Guillemot, Coulter-neb [puffin] Puffin, etc. The chief Climber is commonly call'd Gingich, and this Name imports a big Man having Strength and Courage proportionable. When they approach the Rock with the Boat, Mr Gingich jumps out first upon a Stone on the Rock-side, and then, by the assistance of a Rope of Horse-hair, he draws his Fellows out of the Boat upon this high Rock, and draws the rest up after him with the Rope, till they all arrive at the Top, where they purchase a considerable Quantity of Fowls and Eggs. Upon their return to the Boat, this Gingich runs a great hazard by jumping first into the Boat again, where the violent Sea continually rages; having but a few Fowls more than his Fellows, besides a greater esteem to compensate his Courage."

A century later, in 1794, MacQueen wrote of Mingulay and Berneray:

"The inhabitants catch some of them [the birds] in the rocks, which they think very good eating, and from which they get very fine feathers, these feathers they sell for 6d the lb in the country [Barra] as they never had them in such quantities as to send them to a public market."

In 1820, the feathers were fetching 9d per pound (4p per 452g). Several men were recorded as selling large quantities at a time (to whom is not recorded), though none so large as the 109 pounds (49 kilos) sold in Greenock by a man from Pabbay, who had probably got them from Mingulay[2].

The sale of feathers, for beds, was mentioned again in 1840[3]. There is a tradition that at about this time Mingulay boats sailed to the Isle of Arran in the Clyde with feathers and salted birds, and returned with salt, flour, paraffin and drugget cloth (a mixture of linen or cotton, and wool). Arran did produce salt and cloth at this time, so the tradition may be true.

Birds, mainly young shearwaters (*fachaich*), were also used to pay rent to MacNeil at one time, as we saw in chapter 4; and according to John Finlayson, "Fulmars were so good that MacNeil the chief had to be supplied with some."[4] In more recent times gulls' feathers were rolled into flies for use in fishing from the shore with rods. Parts of the birds may have been put to other uses; in other fowling islands, for instance, bones were made into pipe stems, stomachs into tobacco pouches, beaks into thatching pegs, and the skins of necks were made into footwear[5].

Only in later years do we have details of species caught and catching methods, from the tape recordings, and from the naturalists Harvie-Brown (who quoted information from John Finlayson), Elwes, and Walker. The main species caught were guillemots, razorbills, puffins and cormorants. Some of the Gaelic words for the birds were specific to Mingulay, or variants of terms in wider use, such as the general word for birds, *peataichean*; they are given here in their singular form[6].

Guillemots (*langaidh*) and razorbills (*duibheineach*) are cliff dwellers. They take up residence on ledges in May and lay a single egg on the bare rock. Finlayson wrote:

"The female guillemot often allows itself to be caught by the hand, but that only at the time when the young one is nearly being hatched. The guillemots and razorbills are so blinded by their affection for their young that, during the week before and the week after the little ones are hatched, they allow themselves to be captured in hundreds. The way of capturing them practised in Mingulay is by a lasso [noose] of horsehair stuck to the top of fishing rods[7]. There is no use trying to lasso guillemots on a shelf visited before. In this case the bird is educated and

will not allow itself to be taken. I let down a climber years ago to a shelf never visited, and he captured all the birds with his hand without loop or lasso."[8]

The noose was known as the *dul gaoisne* ('hair loop'), and the method, known as *ribeadh* ('snaring'), was used in many fowling islands (see plate 13). Puffins (*peata-ruadh* or *bùigire*[9]) sitting on ledges could also be taken in this way; they could also be dragged out of the burrows on the cliff tops or ledges in which they nest, by hand[10]. Young kittiwakes (*seagaire*, old ones *crahoileag*), also cliff dwellers, were regarded as a 'favourite dish', according to Elwes in 1868[11].

Another method of catching birds was used when a strong wind blew against the cliff face and was forced upwards, particularly up gullies in the cliff. Birds trying to settle on ledges were whirled about, in such a way that a man, sitting or lying on the cliff top with a wooden pole about five metres (15 feet) in length, could strike the birds from below. A blow on the body would not harm the birds, but a hit on the head would stun them; they were thrown back to the cliff top where another man wrung their necks. This method was known as *stearradh*[12], and was also used by fowlers from Lewis on the Shiant Islands in the Minch[13], and on Ailsa Craig in the Clyde[14].

Eggs could be taken in the knowledge that the birds would lay again. Finlayson continued: "all the species lay several times again if their eggs are lost. I have seen the same shelf robbed three times of its eggs. The time allowed between each lifting may be fifteen or sixteen days."[15] This would have had the advantage of prolonging the breeding, and catching, season, which ended with the departure of the majority of the birds in July. Sgeir nan Uibhein (correctly Uibhean, now normally spelt Uighean), Skerry of the Eggs, a low islet off the north east coast of Mingulay, was presumably a source of eggs.

Although Martin and Finlayson mentioned the use of ropes, in general the fowlers "do not seem to have used ropes as they do in St Kilda, but to have clambered among the rocks like goats", as Alexander Carmichael wrote in 1883. His description of how one of the fowlers, Roderick MacNeill, did this has been quoted in chapter 3. It is not perhaps surprising that "this desperate robbery", as the Rev Alexander Nicolson described it in 1840, "has cost some of the natives their lives." Accidents were rare, however; only one death in the last fifty years is known to have occurred while fowling, that of Finlay MacNeil, aged eight, in 1878. He was collecting eggs on the low cliffs at the north east corner of the bay, and fell into the sea. The accident was witnessed by members of his family, including his sister, who never got over the shock. Another reason for descending the cliffs was to retrieve sheep which had wandered along grassy ledges, and would end up in the sea if not rescued.

Catching cormorants (*sgarbh*, young ones *odhragan*) required different tactics. These birds occupy the lower levels of the cliffs and coastal rocks, and are more accessible by boat. Michael MacPhee described how the men would go out at night with oars covered with cloth to quieten them. Once the sentinel cormorant had been dispatched with a twist of the neck, the rest could be killed while asleep[16].

We have two figures of numbers of birds that could be taken: 600 in six to eight hours using the pole method in Berneray in 1868[17]; and 2,000 guillemots in a day's raid on Lianamul by men from Pabbay in 1887[18]. There are no detailed figures such as exist for St Kilda, where over 100,000 birds were taken annually, and tens of thousands of eggs weekly during the season[19].

Some of the birds were cooked and eaten fresh; Walker described how they were "plucked, boiled, and the flesh gnawed off by the men, but is not much relished by us, as it is tough, red and fishy-tasted: the eggs when fresh are delicious, those of the razorbill and guillemot having a rich orange yolk, and the white of a semi-transparent opal colour." Most of the birds were preserved for use in the autumn and winter. Young cormorants were singed and salted, and dried "as hard as a tangle", said Mary Campbell[20]. Other birds were plucked and hung to dry, presumably in the houses and barns. In earlier times they may have been dried in small stone huts, the remains of which can be seen in places near the cliffs, perhaps comparable to the 'cleits' of St Kilda. Roderick MacNeil reckoned dried puffin to be 'as good as smoked ham'[21]. Another opinion was that young puffins were especially tasty, also old ones if boiled for an hour[22]. Puffins were not always so good; in 1899 John Finlayson wrote: "This season the young puffins were in such a lean condition as to be unfit for the kitchen. One year all birds were inedible – too dry, even dogs wouldn't eat them. This is due to scarcity of spawn on the fishing grounds."[23] The eggs were preserved in barrels, in salt.

Fowling declined in the last decades. Carmichael said in 1883 that "the people do not now kill many birds, being too much occupied otherwise"; by this he must have meant fishing, which coincided with the fowling season. Harvie-Brown said in 1887 that an old man, Rory Campbell, still occasionally went down the cliffs, but was the only one who did[24]. Ten years later John Finlayson wrote: "Up to ten or twelve years ago, people here made a trade of getting birds and eggs from the rocks. There are no professional climbers now. Long since I dropped it."[25] The islanders are unlikely to have known that after 1869 most of their fowling operations were made illegal by the passing of the Preservation of Seabirds Act, which outlawed the killing of all seabirds except young unfledged ones, between April and August. The

Act was aimed at bird hunters in search of feathers for ladies' hats, but Mingulay's remoteness preserved it from the raids suffered by other bird stations. No voice was raised on behalf of the islanders to exempt them, as happened in the case of the St Kildans[26]. Fowling did continue, however, as the islanders recorded on tape talk about it in detail. Alexander MacKinnon is remembered as being a fowler in the last years. Robert Adam and his companions performed a useful service on their visit in June 1905 by catching birds (see plate 13) at a time when most of the men were away fishing[27].

8

The Village:
Walls and Work

The village was the centre of island life. It lies at the head of the beach of Mingulay Bay, astride the main stream running into the bay. The grey stone walls remain, like the bleached skeleton of a long-dead animal, and, with the help of early maps and photographs, the tape recordings, and visitors' accounts, it is possible to flesh out the bare bones and to say a good deal about it and the domestic work of its inhabitants.

The village occupies an ideal settlement site: the ground is firm and dry, being gently sloping boulder clay, the southern part at least is relatively sheltered from the south westerly winds, and it is close to water and a landing place for boats. The site had probably been used for hundreds, if not thousands, of years, though not necessarily continuously. Compared to most Outer Hebridean settlements, in which houses were, and are, scattered on crofts or wherever the land permitted a house to be built, the village is large and exceptionally compact on account of the limited space available. Enclosed on most of its landward sides by rising ground, and clinging to the edge of the beach, it is easily imagined as the "picturesque huddle of rude dusky huts" seen by Muir in 1866. Like the village on Hirta, St Kilda, it is tremendously evocative of a way of life gone for ever; but unlike the latter, planned and built under outside influence, it is a truly Hebridean township.

The village in its present, final form consists of about fifty buildings, associated walled enclosures, the graveyard and the chapel; along the road to the landing place southwards there are about ten more buildings and the school (see map 3)[1]. The present layout of buildings presumably originates from the population expansion of the first half of the 19th century, and was established by the time of the first Ordnance Survey of 1878, after which there were only minor changes. It evolved haphazardly, with little regularity or consistency in the position of buildings, though the majority are aligned down-slope. The isolated buildings south of the main village may have been built at a relatively late date, when the best sites had been taken. Those west of the school appear on a map of 1861-3[2], but the house next to the road doesn't; John Sinclair (Iain Dhunnchaidh) is known to have occupied this house (plate 15) in the last years, and he probably built it himself when he moved to Mingulay from Berneray in about 1868.

The enclosures around the houses served as stackyards for the peat stacks, and as vegetable gardens, and some of them were built of peculiarly massive upright blocks. The early photographs show a network of paths, now disappeared; the road to the landing place, however, is still very much in evidence. The road is surprisingly wide and well built for its comparatively short length, and for the small population it served; and the terrain it crosses is not particularly rough. It seems unlikely that the islanders would have built it on their own initiative, and it is possible that, as suggested in chapter 4, it was built during the famines of the 1840s when many public works were undertaken in the islands.

With the exception of two gabled houses of 'modern' type, the domestic buildings – houses, byres for cattle, and barns – are variants of the traditional Barra Isles type. Contemporary observers compared the Barra type unfavourably with houses in the islands to the north, with such phrases as "a disgrace to a civilised country", "the worst in the Hebrides", and "of a most miserable description."[3] But the houses were very practical and well adapted to the conditions. The thick drystone walls were built up to the same level all round, the doors being about 1.6 metres (5½ feet), or less, high, and topped with lintels. The walls had an outer and inner face of stone, with a core of smaller stones and earth. The outer face leant inwards and the corners were rounded to withstand the weight of the roof. The rounded (hip-ended) thatched roof was supported by driftwood rafters which rested on the inner face of the wall, leaving a terrace running round the wall top and ensuring that there was no overhanging roofing for the wind to play havoc with. It also meant that the rain drained into the wall, leading to permanent dampness. The rafters and smaller timbers were covered first with a layer of overlapping turfs, then a heavy thatch of straw, or marram grass from Pabbay (as in plate 12); the thatch was then secured with ropes of marram (superseded by hemp in later years), which were weighted with stones. The thatch was renewed every year[4], and the old thatch and turf, its underside covered with soot, may, as in Barra, have been spread on the agricultural land as fertiliser. A small building in plate 12 is roofed only with turfs, or peats, like tiles.

This form of construction was determined by available materials and the climate. The hip-ended roof was the only option in an area where wood was scarce and inadequate for a gabled, high-pitched and more lightly thatched roof, which would anyway have been unsuitable for the conditions. The crudeness of the construction meant that buildings could be modified, rebuilt, or added to easily. To add a barn, byre or house to an existing one, only three walls had to be built, the fourth being there already. Most buildings are in fact in groups, varying from two – such as house and byre – to ten, such groupings often being family units. Many cases of elderly parents living in houses built onto their adult sons' or daughters' houses are known. The form of construction also means that it is very hard to date buildings (with the exception of the improved houses described below), except to say that one might be older or younger than its neighbour. It is unlikely that any of them are of great age. Comparison of the earliest maps and photographs with the later ones and with the present remains shows that many buildings were modified or rebuilt, or new ones built on new sites in the last twenty years; there were some changes even after 1901. The last inhabitants of most of the houses are known[5]. Occupancy of buildings seems to have changed surprisingly often, and families were not necessarily fixed to particular buildings or their sites.

Until the later 19th century the houses would have had no windows or built-in fireplaces and chimneys; this type of house in the Outer Hebrides is often called 'black house', though this term was not local, and there is no one definition of it[6]. Windows appeared, if the censuses are reliable, between 1861 and 1871, when most of the twenty-five houses had two windows – to be precise, two rooms with windows – where there had been none ten years earlier (or perhaps the definition of the term had changed). Windows were described by Jolly in 1881 as "small openings, often without glass", which must have been in the wall-top or at the base of the thatch. Later, some houses were provided with more substantial glazed windows, like those seen in the 1905 photographs (one can be seen in the 1887 photograph, plate 1); thirteen out of twenty-seven thatched houses in 1901 can be seen to have been improved in this way. Fireplaces – with stone or wooden lintels – and chimneys were also a late development. As late as 1883, according to Jolly, the fire was "in the middle of the clay floor, and there is the usual hole in the roof for the smoke, which as frequently escapes by the door or oozes through the thatch, and gives the dwelling, as MacCulloch truthfully puts it, the look of 'a melon bed in heat'."

Some chimney stacks can be seen in the 1887 photograph, and by the time of the desertion twenty-two houses had fireplaces and chimneys in one end wall, sometimes in both end walls. There were other improvements in later years, such as the use of dressed stone, and mortar. These were probably inspired by the building of the new schoolroom in 1881, and later the schoolhouse and the chapel, the stone for all of which was quarried using drills and wedges. The front of one of the houses west of the school was rebuilt using massive quarried blocks.

Two accounts of the interior of these 'unimproved' houses are known. Theodore Walker and his brother stayed overnight in what he called the "chief hut" in 1869. He noted the "peat fire on the earth floor, filling the hut with blue eye-smarting reek, through the gloom of which one sees the grandfather and grandmother crooning over the fire, two calves, a fat young grunter and sundry fowls, two cats and a dog." They ate "haddock, with sea-oat cake and sour milk", and slept on beds of straw and heather.

Mrs Murray provided a more detailed account, in the autumn of 1888. *"An old woman at her time-blackened spinning wheel, sitting on a lump of the naked rock beside the peat fire, which is burning brightly without smoke, in the middle of the clay floor; two children healthy and brown beside her, playing with a kitten; a hen mother and some chickens busy foraging for themselves over the clay floor; a small pig scratching his back under the bench of driftwood supported by turf on which we were sitting. A little table, but no dresser; one small chair, one three-legged pot, and a kettle, not to omit the never-failing friend of every old wife in the kingdom, the brown teapot standing by the fire. What more? A quern or hand-mill on the table, in daily use still in an island where there is no population to support a miller, and where the meal is still prepared by two women grinding it painfully in this primitive way. Three stout kists [wooden chests], the property of the girls of the family who had just returned from the fishing at Peterhead. This is about all. Most of the houses have separate byres, which are cleaned out twice a year, but this dwelling was one in which the cows were tied up along with the family in the same end of the cottage in four stalls between the fire and the door. During our visit the cows were in the fields, but there was plenty of evidence to show where they lodged at night."*

In time, we can assume that most, if not all, cattle were driven out of the houses into their own winter quarters, and there is no mention of cattle in houses in the last years. This was one of the requirements of various public health acts which were being enforced, with some success, in Barra in the 1890s[7]. Byres were usually tacked onto houses, often, as Mrs. Murray observed with distaste, "above the level of the dwelling, so that the whole drainage had to soak through it into the house below." Perhaps fifteen to twenty of the smallest buildings in the village can be identified as byres. The byres or cow ends of the houses, were used as toilets, and the beach was also used. Intermediate-sized buildings would have been barns, which most of the twenty crofters had; a few can be identified by the hole in the wall opposite the door which was opened to create a through-draught when grain was being winnowed. There were also a few stables and workshops[8]. Other buildings which were not obviously houses, having none of the 'improvements', were dwellings even in the last years, and even more of these must have been lived in earlier; thirty-four houses were recorded in the 1881 census.

Two houses were built in 'modern' style towards the end of the community's life. One, in the village below the chapel, was built by John MacKinnon, the joiner, sometime after the 1887 photograph was taken and probably before 1898[9]. It was well built of dressed stone and mortar, and was gabled, having had a felt roof. The other, near the school, was even more modern in that only the gable ends were built of stone, the side walls having been of wood and corrugated iron. Tradition has it that this was built for Donald MacPhee (Dòmhnall Bàn) on his marriage, but as this was in January, 1907, when the evacuation of the island had just begun, it is likely that the house had been built some time before. Perhaps MacPhee had an inkling of the forthcoming exodus, and only had the gables built of stone, but this style of house was becoming common in Barra. A 'mass stone' was built into one of the gable ends, perhaps got from the site of the Cross nearby. The free-standing gables were so well built that they stood, unsupported, until a severe gale flattened them in 1989.

These improvements in housing reflect the general trend in the islands at this time, though Mingulay seems to have been in advance of Barra in this respect; there, the central hearth was still common in 1901, and cattle were still in many houses as late as 1907[10]. Many of these improved houses were built after the photograph of 1887 was taken, and the old schoolroom was rebuilt into a house after the new school was built in 1881. There are various possible reasons for this trend, as we have seen. The building of the school and chapel in modern style would have been a stimulus. Legislation such as the 1886 Crofters Holdings Act gave crofters security of tenure of their houses, which they now had an incentive to improve; and there were various public health acts from 1867. There was also increasing contact with the mainland, and the fishing industry created some prosperity.

The improved, cattle-free houses measured between 8 and 12 metres (26-40 feet) long and about 4 metres (13 feet) wide internally, and were divided into three rooms by wooden partitions. Inside the door, which was roughly in the middle of a long wall, was a small entrance lobby leading to the kitchen/living room on one side and the bedroom on the other, with a small bedroom between, reached from one of the other rooms. In the kitchen there was a bench under the window, a dresser, full of dishes, a table and a few upright chairs. Cooking and baking were done over the fire[11]. The photograph of the interior of the house of John MacLean (Barnaidh) (plate 14) shows that the wall, which must have been rendered, was covered in newspaper which MacLean probably got from the east coast of the mainland when fishing there. This house was one of those built after 1887. In the bedrooms the family slept in box beds, perhaps fitted with roofs to keep out rain, and curtains to keep out draughts, and there were several people to a bed. Lighting was provided by means of the *crùisgean*, a simple lamp using fish oil. These were made of iron or tin, and used rush wicks. In later years paraffin lamps were used[12]; paraffin was got from Arran as early as 1850.

Furniture, spinning wheels and other items of wood were made locally from driftwood. All the men were practical, but the best known carpenters were the MacKinnons, Donald and his son John. John had a 'sawpit' made of boulders on the shore below the school for sawing up driftwood, and he had a workshop in the village. He also made his own clothes, which was unusual for a man[13].

The house was the centre of various activities – mostly carried out by women – such as food preparation and cooking, and making cloth and clothing. Food varied according to season; the staples were fish and seabirds (fresh or dried in both cases), seabirds' eggs, milk and milk products, potatoes, and grain in various forms. Mutton, chicken, eggs, seaweed, cabbage and other vegetables were also eaten. Ealasaid Sinclair said the people were never hungry in her day. Sheep were slaughtered in the autumn and the meat was salted for winter use. All edible parts were eaten – the stomach was used for puddings made with oatmeal, onions and suet. At one time cattle were also slaughtered in the autumn, when the meat, salted, would be shared out among the community. Chicken was eaten on St Michael's Day and Shrove Tuesday, when it was made into a soup with husked barley[14].

Most food was boiled in pots hung over the peat fire; bannocks and scones were baked on girdles – flat iron pans – hung over the fire, or on a flat stone on the edge of the fire, as illustrated in plate 14. Bannocks were made from both barley and oatmeal; older people preferred the oat bannocks. A savoury and nutritious variety had cod liver mixed in. Soda scones made with imported white flour were also made; Ealasaid Sinclair said these were better made on a stone by the fire than on a girdle. Making the day's bannocks was the first job in the morning, after stoking up the fire; the previous night the glowing embers had been covered with ash – 'smooring' as it was called – to keep them alight. Robert Adam described his experience of Mingulay bannocks – the very ones, perhaps, in his photograph (plate 14):

> *"Our bread consisted of a huge girdle-scone an inch thick. So thick that, after being baked on the girdle, this round, flat object was allowed to finish the baking*

process by a long lean against the sooty kettle in front of the peat-fire. These mighty comestibles, when new, were easily chewed. A day or two old, they resembled crepe rubber, fearfully tough. How we were able to eat them then was by soup made of seafowl. When softened in this highly concentrated meat-juice, they presented no dental difficulties."[15]

Nan MacKinnon told a charming story about small oat bannocks called *bonnaich boise*, 'hand bannocks', which her mother, who was from Mingulay, used to make. When she had finished shaping the bannock, she used to put a small mark in the middle of it with her thumb. She explained why:

"Before there were chimneys in the houses, they had a smoke- hole in the middle of the house, and this day, this woman had made a bannock; this was in the time of the fairies. And she'd made a bannock and set it up against the fire. And the fairies came to the door and she kept the door barred against them. And they looked down through the smoke-hole, and saw the bannock. And the fairies called down the smoke-hole: 'Little bannock with no dimple, rise up and open the door for us.'

The little bannock started moving and rolled away from the fire and struck the door, and the door opened and the fairies swarmed into the house. And ever since, every bannock they made they had to put a dimple in it with their thumb, and as long as there was a dimple made in it with their thumb the fairies could do nothing to it."[16]

Milk, besides being drunk, was made into butter and crowdie. To make butter, milk was put in a butter churn, a cylindrical vessel a metre (3 feet) or more in length, and agitated by means of a plunger pushed in and out until the butter separated out. As with other repetitive and rhythmical activities, this was done to the accompaniment of songs. Crowdie was a kind of cottage cheese made from buttermilk, the curds being produced by warming the buttermilk gently. Mrs Murray found that the milk and cream she was given in the Barra Isles sometimes " tasted so of peat that we could hardly make it palatable."

Food was eaten off chinaware in the late 19th century, and dishes were displayed on the dresser as well. The fishermen got it from the east coast when they were there fishing. Before that, wooden bowls were used, as noted by Miss Bird, a visitor to Berneray in 1863.

Various naturally-occurring foods were eaten. Shellfish – cockles, mussels and limpets – were eaten in early times, and very probably more recently in times of hardship, though not in Catherine MacNeil's time. Sand eels were eaten, as we have seen. Seals and whales may have been eaten if found stranded, though there is no mention of this in recent times, and the name of an inlet on the west coast may suggest that whales, or a whale, was caught or found there. Seals may have been caught, as they were in Barra, according to Hall in 1807. Silverweed, which grows in sandy soil around the bay, and seaweeds such as dulse, may also have been eaten in times of hardship. Edible mushrooms grow in profusion, and to an enormous size, on the more fertile ground, but these were, said Harvie-Brown, "contemptuously left alone by the natives, and called *balgan buachair*, i.e. 'spots made by dung'". Only John Finlayson, the teacher, seems to have appreciated them: "They are excellent for clearing down any flatulency or stomach burden. They are real cathartics and though I always go to extremes in their use, there is nothing like surfeit or nausea as a consequence." Cattle liked them too, and Finlayson "once had a race with a cow for a brilliant mushroom ahead of us."[17]

Alcohol – whisky and wine – was drunk on special occasions such as weddings, and no doubt at other times too. It was Mrs Murray's opinion that the people had "plenty to spend on tea, whisky and tobacco." There was a whisky still in Pabbay at one time, and a jar believed to have been used for carrying its produce to Mingulay survives. Pipe-smoking was common among the men, and running out of tobacco during bad weather when it was impossible to get to Barra is said to have contributed to the men wanting to leave Mingulay[18]. At such times they would sniff the newspaper the tobacco had been wrapped in as second best.

An important part of a woman's work at home, especially in winter, was spinning, weaving, and making clothing. "They manufacture all their own clothing from the wool of their sheep," wrote Jolly in 1883. The fleece, sheared in summer, had to be washed in the stream, dried, and carded (to straighten the fibres) before it was ready for spinning. Before the mid-19th century, when spinning wheels were introduced to the Hebrides, wool was spun using the spindle. This was a shaft of wood, weighted at the bottom, which was spun, drawing the fibres into yarn. The spindle could be suspended from a distaff, a longer shaft of wood held in the crook of the arm, enabling the woman to spin while walking. By the end of the century, most households had a spinning wheel, made locally by the MacKinnons, who also sold them in Castlebay[19]. Donald made a set of eight from a single piece of oak driftwood, without using nails or screws, in about 1859 (see plate 22). Several of the MacKinnons' wheels survive.

Once spun, the yarn could be dyed in large pots using natural dyes derived from plants, lichens and seaweeds; and then woven into cloth. Not all the households had looms; Michael MacPhee said that only two, one all-female, had them, but they served the whole community[20]. Finally, the finished cloth had to be waulked (fulled or shrunk). The cloth was first soaked in human urine, to fix the dye, then laid on a broad bench or table with a row of about six women each side. The women on each side moved alternately, simultaneously crushing and kneading the cloth against the table. The action was conducted in a disciplined rhythm to the accompaniment of songs specially devised for this purpose. It started slowly but gathered speed until it reached a feverish frenzy. The 'leader' measured the progress of the shrinkage at intervals, using the middle finger as a measure[21]. Ealasaid Sinclair said there might be a waulking in each house in turn, say one every week of the winter. Mary Campbell said a waulking would start at four in the afternoon and might continue till three next morning, the women working in shifts. In one house, known as the *taigh-ceilidh* ('ceilidh house'), girls learned the waulking songs from the old woman who lived there. The waulking women were the best singers in Mingulay[22]. One of these was Nan MacKinnon's great aunt, Effie MacKay (Oighrig Iain Mhìcheil, maiden surname MacNeil, born c. 1837)[23].

Alexander Carmichael, the folklorist, witnessed a waulking in Mingulay in 1866, at which he

> "*asked a beautiful girl to sing a certain song over again. She blushed and looked confused and abashed, and the women looked in an embarrassed way at one another. The leader said that were they to sing the same song twice at the same waulking the cloth would become thin and streaky and white as* rùsg na caora, *the sheep's fleece, and there was no knowing what mischief might not befall the wearer of the cloth or the singer of the song. The hands of these girls were small, the fingers tapered, the arms muscular, the girls themselves of medium height, strongly made, well formed, and well mannered.*"[24]

Cloth of varying thicknesses was produced. Lightweight, undyed cloth (*clò bàn*, 'white cloth'), was used for men's underclothes. Lightweight cloth was also used for plaids, shawls and blankets. The heavier tweed (*clò gorm*, 'blue cloth') was used for men's trousers and waistcoats. In later years women wore skirts and blouses of imported drugget, a mixture of linen, or cotton, and wool[25]. Jolly wrote:

> "*The people seemed generally well clothed, wearing a thick, strong, heavy woollen stuff. The boys were clad chiefly in trousers and woollen shirts alone, sometimes with vests and cravats, but seldom with coats or jackets. Most of them had no bonnets, and their hair was matted into a coarse, thick felt, which formed a perfect, if more suspicious, substitute. The girls were better dressed than their brothers. They wore various materials, bright colours being much appreciated, as in all primitive communities, and many of them were clean and tidy.*"

Women's dress is well illustrated by plate 11. The woman and the girl are wearing skirts, blouses, and the small head-shawl (*beannag*), which could be worn as a scarf around the neck or over the head. In some parts of the islands women wore the latter round the neck before marriage, and over the head thereafter. Women would have worn the great plaid (*plaide mhòr*) as an outer garment, covering the head as well; and, when in mourning, most of the face too[26].

Fishermen wore blue knitted jerseys, as seen in plate 4. The patterns varied from island to island, which meant that, should the wearer drown, his home could be identified. In wet conditions they wore long smocks of oiled canvas.

All the men in the 1905 photographs are wearing boots, as is Catherine MacLean, and the younger children are barefoot. James MacNeil was described as a shoemaker in the 1851 census, though not again. He wouldn't have had any custom from at least one islander, his father-in-law, Rory Rum the storyteller, who was said in 1860 not to have worn shoes for fifty years.

The islanders were therefore largely self-sufficient not only in food, as seen in previous chapters, but in clothing, building materials, and furniture. Various items would always have been imported, such as anything made of iron, and in later years more and more items and commodities were imported as contact with the mainland increased and there was more cash to spend.

9

Sickness and Death

*"One of the features of the Barra population was its physical excellence
and powers of physical endurance. It is astonishing to me how one can
reconcile this with their struggles, their low standard of nutrition and their
indifferent sanitation."*

So wrote Dr Donald Buchanan, a native of Barra and a doctor, in 1942.
Dr Ogilvie Grant, medical officer for Inverness-shire, was in no doubt
about the principal cause of ill-health among the islanders. After a visit to
Mingulay in 1892, he wrote:

> *"There I saw that sad scene, alas, so common, a young man dying of
> consumption, and when I left his bedside and breathed as pure an air as exists
> in the wide world, I felt that here perhaps another human being was being
> sacrificed to insanitation."*[1]

Insanitary living conditions were a principal cause of the vulnerability of
the islanders to infectious diseases such as typhoid, measles and influenza.
Numerous outbreaks and deaths are recorded in the later years. Dr Grant
again:

> *"The difficulties peculiar to the treatment of infectious diseases in the island
> districts are very great. The poverty of the districts has to be considered, their
> congested state, the ignorance and prejudice of the people, and their neglect of
> the most rudimentary attention to sanitation."*[2]

Mingulay certainly was 'congested', as far as the village was concerned. The
houses were closely packed together, and there were up to eleven people to
a house. Until the later years, cattle shared the houses in winter. Sanitation
was non-existent; the only privies were at the Board school, where the risk
of infection spreading among the children was high. Household refuse was
dumped outside the houses; in 1893 the county Sanitary Department issued
all households in Uist and Barra district with a written notice instructing
them to remove "offensive middens, ashpits and dungheaps" at least twenty
yards from houses and wells, and to provide separate accommodation for
cattle[3]. It is unlikely that such instructions were taken much notice of in

Mingulay, and as far as the cattle were concerned, people had begun to build byres already. A "dung heap" was mentioned by Harvie-Brown as being the last resting place of a snowy owl which had been shot early in 1887, for the remains of which the portly naturalist made an unsavoury and unsuccessful search on his visit the following summer. Contamination of water supplies, so common in Barra, was not a problem in Mingulay, where "most of the inhabitants", Dr Grant was told, "take their water for domestic purposes from Linique, well up the brae"[4]. Linique (derived from *lianag*, a green spot) was a pool above the chapel, on the small stream running past it into the bay. There appears to be a well between the house and stream in plate 12.

A well documented case of typhoid occurred in 1894 in the family of Donald MacPhee (Dòmhnall Dhòmhnaill Iain) and his wife Catherine (Catriona Ruairidh Eachainn). John Finlayson, the teacher, reported as follows:

"In July last typhoid generated somehow or another at Castlebay. A girl from this island unfortunately went across and put up for the night in the house where the fever was. She did this without knowing it was typhoid the children were sick with. The girl came back to this island, taking the disease with her. The people here got alarmed, and those houses nearest the infected family were deserted. The house was well kept isolated. In due time all the other members of the family, six in number, were infected. The father kept up as long as he could, but he should have been in his bed a week before. He could be seen walking out like a drunken man. I saw him fall down in the sand. He took to bed and died two days after. Alas, there was not a person in the island who would put him into the coffin."[5]

Dr MacRury, who arrived from Barra shortly after MacPhee died, continued the story:

"On learning that none of the inhabitants, in spite of my persuasions, would enter the house to give assistance in putting the dead man in his coffin, I offered to do this myself, but found that the coffin could not be ready till next day, and as I could not wait so long the Reverend Mr MacKenzie then volunteered to do this, as he said he had to return to the island next day to discharge some professional duties."[6]

The case illustrates the dread of infection prevalent in the islands, which we have met already in the story of the 'plague'. This attitude was not understood in the south; an English newspaper, the *Daily Chronicle*, seized on the story, criticising the "unkindly islanders" for their "failure to act with common decency or courage." It also shows the islanders' attitude to such occurrences to be on a spiritual rather than practical level, for when Donald MacPhee was dying, the islanders went to Barra to fetch the priest, not the doctor. They met Dr MacRury by chance, and he went with them; before returning to Barra, he instructed one of the daughters on how to look after the other patients and later sent medicines and disinfectants. When Catherine MacPhee died two days later, again nobody would go near the body to put it in a coffin. Help was sought from Barra, and the sanitary inspector, Donald MacLean (nicknamed 'an Sgarbh', meaning 'the Cormorant'), came to do it. Dr MacRury commented on the case: "That such a state of matters should exist in any part of Great Britain today is scarcely credible."

In January 1898 measles was brought by someone returning from Glasgow. Three adults, children of Malcolm MacPhee (Donald's brother), died, "which disposes the people", wrote John Finlayson, "to look upon the whole thing as a mysterious visitation and plague." This time new legislation allowed Dr Grant to send a nurse, Nurse King, to the island; she believed that "the deaths are simply due to not being properly nursed, want of cleanliness, and overcrowding."[7]

There were numerous outbreaks of influenza, some fatal, and in 1899 John Johnston recorded in the school log book that an "epidemic of mumps aggravated by an epidemic of harvest work reduces attendance." He had trouble informing the doctor, so as to get the requisite certificate to close the school. Dr Grant stressed the importance of ventilation in the schoolroom, in order to reduce the risk of infection spreading among the children.

Smallpox may have visited the island at one time, but this was gradually eradicated throughout the country following the introduction of compulsory inoculation in 1864. Children were vaccinated between the ages of six months and three years[8], and the Barra doctor would visit the southern islands periodically for this purpose. By 1906 the high cost of this was met out of the parish rates, which, a government report noted disapprovingly, the Mingulay people themselves never paid[9].

Another cause of ill-health in the islands was dampness, which was largely responsible for lung diseases such as tuberculosis, pneumonia, pleurisy, and whooping cough, which were often fatal. Dr Grant blamed, firstly, the coldness and dampness of bedrooms, and the contrast of these conditions to the heat of the living rooms from which the people retired to bed; and secondly, trudging over sodden hills to fetch peat, herd or milk cows, etc[10]. Fishermen spent long periods in wet clothes, and as a result, suffered from rheumatism as well[11].

Most deaths in Mingulay occurred without a medical person being present, in which case nothing more specific than, for example, 'senile decay', or simply 'unknown' was given as the cause of death in the death

Plate 1. 'A picturesque huddle of rude dusky huts': the earliest known photograph of Mingulay Village, taken in 1887. The tide was unusually high.

Plate 2. The same view, 1987. There were a number of building developments in the years after the earlier view, and the sand began to encroach on the village after its desertion.

Plate 3. *The four hills of Mingulay from the north east. Mingulay lies between Berneray, left, and Pabbay, right.*

Plate 4. *Mingulay men in Vatersay, August 1909. Left to right: Hector MacNeil, Angus MacNeil (Beag), John MacKinnon (the joiner), Michael MacNeil. The latter two had not left Mingulay permanently by this time; Michael MacNeil was the last to leave in 1912.*

Plate 5. *The chasm between Mingulay (left) and the stack of Lianamul.*
Sheep grazed the stack's summit, and seabirds were caught on its precipices.

Plate 6. *Skipisdale, Mingulay's formerly-inhabited southern valley. In the foreground is a sheep pen built in the 1920s, and across the sound, Berneray, with the lighthouse of Barra Head.*

Plate 7. *The schoolroom (roofless), built in 1881, and the schoolhouse, added in 1894. To the left is the privy-block. Photographed in 1984, before the schoolhouse was re-roofed.*

Plate 8. *Malcolm MacPhee building a peat stack on the slopes of Carnan.*
MacPhee apparently blinked during the exposure. 1905.

Plate 9. *A crofter and young cattle above the village. The mill can be seen in the valley*
bottom on the right. 1905.

Plate 10. *The croftlands inland from the village, created by generations of toil. On the right, the rounded bulk of Carnan, on the left, Hecla. 1922.*

Plate 11. *Peat cutters on Carnan. 1905.*

Plate 12. *Houses in the northern half of the village. In the foreground is John MacLean's house, and the furthest was occupied by the teacher John Finlayson. 1905.*

Plate 13. *Fowling with a noose on the end of a rod. On the right is the stack of Arnamul, and beyond, Gunamul and Dun Mingulay. The figure is the photographer's companion. 1905.*

Plate 14. *The interior of John MacLean's house showing bannocks cooking, as described by Robert Adam. 1905.*

Plate 15. *John Sinclair's house on the road south of the village (which lies below the ridge in the middle distance). Beyond is MacPhee's hill. 1905.*

Plate 16. *The Chapel House, built in 1898. The upper floor was St Columba's Chapel, the lower, the visiting priest's quarters. 1905.*

Plate 17. *The graveyard, where countless generations are at rest. 1922.*

Plate 18. *Three of John MacLean's children outside their home: Catherine, centre, Mary, right, Allan in front. The other girl is unidentified. 1905.*

Plate 19. *Men preparing to launch a boat into an exceptionally calm sea. The lack of a boat slip or anchorage contributed to the decision to evacuate. 1905.*

Plate 20. *The derrick, erected in 1901. The jib, seen resting above the steps, swung out to hoist loads from boats. It was an ill-conceived scheme which turned out to be practically useless. 1905.*

Plate 21. *'Rory Rum the storyman', Roderick MacNeill, painted by J F Campbell in 1871.*

Plate 22. *One of eight spinning wheels made in 1859 by Donald MacKinnon, from a single piece of oak driftwood.*

register. There were occasional accidents, such as drowning or falling from cliffs, and we can assume that there were deaths of mothers in childbirth, though none are recorded. Infant deaths were common: of fifty-one babies born between 1890 and 1908, eight died when anything between a few minutes and over a year old. Compulsory civil registration of deaths, certified by a doctor, began in 1855, but it was seventeen years before the first death in Mingulay was certified. There had been a doctor, in private practice of course, resident in Barra since about the middle of the century, but it was not until 1890 that the foundations of a publicly-funded medical service were laid, in the form of a medical officer for Inverness-shire. He was concerned about the large number of uncertified deaths, which were due to the unwillingness or inability to pay a doctor for his services as much as, in Mingulay's case, to remoteness, and the islanders' attitude[12].

A total of 125 deaths were recorded in Mingulay between 1855 and 1909. Some elderly people from Mingulay may have died in Barra, for tradition has it that people would go to live with relatives in Barra in their old age to be sure of getting the last rites from the priest on their death. The last death occurred in March 1909 (Mary MacPhee, Màiri Iain Mhìcheil, widow of John), but the last person to be buried there actually died in Sandray, as we will see.

The dead were buried in the little graveyard by the stream in the middle of the village (plate 17). This is a low oval hillock enclosed by a wall, with an entrance on the west. The graveyard had been used for centuries, being the site of the medieval St Columba's Chapel and graveyard. There are today about fifteen identifiable gravestones, merely unshaped slabs set vertically into the ground, and forty to fifty other stones which may be gravestones; and no doubt there are more under the sand which has overwhelmed the eastern edge of the graveyard since the desertion[13]. There are two free-standing concrete crosses, one a memorial to John MacPhee (Iain Dhòmhnaill Iain) who died of influenza in 1900, inscribed with 'in loving memory'. A third concrete memorial is substantial and very elaborate, unlike any in Barra; it can be seen in plate 17. It has an unfinished twin lying in an enclosure at the southern end of the village, where it must have been made, but it was never erected. They are obviously a pair, and must be relatively late, as the one in the graveyard does not appear in the 1905 photographs; but it is not known whom they commemorate. Three wooden crosses in plate 17 seem to be the same as the three white ones in plate 1 of 1887.

If there are, say, fifty to seventy marked graves, there must be a great many more unmarked. There were at least 123 burials in the last fifty-five years, and perhaps hundreds before that; because of the graveyard's small size, later burials must have cut earlier ones. Many of the stones are in groups, presumably family groups, and the closeness of some on an east-west alignment suggest infant graves.

T S Muir was informed, by Miss Oswald of Barra Head Lighthouse, that (in 1866) the graveyard was "in a most ruinous condition; there has been a wall of loose stones around it, but the cows and horses are allowed to graze in it, and it is covered with weeds. There are no tombstones in it more than some rude ones at the heads of graves." By 1905 the wall had been topped with a barbed wire fence, but the weeds were still lush.

To return to the living: the islanders, of course, had their own forms of treatment using naturally-occurring substances; boils and sores, for example, were treated with a poultice of dock. Martin Martin mentioned "a sort of Stone, with which the Natives frequently rub their Breasts by way of prevention, and say it is a good Preservative for Health." Some forms of treatment were based on superstition, and Jolly wrote of the treatment of the so-called 'king's evil', or scrofula (tuberculosis of the lymphatic nodes). He met a boy from South Uist travelling to Mingulay.

"It seems that in Minglay there lived a native, who was the last of seven sons in direct male descent without any intervening daughter. According to popular notions, this endows him with a power of curing the malady, like the once potent 'royal touch' which gave name to the disease. The supernatural physician enjoyed great local fame for the many cures believed to have been effected by him. He had already seen the boy twice, and this was the last visit that was necessary for completing the cure. It appears that he operated on the patient with no human eye to see, but merely recited a 'rhyme' or charm over the sore. He charged no fee, though a piece of silver must be presented as essential to good luck."

The belief in the powers of a seventh son (of a seventh son) was common in the Outer Hebrides well into this century. The silver was usually a sixpence hung around the patient's neck.

Women in childbirth were attended by 'midwives', who, although scorned by the medical authorities, were well regarded locally. There is even a tradition of a Mingulay woman, who had gone to live in Barra, returning to her native island for the birth of her baby in the 1860s. According to Nan MacKinnon, it was believed that the 'gift' of midwifery was passed down from mother to daughter, and that an ancestor of the last midwife, Anne MacNeil (Anna Ruairidh Dhòmhnaill, daughter of Roderick MacNeill, the storyteller, and Flora MacNash), received the gift from a supernatural man she met one night in Barra.

"No wife or mother died there in childbirth while she was there. . . she would stay

up with them for three whole nights running on her own. Nobody dared to give drink or food or anything to the woman in child-bed, as they called childbirth, but herself. And when the three days were up and when she was certain that she was on the way to recovery she wouldn't come so often at all then, but she would call to see her each day after that."[14]

Anne MacNeil continued to attend births into old age when she could no longer walk. She moved to Sandray in about 1909 to be with her son John and daughter Flora Gillies, and died there in April 1910. There being no burial ground in use on the island then, her body was taken to Mingulay for burial, the last one there[15].

Another midwife was Isabella MacLean, who registered births she had presumably attended.

In general, then, Mrs Murray was right when she said that in spite of the various "defiances of the laws of sanitation. . . the people in Mingulay are a healthy, long-lived people."

10

The Ladies' School

"In the education of the children, Minglay has long been singularly fortunate."

So wrote William Jolly in 1883, referring to the fact that Mingulay was the only one of Barra's satellites to have a school. Not only were the islanders fortunate; the historical record has benefited from the records of both the schools which served the community in its last fifty years.

Until 1872, when education in Scotland became a state responsibility, basic education in the Highlands and Islands had been provided sporadically by various religious and philanthropic bodies. For a few years at the end of the 17th century Barra boasted one of only two Catholic schools in Scotland at the time, its main function being to train young men for the priesthood. A contemporary observer scornfully remarked that Catholic parents in the west of Scotland would sooner send their children to Jamaica than to Barra. At the end of the 18th century, the Society in Scotland for the Propagation of Christian Knowledge, founded to counter Catholicism and the Gaelic language, set up a school. Then, in the early 19th century, the Gaelic Schools Society, which taught the reading of the scriptures in Gaelic, provided itinerant teachers in Barra, and even, briefly, in Sandray[1]. By 1865 Barra had four schools: the parish school, a Church of Scotland Ladies' Association school and two run by a new organisation, the Ladies' Highland Association. In the report on education in the Hebrides of that year, it was stated that "The educational state of Barra appears to be behind that of any other of the Western Islands, not excepting St Kilda."[2]

In 1859 Mingulay became the only other island in the Barra group to benefit from a permanent school, when the Ladies' Highland Association, also known as the Free Church Ladies' Association (Edinburgh branch) established a school there. This Association had been founded in 1850, seven years after the establishment of the Free Church of Scotland by disaffected ministers of the Church of Scotland. The reasons for the break were complex, but the power of landlords in appointing ministers, and the consequent failure of most ministers to condemn evictions by their patrons, were important factors.

The Association had three principal objectives. Firstly, to attempt to improve the conditions of the population of the Highlands and Islands after the terrible famines of the 1840s by providing schools (and, in poor districts, clothing to enable children to attend). Secondly, to use the schools as a training ground for the young men being trained for the ministry in the new Church. And thirdly, "to bear upon the popery [Catholicism] which still exists in some Highland districts." Schools were established throughout the region, in Catholic as well as Protestant areas; Mingulay was the only solidly Catholic island to get a school, and the most remote. They were known locally as *Sgoil nan Leadaidhean* (The Ladies' School). The organisation was funded by private donations; fees were not charged, but local people were expected to contribute to the provision of buildings, and food for the teachers[3]. We are fortunate in knowing a good deal about the Mingulay school, which features in some of the annual reports of the Association[4].

Mingulay seems to have got its school largely by accident. In 1857 one of the Barra Head lightkeepers appealed to the Association for a teacher. He "promised that half the salary would be raised by the people, and that about 70 children would attend", most of whom would have come from Mingulay, as Berneray's population was much smaller. A benefactor, William MacKerrell of Great Malvern, promised £20 per year for the first three years (in fact, his support continued for many years). Lack of accommodation and the remoteness of the island prevented the school being opened the following year, and by early 1859 it was too late:

> "The light keeper, expecting to be removed, withdrew his offer of aid, and most of the people were in the adjacent island of Mingalay, where nobody could be found to make any preparation for the teacher, or to promise to encourage or to aid him. It was felt to be a very perilous and difficult experiment to send a young man to so remote a place where nobody could read, and all were Roman Catholics. . . however, a young man being found willing to make the trial, he was sent in May, and was so well received, that in a few weeks he had a flourishing school of about sixty scholars, was lodged by the people as comfortably as they could, and in August, when the barn was required in which the school had been taught, they offered to build a new house if a little aid could be given them for timber for the roof and windows, for which they had to send a boat to Fort William. Stormy weather, and the exposed situation of the island prevented anyone from visiting the school; but the progress the children have made has been very encouraging, and this arduous enterprise has hitherto succeeded beyond the most sanguine expectations." The pupils included "full-grown men, and children from adjacent islands, boarded there on purpose to enjoy the advantage of the school." The people said that "there has been no school from the creation of the world till now."

According to a tradition current in Barra, the teacher, John Finlayson, was destined for Berneray and was taken there by an islander, Duncan Sinclair, who would have been among those calling for a teacher. However, on the journey from Barra a storm blew up and they had to seek shelter at Mingulay, where Finlayson saw that there were many more children than in Berneray, and so he decided to establish the school there.

Finlayson's early days cannot have been easy: he was the first outsider known to have lived there, and brought with him the values of the outside world and a foreign religion. Muir speculated on his task on his arrival:

"The labour of breaking in even so merely a handful of utterly uncultivated homespuns must have been dreadful. It is supposed that [Finlayson] went forth to the task sufficiently apprised of the material upon which he was to operate; but if not, his earliest encounter with his sucklings-elect must have somewhat suddenly perfected his knowledge. Upon his landing in Mingula, the tiny vagrants crowded round to see the school they had been told they were going to have. They thought he had it with him packed up in his trunk!"

The school was visited, and the children examined, at intervals by supporters of the Association. The first of these, in 1860, reported that the thirty-three pupils "showed considerable acquaintance with Scripture, and had made good progress in acquiring English, though, like the other Barra schools, the work was elementary." Three years later twenty-four children could read the Bible, and could write letters to their teacher during his periods of study at college in Edinburgh. The intelligence and ability of the children impressed the visitors, such as a Mr Ross in 1868:

"The Bible lesson was remarkably well read by every one of the eighteen who were present, and they translated the chapter, verse by verse, with the utmost ease into Gaelic. The examination upon the lesson was conducted in English, and as readily answered by the pupils in English also. They repeated portions of the Psalms in both languages, and their spelling and translation from English into Gaelic, and vice versa, was well done. The writing was wonderfully good, and to appearance bore no trace of having been spoiled by the steel pen. Many of the children were this year able to write letters to friends absent for work in the south and east. A number of them performed sums in the advanced rules of arithmetic."
In 1865 there were *"seventeen boys and ten girls; the latter were tolerably well dressed, for our visit was expected. The boys were very quaint in their rags – petticoats or sacks. One piece of dress was thought sufficient for a child, and the feet were all bare."*

The Bible, reading, writing, English and arithmetic are the only subjects mentioned, but others may have been taught; in Barra these included history, geography, Latin, grammar. The children had books, and the London Tract Society was so impressed by the reports of 1865 that it donated a number of books, including a Gaelic translation of *The Pilgrims' Progress*, to the school. John Finlayson was much commended; his work must have been helped enormously by his knowledge of Gaelic, a facility which not all teachers had, but it was to be used only as an aid to learning English. The Association had high hopes of Finlayson: John Cowan, on his departure from his visit in 1865, "commended him to the care of Him who has strengthened him, in the midst of much discouragement, to do what I believe will be a great work for Him."

The first school building was situated on its own on the northern edge of the village, overlooking it[5]. It was, said Muir in 1866, "externally in no way distinguished, excepting in length, from the neighbouring huts." In 1865 "there was no glass in the windows and many crevices in the roof through which the sun's rays slanted, helping to lighten up the room" (and let in the rain?). Muir described the interior as "a rather sparingly-illuminated apartment of some length, furnished with a few desks and forms", an improvement on 1860 when "writing was performed on a plank or seat, the children kneeling in the sand." The children normally wrote in copy-books, but in 1865 these had not arrived, so roof slates saved from a wreck were used, the children writing with stalks of pipes instead of pencils.

Muir was horrified by Finlayson's own accommodation:

Finlayson *"led us to the lower end of the apartment, and there, pushing aside a suspended curtain, ushered us into what was at once his sleeping room and parlour. Jacques's 'O knowledge ill-inhabited! worse than Jove in a thatched house!' came into my head as I looked around the solitary magister's ultra-economised sanctum – its earthen floor, deal chair or two, chest, and low roughly fashioned bedstead, covering fully one-half of the area. How it was that anyone at all smoothly brought up could stand out such a life of privation, I could not comprehend. Perhaps, as a Highlander, the poor probationer was in some measure to the manner born; and most likely Hope, the blessed partner of the downcast, soothed him o' nights with visions of vacant pulpits, into some one of which at no distant day or night he might peradventure happily be lifted; but for all that the good ladies should, I thought. . . have gone the length of at least making his lonely cell somewhat roomy and comfortable."*

But this must have seemed like luxury to Finlayson, for in 1861 he was lodging with Donald MacKinnon, the constable, and his family of eight children[6].

In terms of its educational function, "the teacher and school are highly appreciated by the people," wrote Ross in 1868. So were the visitors, such as one in 1865 whose "distribution of comfits and toys gave great joy, and a few of the parents who were present cast on us looks of wonder and gratitude." But the missionary function of the school must not be forgotten. The 1859 report reads: "The success of this school proving, as it does, that a wide and effectual door is open for diffusing gospel light in all parts of Scotland where Popish darkness still prevails, Christians will surely be stimulated to remove what is indeed a reproach – the fact that there are districts in our land which the Reformation never reached." A visitor to the Barra school in 1857 described "the young in that benighted spot" as "a crooked and perverse generation." Given such attitudes, and the Free Church's strict austerity and condemnation of all forms of entertainment and other aspects of culture, conflict was inevitable. In the early years, the Association was content with religious instruction during school hours, but in time it wanted more than that. The 1864 report says:

> "It is necessary to be very cautious in giving any report of the work of the Association in the Popish islands of Barra and Mingalay. The school in the latter island is as well attended as formerly, the priest offering no opposition to the day-school, but rather encouraging the children to go. It is otherwise, however, with the Sabbath-school, where proselytizing is feared. But 'we have need of patience'. . . The people have been warned that unless attendance is secured on Sabbath as well as week-days the school may not be continued."

This 'caution' was repeated in 1866, with a rather sinister reference to "direct cases of conversion" in the Catholic islands; but it was not until 1871 that the threat to close the school was carried out, as we learn from the report of that year:

> "In some of the work in the Popish districts there has been much interest, and some hopeful promises of success, whilst in other places faith and patience have been tried by bitter disappointment. The school in the island of Mingalay. . . was found lately in so unsatisfactory a state that the Committee were advised to drop it for a time, perhaps to be resumed at a future period under a new labourer. It cannot be said to have been useless, when all the young people in the island, none of whom knew a letter before, can now read the Word of God both in Gaelic and English; but the influence for good on the population has not been what the Committee fondly hoped to see."

Viewed in isolation, it is hard to be certain exactly what the writer of these words was getting at, apart from pointing a finger at Finlayson. But, considering previous and sometimes equally nebulous comments, it is likely that the refusal of the people to accept the Sunday school, or to be converted, were the main reasons for the Association's decision. For this one can only blame the Association's own naivety in thinking these aims could be achieved in such a close-knit Catholic community; Mingulay was not directly comparable with Barra, where Sunday schools were accepted, and where there were a few Protestants. The implicit criticism of Finlayson therefore seems unfair, but there may be more to it than the Association let on. So what about Finlayson?

John Finlayson was born in 1830 in Lochcarron, Ross-shire. His father, Finlay, was a tailor who joined the Free Church on its formation, and was keen to see a son of his "wag his head in the pulpit."[7] He attended Edinburgh University, but never graduated[8]. His appointment to Mingulay was his first with the Ladies' Highland Association, who must have considered him equal to perhaps their toughest post. He was a shy, scholarly man – not, one would have thought, a proselytising type – and a conscientious teacher. A witty uncle once referred to him as 'the Philosopher at Patmos'[9], likening him to the Apostle John who was exiled to that Aegean island; to the islanders he was known – in later life – as *an Sgoilear Glas*, 'the Grey-Haired Teacher'.

Originally the schools were intended to operate for only half the year, as the teachers were expected to spend the winter months at Free Church College in Edinburgh as part of their training for the ministry. Finlayson managed to do this some years, such as in 1863, when there was uncertainty as to whether he would return; the islanders offered to repair the school roof as an inducement. Other winters he remained, with no contact with the outside world. John Cowan wrote of his meeting with Finlayson on the former's visit in 1865:

> *"As we gained the sandy beach, a solitary figure was seen approaching, accompanied by his dog. It was your teacher, our friend Mr Finlayson, and our meeting was one that touched his heart and ours, for words we had few, but we warmly pressed each other's hands. It was like Robinson Crusoe visited for the first time after his solitary residence in his island."*

If it was Finlayson's original intention to become a minister in the Free Church, it was not to be his destiny, for he spent the rest of his life in this remote Catholic community. In November 1871 he married an islander, Jane Campbell (Sìne Dhòmhnaill Nèill), and it is tempting to speculate whether this had anything to do with the school's closure. The marriage would have been unacceptable to the Association, being incompatible with their religious

105

mission, and Finlayson's position would have become impossible. He may also have been criticised for not producing results in the narrow sense of converts. He decided on marriage and Mingulay rather than ministry, and the wedding took place not long after the closure of the school – if we assume that he was no longer in post at the time of his marriage – for the school was still open in July 1871 [10]. The wedding was held, unusually, in Mingulay, and was a Catholic ceremony. He was then forty-one, she forty-five; they had no children, but later brought up a great-niece of hers, Maria Campbell (Màiri Dhòmhnaill Chaluim), born in 1878. It was not unusual for childless couples who could afford it to offer to bring up a child of less well-off relatives. Finlayson was not alone in not 'finishing the course', for over the years only a quarter of the teachers reached the pulpit [11]. Finlayson's younger brother, Alexander, also began the training, but later gave it up to study medicine [12].

The Association did not resume the school, perhaps because it discovered, in time, that a government school was planned there. But the story does not end here: ten years later, long after the new school had opened, the Association expressed a willingness to take over its running, as it had agreed to close its school at Northbay, where Barra School Board wanted to have its own school. Nothing came of the suggestion, and the Association's presence in Barra finally came to an end [13].

It is hard to assess the school's success or impact, though the reports suggest that a great deal was achieved. One indicator is the ability of the people to write their own names, shown by the requirement to sign an entry in a register of birth, marriage or death (in the case of the first and last, as an informant). The first such signature was in 1868, and rarely after that; but one has to allow for the lapse of time between acquiring the ability and having an opportunity of using it before losing it through lack of use. This must partly explain Finlayson's comment in his first entry in the log book of the subsequent Board School, four years later, that none of the pupils knew the alphabet. As he must have taught some of the same pupils before, it cannot have been quite true. On a broader level, there is no doubt that the school served to introduce the people to the ways and values of the outside world, which they were to relate to increasingly; and the school must have made the work of its successor much easier.

11
Mingulay Public School

The Education (Scotland) Act of 1872 brought education under state control for the first time, and made it compulsory for all children between the ages of five and thirteen (later raised to fourteen). On the local level, it was administered by school boards which appointed school 'managers' – like governors today – and the school staff. Schools received an annual grant according to attendance, the qualifications of the teacher, and the quality of the teaching, as perceived by the inspector on his annual visit. In poor districts such as Barra, school fees were not charged; education was funded out of local rates and from central government[1].

Barra School Board was duly formed, and opened four 'public' schools initially – three in Barra, and the Mingulay school, much the smallest, which opened in November 1875. John Finlayson was appointed teacher, a choice which, although an obvious one, would not have been universally welcome in the Catholic islands of Barra and South Uist. Finlayson and all the other teachers in the islands were Protestant, and this was resented by the Catholic majority, which wanted religious instruction in schools. This paradox was no accident; it was deliberately engineered by those in power, a tiny Protestant minority headed by the factor (estate manager), and is an example of the discrimination Catholics still suffered. In theory the school boards, which made the appointments, were freely elected by the ratepayers, but in practice the estate authorities ensured, by devious means such as the threat of eviction, that they always had a Protestant majority[2]. This injustice was redressed only when the Crofters Act of 1886 gave tenants security of tenure, and removed the fear of eviction for voting as they wished.

The affairs of the school are documented in the school log book[3], in which the teacher was required to make weekly entries, and the book also contains the inspectors' annual reports, copied in laboriously, and no doubt reluctantly in the case of critical ones, by the teacher. In his first entry Finlayson wrote: "The children, 30 in number, are all beginners, not one of them knowing the alphabet." As already indicated, this cannot have been strictly true, since some of them must have attended the Ladies' School which closed four years earlier; indeed, it is almost a negation of his past labours, though he may have wanted to give the impression that all were starting from scratch. The children were willing and made rapid progress in reading and writing. In the fifth week Finlayson started dividing the pupils into classes, to study at different stages in a scale of up to six 'standards' using set books. Once the school was established, the children were examined in the first standard at the age of seven or eight, and in subsequent ones at approximately yearly intervals. Pupils progressed from one standard to another on the basis of ability, assessed by the inspector at the annual examination. Only a few pupils reached the sixth standard, the next stage being 'intermediate'. This was the last stage offered in any of the Barra schools, so if this was passed, pupils had to go to Glasgow to continue. However, this was impossible financially for most families, bursaries being unavailable, and although a few Mingulay pupils did pass, none went any further.

Subjects taught in Mingulay were basic: reading, writing (on slate and paper), English (with much emphasis, in true Victorian style, on grammar), arithmetic, history, geography, singing, and, from 1885, Gaelic. Religion was not taught; it was left to school boards to decide whether to include it or not, and Barra decided against[4]. For the boys there was navigation, and for the girls sewing, for which a 'sewing mistress' was employed. For some years this was Finlayson's wife Jane, and later a Miss Glancy was employed. She was presumably one of the Barra Glancys, for she paid only short and occasional visits, as a result of which she was replaced by Mary Campbell of Mingulay.

Instruction was supposed to be in English, the existence of Gaelic being ignored by the original Act. (Gaelic was regarded as having no future, not only by the government, but by many parents as well. Emigration was still on the agenda, and Gaelic was useless to emigrants; it was also useless for work on the mainland. Gaelic as a school subject was subsequently permitted, as a result of campaigning by concerned organisations.[5]) Finlayson's use of Gaelic was, however, tolerated by the inspectors, though they gave him conflicting instructions as to how much he should use it.

School ran from Monday to Friday, and there were two sessions per day. The pupils sat on benches, infants at the front. The system of one teacher trying to teach pupils ranging in age from four to fourteen or more in one room cannot have been conducive to learning.

Finlayson and the inspectors were generally complimentary about the children's ability and progress. William Jolly, the inspector in the 1870s, found them "bright, willing, and wonderfully intelligent, earnest to perspiration point and shy to a fault." The inspection and examination were held in the summer, and heralded the annual holiday of between four and seven weeks. The first examination, in 1876, took place in Barra, with Barra pupils. Inspector Jolly described it:

"On turning round into the valley of Borve, where the school is, my attention was arrested by a group of bonnetless bairns, romping on the banks of the stream which enters the sea close by. These were the Minglay children, both boys and girls, who had been brought by their teacher in an open boat, over the dangerous seas between, to be examined. The shock-headed creatures acquitted themselves surprisingly, beating with ease their Barra comperes."

Subsequently, the Board took the more logical step of sending the inspector to the pupils, although in 1877 bad weather prevented his visit altogether.

The inspectors would also have examined the attendance register and admissions register. During the years 1889 to 1894, for which an admissions register survives, numbers enrolled annually varied between thirty-eight and forty-eight, the age range was four to fourteen, and there were more girls than boys. One of the pupils came from Berneray, where there had been a 'sub school' in the 1880s, and another, though from Mingulay, had attended that school (Flora Sinclair, who would have stayed with relatives in Berneray). Two were from Pabbay, the children of John Campbell, originally of Mingulay. Four had previously attended Castlebay school, and the parents of one of them still lived in Castlebay. Two children, James and Annie Murphie, were born in Glasgow and lived with their Mingulay grandmother, Anne MacNeil (the midwife). James was nearly seven when he was admitted to the school in 1890, which may be when he arrived in Mingulay, as he had not attended a previous school.

The performance of the children at the examination was not only of interest in itself; it was regarded as a measure of the performance of the teacher, which partly determined the amount of the annual grant awarded by the Board. Attendance was also taken into consideration. Irregular attendance was an obstacle to progress, and an exasperation to Finlayson and his successors. Its main cause was the withdrawing of children by their parents for croft work in the summer months, and in the early years it fell to Finlayson to remind parents that their children's attendance was compulsory. In later years he was relieved of this irksome duty by the Board's 'compulsory officer'. Other causes of irregular attendance were bad weather (even though the school was no distance from the houses, the children had no adequate protective clothing) and the occasional epidemic, the worst of which was a measles outbreak in 1898, when the school was closed for three months. There were a total of twenty religious holidays throughout the year. In 1886 the Board reduced the grant merely because a small mistake by Finlayson in the attendance register had cast doubt on their accuracy and led to accusations of fiddling. Finlayson was then subjected to the humiliation of more frequent checks by the school managers, such as Father James Chisholm of Castlebay, who looked in during pastoral visits.

The first six years of the school's life were spent, in Inspector Robertson's words, "in a hovel with appliances more in harmony with the premises than with present requirements." In 1878 it was on the same site as the earlier school, although it apparently began somewhere else as the log book records a change of schoolroom in 1877. William Jolly described it:

"Their old school at Church Bay was one of the small thatched huts of the island. It consisted of a thick wall of rude stones five feet in height, and the low entrance was formed of the door of a ship's cabin, floated in from some wreck. The interior was dimly lighted by two small windows, and was open to the sloping rafters. The floor was covered by a layer of light-coloured sand from the adjacent shore. The walls showed the rough stones of which they were built, and were quite bare except where a newspaper was hung, on examination day, behind the inspector's seat. The whole apartment was, however, beautified by various natural gifts from sea and land. Every crevice had a wild flower inserted in it, and these united their varied hues with pleasing effect, and shed a refreshing odour through the close, little hut. The window sills also were stuck full of coloured shells, while a string of seabirds' eggs hung in graceful curve from side to side of the room. The seats were formed of ships' planks resting on stones set all round the walls, and the only two desks consisted of flat boards nailed to uprights driven into the ground."

This delightful account says much for Finlayson's love of nature and imagination, and for the broad-mindedness of the inspector, who clearly appreciated it.

In the summer of 1881 the 'hovel' was replaced by a fine new building on a new site, next to the road between the village and the landing place (plate 7). The building, the first modern one in Mingulay, was a single rectangular room built of dressed stone and mortar, with a slate roof. It had large windows high up in the walls, fitted with blinds, and was lined internally with match boarding (linoleum was later placed on the walls, which the children enjoyed drawing on). Heating was provided by a coal burning stove. The furnishings were desks and forms, and a desk and blackboard for the teacher. The school was designed to accommodate an average of thirty pupils[6], but when numbers rose later they must have been rather squashed. The original grant for the building was £494. In 1894 a modest teacher's house was built on to the schoolroom, providing a standard of living previously unknown on the island. The buildings were then surrounded by a generous square enclosure, against one side of which a magnificent set of three privies (quaintly termed 'offices' in Scotland at the time), which were doubtless a great curiosity to the islanders, was erected. The new facilities must have transformed the process of education in the island and increased the regard in which it was held.

John Finlayson retired in June 1897. He was sixty-six, and may not have been in good health; illness had kept him off work twice in the previous few years. The log book and visitors' accounts show him to have been a gentle and conscientious teacher, rarely critical of the pupils; but the inspectors' reports were not on the whole very flattering, and he cannot have got much satisfaction from them. He seems to have lost heart somewhat in later years, as his entries in the log book tail off into one-liners. But he was undoubtedly a good teacher, and he contributed to the islanders becoming articulate participants in the modern world; it was he who taught most of those who fought, and eventually won, the battle for better living conditions.

Finlayson was regarded with respect and affection by the islanders, and that is how tradition remembers him; and one would expect, from one who had married into the community and devoted his working life to it, that the feelings were mutual. But they do not appear to have been, in later years at least. Letters he wrote to his friend J.A. Harvie-Brown, the naturalist, show little sympathy for the crofters' values, aspirations for better living conditions, and religion; and it is hard to believe that, although a retiring person, he kept his feelings secret from all but his distant friend. Perhaps he knew Harvie-Brown would have been receptive to such comments, and thus his emphasis on them may not be a fully accurate reflection of his attitudes. So what drew him to Mingulay and kept him there? The answer lies in his letters: it was the fishing "and the sport it afforded that fascinated me about Mingulay, not the people"[7]; also the birds, the plants, and the isolation.

Finlayson's correspondence with Harvie-Brown began before the naturalist visited Mingulay for the second time, in 1887, in the course of gathering material for his book on the fauna of the Outer Hebrides. Harvie-Brown clearly regarded Finlayson as a valuable informant on the island's birdlife, and quoted extracts from the early letters in his book. Finlayson, in turn, valued Harvie-Brown as a real friend, confidant, and fellow bird enthusiast, something he seems to have missed on Mingulay. Finlayson expressed his views on human affairs on Mingulay, as we saw in chapter 4, and also in the wider world, in which he maintained a lively interest through *The Scotsman*; his comments reveal his political views to have been Conservative. A strong sense of humour comes across in the letters, and Father Allan McDonald of Eriskay, who knew Finlayson in his later years, wrote that he was "entertaining and sociable"[8], while Harvie-Brown appreciated his "good companionship and genial conversation." These are not quite the impressions one has of him from other sources, but in the company of the rare visitors, especially fellow intellectuals, this is how he appeared.

Finlayson enjoyed his retirement: "I have nothing to do now but play and admire nature," he wrote in 1899, adding, "I am now master of 100 flowering plants. Last year I had the assistance of Miss Freer from London."[9] She wrote of him: "He has books, and is quite an accomplished botanist, having observed and classified the flora of the island without knowing the names of a dozen flowers." She also noted that "his one luxury is tea – which he imports – of the very best". Finlayson spent several winters on the Earl of Dunmore's estates in Harris, apparently for the sport[10].

Finlayson died in March 1904, and Harvie-Brown was informed by his grief-stricken adoptive daughter, Morag Campbell Finlayson, as she signed herself[11]. She mentioned that she and Finlayson's widow Jane (who died the following year) were in touch with his younger brother Alexander, who was a doctor in Munlochy, Ross and Cromarty. Being a Protestant, he could not be buried in the islanders' graveyard, and so his body was taken to Barra. This is a translation of what Ealasaid Chaimbeul wrote of his final journey in her Gaelic autobiography:

> "With great sorrow and sadness, the brave men departed with the Grey-Haired Teacher's remains bound for burial at the old graveyard at Cuithir in Barra, beside the people of his own religion. It is understood that the weather got so wild on the way to Castlebay that they were forced to lash the coffin in a vertical position to the mast – otherwise it would have been swept out to sea – and because of this, even on his last journey, the mortal remains of the fine man looked over those to whom he had given their first knowledge of education."[12]

The story is told that the party arrived at Castlebay too late to continue on foot to Cuithir. The only place they found to leave the body overnight was the bank, so they left him there as a 'bank deposit' until the following morning.

Finlayson was succeeded by John Johnston, *an Sgoilear Bàn*, 'the Fair-Haired Teacher', aged nineteen. He was born in Mingulay but was brought up in Barra, and had been a 'pupil teacher' for all of four weeks at Castlebay school. The appointment of a Catholic at last should have satisfied everyone, the more so as he was a local man. Johnston's performance during his three years' service was considered satisfactory in difficult circumstances, which included epidemics of measles, mumps, and influenza. The "epidemic of mumps", recorded Johnston in October 1899, "aggravated by an epidemic of harvest work reduced attendance". However, Barra School Board felt he needed more supervision, and in September 1900, only two months into the school year, he was transferred to Barra. Exactly what supervision was needed was not elaborated, but he is known to have visited Castlebay frequently. He had his own boat, and the story is told that one evening he started rowing home to Mingulay only to wake up next morning to find the boat still tied to Castlebay pier! The Barra storyteller, the Coddy, told a story about how Johnston once fell overboard on his way back to Mingulay, and on getting back in, had to strip and dry his clothes before arriving in the bay[13]. When he was away during the week, he would open the school on an equivalent number of Saturdays to make up. This was not approved of by everybody – Malcolm MacLean (Cadaidh), for instance, thought croft work was more important. Johnston was interested in navigation, which he studied while in Mingulay; but he remained a teacher, firstly in Barra, and then in some of the Inner Hebridean islands before returning to teach in Barra, where he is remembered with great respect.

The Board now wanted a woman teacher, but it must have had a good deal of trouble recruiting one, for it was a year before Miss Margaret Haggerty, from Liverpool, took charge in October 1901. Miss Haggerty earned a high grant (from central government) for the school by virtue of her teaching qualifications, and saved the Board money by virtue of her sex: women teachers' salaries were appreciably lower than men's. Her entries in the log book and the inspectors' reports show her to have been very professional, and she must have been very able, for she presumably had no Gaelic.

Miss Haggerty resigned in December 1903, and the following month Mrs Sarah MacShane, a qualified teacher and a Catholic, took over as the last teacher. She was born Sarah Tinney in Beauly, Inverness-shire, about 1873, but the family later moved to Barrhead, near Glasgow, where she trained as a teacher. She married Edward MacShane, a railway worker, in 1898, and their first child, Peter, was born about 1902. In Mingulay, Peter was looked after by local 'childminders' while his mother was at work. He was a naughty child, and when the women told his mother, in Gaelic, how he had behaved, Peter, who had picked up some Gaelic, would 'translate' these bad reports into glowing ones. Mrs MacShane was musical and a good needlewoman, and these helped her to be accepted by the islanders[14]. She introduced the novelty of "concerts with a charitable purpose" performed by the children, and balls, in the schoolroom. On one of these occasions, Mary Campbell said, one of the Barra Head lightkeepers brought a gramophone, the first one seen on the island. Malcolm MacLean (Cadaidh) thought that anything that sang like a person must be the devil's work, and refused to listen to it[15]. Mrs MacShane gave prizes for best attendance, and gave Christmas cards to the children. The inspectors' reports show that she performed satisfactorily, though they had become very brief by then. She was a strong-willed woman, as her determination to work at the same time as raising a family, unusual at that time, shows. She could also be quite formidable: in her attempts to get a croft on Vatersay, where the family moved in 1910, she wrote to the Secretary of State for Scotland when she had no success with local officials, but still got nowhere[16].

Mrs MacShane gave birth to five children during her years in Mingulay and Vatersay. Two of these were born in Mingulay, Eleanor in November 1906 and John in October 1908, John's being the last birth ever to take place in the island (the last native islander, Marion Sinclair, Mòrag Iagan Iain, was born in August 1907). She described herself in the log book as 'ill' around the time of Eleanor's birth, but didn't take a single day off for John's. She asked Donald Martin, the Castlebay priest and future Bishop of Argyll and the Isles, to be Eleanor's godfather. Eleanor later became a teacher. Mrs MacShane's husband, Edward, took on two crofts which became vacant when their owners left the island and were not required by other islanders.

In 1907, just as families began to leave for Vatersay, Mr Coats of Paisley donated a library of books to the school (and later, a school bag for each child), as he did to many others. The lending register shows that there were various English classics, such as *Robinson Crusoe, The Arabian Nights, The Pickwick Papers*; but, with the exception of Maggie MacMillan, who borrowed practically everything, not many children made use of them, even when they moved to Vatersay. A book on electricity was not amongst the more popular titles. One book was "returned in a disgraceful condition."

A curious incident occurred in October 1909. A bull was 'interfering' with children on their way to and from school, and their parents threatened to keep them away. Mrs MacShane reported the business to the police, and a policeman came from Barra. This seems to be a rather odd way of dealing with a situation which, one would have thought, the islanders could have solved themselves; but of course there must have been more to this story than Mrs MacShane recorded in the log book!

The school's decline set in when the emigrations to Vatersay began in 1907, reducing the school roll from twenty-five in 1906 (as it had been in 1901) to just seven at the end of 1908. Despite this, the school struggled on with a handful of pupils – the number varied, as there was a lot of coming and going between Mingulay and Vatersay and Sandray – until Barra School Board decided that its operations should be transferred to Vatersay. It finally closed on the 27th of April 1910, when there were nine pupils, and Mrs MacShane was on duty when its successor opened in Vatersay two months later. Some of the Mingulay children had missed three years of school by then.

As in the case of the Ladies' School, it is hard to assess the impact of the Board School, especially as so many other changes were taking place in the islands at the same time. Mary Campbell said they learned to read and write, but didn't learn much otherwise[17]. As to the ability to sign their own names, it is surprising how few people did so in the registers of births, marriages and deaths even in the last years when most people would have been to school. Many of the 'signatures' on the petition for improved landing facilities in 1896, and the deed of agreement concerning the derrick in 1901, were clearly written by other hands. Regarding knowledge of English, a potential indicator recorded in the censuses from 1881 is of limited use. People who were "in the habit of making colloquial use of the Gaelic language" were recorded in 1881; not surprisingly, all but four were in this category, which reveals nothing of actual ability in English. The censuses of 1891 and 1901 recorded whether only Gaelic, or Gaelic and English, were spoken; again, not very revealing. The 1891 figure for the latter category was five, including John Finlayson and the two children from Glasgow. The 1901 figure was seventy-seven, but it is impossible to evaluate its significance or to compare it directly with the previous one. The school inspector in 1899 recognised that "the teacher has unusual difficulties to contend with in imparting instruction to children who never speak a word of English." When John Johnston arrived he found that "after reading a paragraph fluently they have little idea of the meaning."

On a broader level, education was one factor in that inevitable process, the islanders' growing contact with, and knowledge of, the outside world. The story of the desertion might well have been different without it; education was a factor in the desertion, and in that sense the school contributed to its own redundancy. On the negative side, education contributed to the loss of their culture: as J L Campbell wrote of Barra in 1936, those people who had grown up before the 1872 Education Act came into effect retained more of their culture than younger people[18]. Mrs Murray's prophecy of 1888, that Finlayson was "busy with his English standards and methodical training to turn this remote and interesting island into as commonplace a village as any in our own neighbourhood" (Cardross, on the Clyde), was not to be fulfilled.

12

A 'most devout group of Catholics'

"The population of Miulaidh [Mingulay]. . . was the most devout group of Catholics I have ever known."

This was written by Donald Buchanan, a native of Barra who had spent many years in other parts of Britain, in 1942, and shows the strength of the islanders' faith, a faith that was fundamental to their lives.

The early history of Christianity in the Barra Isles has already been discussed. When Sir Donald Monro, archdeacon of the Diocese of the Isles, visited the area in 1549, he found the Church apparently flourishing, with chapels in many of the islands, and he gave no hint of the impending Reformation. Over most of Scotland this momentous upheaval, culminating in 1560, brought to an end a thousand years of Catholicism, first the Celtic monastic tradition, latterly the Roman diocesan system. The southern Outer Hebrides were among the few places where the old religion lived on.

In the decades after the Reformation, there was a general breakdown in church organisation; although the isolation of the islands preserved them from the ravages of Protestant persecutions, priests could no longer operate. The Catholic Church was curiously slow to respond to the threat of its total annihilation in the Highlands and Islands, and it was not until the 1630s that Irish Franciscans were sent there to 'reconcile' people to the old religion and perform marriages and baptisms. In 1636 Father Cornelius Ward "spent a month working in the isles of Barra, Feray [?Fiaray] and Barnaray. . . though the people of the Hebrides may be rough and uninstructed, they have not entirely forgotten the traditions of their fathers, as they always show great affection for the mass." The following year he worked "in the Bishops' Isles. . . where no priest had set foot since the Reformation"[1]. In 1654 another priest, Dermot Duggan, arrived in Barra, where he found "a people so devout and anxious to learn that I was astonished. It was enough to teach one child in each village the Pater, Ave and Credo; in two days the whole village knew them – children and adults."[2]

116

The conditions under which these early missionaries laboured were tough but must have been rewarding. Father Duggan described his work in the islands:

"I have to employ two men; one helps me to row when I travel from island to island, and carries my Mass-box and my scanty luggage overland. . . the other man helps me to teach the Pater, Ave, and Credo, and serves my mass. . . we take only one meal a day, of barley bread and oaten bread with some cheese or salt butter. Sometimes we spend whole days without a meal because we cannot procure anything."

He called for "good apostolic workers acquainted with the language and prepared to bear with hunger and thirst and sleeping on the ground"[3].

Father Duggan spent five years in the islands, and had reconciled people as far north as Benbecula, when he died. The islanders have remained steadfast to this day, despite discrimination and attempts at conversion such as we saw in the last chapter. One happy by-product of the survival of Roman Catholicism was, as related in chapter 3, the survival of traditional culture, which in the northern Outer Hebrides was oppressed by the more austere Protestantism.

A later worker, Father Francis MacDonel, complained of the difficulty of working in the Barra Isles:

"The Sacred Congregation only gave me one vestment, when two were very necessary, for the journey has often to be made from island to island, and there is great danger and difficulty in taking vestments between the five islands where there are Catholics. Indeed there should be one set of vestments in each island."[4]

Whether Mingulay's medieval chapel was in use at this time is uncertain. Bishop Nicolson, writing of Barra in 1700, reported that there were "six other inhabited islands, and there is a chapel in each." Mingulay must have been one of these, but there is no indication as to whether the chapels were in use or intact. Nicolson said of Cille Bharra, Barra, that there were the ruins of "two or three churches and a priory"; St. Barr's chapel was in ruins in 1625, but was still used for worship[5]. There is no subsequent reference to the chapel in Mingulay (or any of the other southern islands), and it was not until the end of the 19th century that another one was built. Mingulay's other site which had religious associations, Crois an t-Suidheachain, has already been mentioned.

By degrees a continuous succession of priests was established in Barra, which survived even the renewed persecutions of Catholics after the 1745 Jacobite uprising, and the conversion to the reformed faith of the MacNeil chiefs themselves. The MacNeils had been forced into this by the anti-Catholic legislation passed after the uprising. A story concerning James Grant, priest in Barra at the time of the '45, is quoted by Goodrich-Freer. Grant had sought refuge from the government soldiers, in Mingulay, from where he tried to escape to the mainland:

"It was at nightfall that he set sail, and when he got to Vatersay he went ashore to enquire news, and heard that the red soldiers (the Hanoverians) were in Barra, so he returned to Mingulay, and went alone to the cave of Hoisp [near the end of the cliff-bound peninsula of Dun Mingulay]. The red soldiers came to Mingulay, and the first two men they met were put under oath at the point of the sword. The first man said he had seen the priest leaving the island the day before, and the second said he had seen him come back and go over the hill. The soldiers struck the first man on the face with their muskets, and his nose was crooked till the day of his death. The other man they took with them, and they got the priest, and he was bound, and brought down to the village, and thrown into a barn near the house where John MacKinnon, son of Donald, son of Neil, now lives. Two young lads came in, one after another, where he was, and he asked the first to bring him some thatch to put under him, for the ground was very wet; and the lad went out, but was unable to return. And he asked the second to bring him an egg, but he too could not return. Thereafter the priest was taken away, and the next thing they heard was that he had been made a bishop" (of the Lowland District, at Aberdeen).

According to tradition, the boy who led the soldiers to their victim was haunted with guilt and heard voices, the priest's voice, the people said, until the day he died. He is remembered as Dòmhnall Mòr nam Bòcan, 'Big Donald of the Ghosts'. He went to New York to escape the voices, but the voices followed him, and followed him back again.

The Barra priest served the southern islands, which he visited, according to MacQueen in 1794, "twice a year, unless by a particular call to visit the sick, and to administer extreme unction" (the last rites). The priest also baptised children on his visits, including children who had already been baptised by a member of the community[6]; this was done if the child's survival was in doubt, to ensure it did not enter the state of 'limbo' in the event of its death. Marriages generally took place in Barra. There were occasional confirmation ceremonies in Barra, at which hundreds of young people from all over the parish were confirmed. At one of these, in 1884, twenty-one youngsters from Mingulay were confirmed by Bishop Allan MacDonald[7]. Confirmations accompanied the opening of Mingulay's new chapel, as we will see. In 1819 a Mingulay man was paying an annual amount for seats in Craigstone church[8]. This is curious, as it must have been rare for Mingulay people to attend the church. People in Pabbay and Sandray also paid these 'dues', as well as Barra people, which was how the Church was, and still is, funded; there was no state funding for the Catholic Church as there was for the Church of Scotland. Seats for two usually cost 2s 6d (12½p); marriages and christenings were also charged for, at 5s and 1s respectively.

The pattern of once or twice yearly visits continued for most of the 19th century, but by the early 1900s the visits had become monthly in summer, and less often in winter[9]. The servicing of the islands could have taken weeks, or not happened at all, if the weather was bad; we have seen how Father Allan McDonald was once stormbound on Mingulay for seven weeks. In the absence of a chapel, Muir was told in 1866, "the people always meet on Sundays and fast days to hear prayers at one of the elders' houses." How this was accomplished when the population was over 150 is hard to imagine. Individuals would lead the prayers; in the last years this was Donald MacPhee (Dòmhnall Bàn).

In 1804 Bishop John Chisholm wrote: "Those in the Western Islands and especially in the islands around Barra are splendid Catholics, who in the innocence of their lives and the firmness of their faith resemble the early Christians, and have the greatest horror of heresy."[10] The strength of the Mingulay people's faith is underlined by the complete failure of the (Free Church) Ladies' Highland Association to get them to attend Sunday school, let alone be converted; and the tolerance they showed by accepting the school contrasts with the intolerance of their beliefs by their 'benefactors'. Families prayed together at night, as was the case in Barra. One member would lead the prayer; there were Gaelic prayer books in Catherine MacNeil's house, which her mother read[11]. The islanders' faith also had its own characteristics which differed from that of the Barra people, due to their isolation and having to take most services themselves: they held prayer meetings on weekday evenings, with one person leading, a practice not found in Barra, and their faith could be considered to have been god-*fearing* rather than god-*loving*, which is a characteristic of that of Barra. It could be suggested that the Free Church school had some influence, but the school was open for only twelve years, there was no Sunday school, and the teacher, John Finlayson, does not seem to have been a zealot. Furthermore, the schools in Barra operated for much longer and Sunday school and other prayer meetings were held.

Mary Campbell told the story of a catechist who was sent to Mingulay to try to convert the people to Protestantism. He asked Ruairidh Dhòmhnaill

(Roderick of Donald, perhaps the storyteller, Roderick MacNeill) if he knew what kind of a place Hell was. The reply was (in translation) "Hell, a deep place, you can't measure it, and if you continue in the direction you're going in, you'll get to the bottom!"[12]. The people were spared the endless stream of fanatical Calvinist missionaries which the St Kildans were subjected to in their last two centuries.

The lack of a chapel, and of accommodation for the visiting priest, was remedied at last in the 1890s, when a building fulfilling both needs was erected (see plate 16). It was built in a prominent position overlooking the humble cottages of the village, as if symbolising the role of the church in the lives of its inhabitants. It was designed and built by John MacIntyre (Iain Mogach) of Barra. Its design was plain, domestic rather than ecclesiastical, reflecting its dual function, unique in the Hebrides; but what it may lack in architectural inspiration, it makes up for in scale. 15 metres long by 8.5 wide (50 x 28 feet), it was large even by Barra standards, and in a small island it is truly incongruous. It was solidly built from blocks of local stone, with a slate roof, and it was well-appointed internally and externally. The ground floor was for the use of the visiting priest and his housekeeper; there was never intended to be a resident priest. It consisted of five rooms opening off a central hall, with fine woodwork and plastered walls and ceilings through-out. This may seem unnecessarily spacious, but it was determined by the size of the chapel on the first floor. This was dedicated to St Columba, like its medieval predecessor. It was a single room, reached by an external stairway, lit by three windows on each side and lined with matchboarding. The altar and altar rail were made in Mingulay by John MacKinnon the joiner. The fourteen stations of the cross were hung on the walls. It is not thought that there were benches; there is no memory of their existence, and the benches of Vatersay church, which was built in 1913, were made in Vatersay (by John MacKinnon). In the last years there was a large bell, thought to have hung somewhere above the chapel steps, but there is no sign of it in plate 16. The bell survives; it was made in Glasgow in 1875, and may have been a ship's bell. Neil MacPhee (Niall Chaluim Dhòmhnaill) made a small sundial on a nearby rock outcrop, by levelling a small area on its top and erecting the pointer in a hole in the middle.

The building of the chapel must have been a huge undertaking, for apart from the stone, and sand for cement and plaster, everything down to the last nail had to be imported. The materials would have been landed on the beach on rafts and carried up to the site by hand. The main structure of the building was complete by 1898 and the whole operation probably lasted for years.

It is paradoxical that for this, the most prominent and one of the most recent buildings in Mingulay, very little historical information exists. It is known that it was the inspiration of the Barra priest, Father James Chisholm[13], and that Tady Glancy, a Castlebay merchant, provided the £700 building costs[14]. But the biggest question – why it was built at all – remains one of Mingulay's many mysteries. It can be explained partly in the context of the creation of the See of Argyll and the Isles in 1878, a re-creation, in a sense, of the pre-Reformation Diocese of the Isles[15]. Hitherto the region had been a remote and neglected part of a much larger see which included Glasgow.

The early years of the new see witnessed a programme of church building and the appointment of more priests. James Chisholm, appointed to Barra in 1883, was responsible for building the Church of Our Lady, Star of the Sea at Castlebay, which opened in 1889. His next project was Mingulay, which he must have decided was in need of a church. In hindsight the timing of this enterprise, so soon before the people left, seems inopportune. Evacuation had already been mooted by then, in 1883, so it may be that the provision of a chapel for these devout islanders was an attempt to encourage them to stay. Another suggestion, based on what tradition remembers of Tady Glancy, is that he saw the chapel as a memorial to himself or to his wife.

One cannot help wondering whether the islanders were involved in the decision, or whether they would have preferred money to have been spent on improving conditions in a practical rather than a spiritual way. From as early as 1890 they were appealing for improved landing facilities, and the derrick they eventually got cost only £200. The chapel building itself could have been simpler and cheaper. But such considerations, had they arisen, would have been academic; the will and the funds were there. There is no doubt that the people would have welcomed the new chapel and more visits from the priest, though they would have preferred him to have stayed. The priest was the most important figure in their lives, and their isolation from him was one of the many reasons for the evacuation.

The first mass in the new chapel, still unfinished, was said on the 19th of June 1898 by Father Allan McDonald of Eriskay. The next day Father James Chisholm, the chapel's founder, arrived with Bishop Smith, Bishop of Argyll and the Isles, and another priest, MacKenzie Saville, and confirmed forty-four children[16].

An early visitor to the chapel was Ada Goodrich-Freer, who went to Mingulay in August 1898 with her companion Constance Moore, together with, according to her, three priests and a doctor. She wrote of her visit:

"We made our headquarters in some rooms under the new chapel in process of building. It was bright August weather, and the scanty furniture was quite

*sufficient for our needs. There was a bedstead and bedding, which, with the aid
of a lavish loan of clean home-spun blankets, we were enabled to distribute into
three separate rooms; there was a board and trestles left behind by the workmen,
and a good cooking stove, with a pot and kettle as part of its fittings. Within an
hour of our arrival we were supplied with chairs, cups, plates, the inevitable
teapot. . . Our companions, the men, both of religion and medicine, found plenty
of occupation, for the people naturally took advantage of their visit to supply
their needs spiritual and bodily.*

*At an early hour next morning Mass was said in the little unfinished chapel,
with such fittings as could be arranged. There were no seats, but we were glad to
bring up our four chairs for the very old and infirm. Almost every adult in the
island was present, except a retired Presbyterian schoolmaster, and outside, a
little group of awe-stricken children silently awaited the dispersion of such a
gathering as they had never beheld."*

Fortunately, this is not the only record of the event, for, as related in chapter
1, Goodrich-Freer's testimony is not entirely reliable. Her companions were
not three priests and a doctor, but one priest, Father Allan McDonald,
together with Everard Fielding, a member of the Society for Psychical
Research, and Walter Blaikie, who was interested in traditions of the 1745
uprising[17]. It is no coincidence that two of the three stories Goodrich-Freer
quotes concern the uprising; it is very likely that Blaikie got Father Allan to
ask the people for such stories at the time of their visit[18]. The implication in
her account that this was the first service in the chapel was also untrue.

The Chapel House, as it is called today, had less than nine years of use
before the people it had been built to serve started leaving Mingulay. How
quickly things changed; and how ironic that Donald Martin, who had
succeeded the chapel's founder as Castlebay priest, was to encourage the
people to leave, as we will see in the next chapter. The priest's monthly visits
in summer continued to the end of 1909, when they became occasional only[19].

The people used a hollow in a rock near the landing place at Aneir as a
source of holy water. It may be this 'well' which is referred to by Goodrich-
Freer:

*In Mingulay is a well, known as the well of Columcille [St Columba], which
the people regard with such special reverence that, left often for months together
without any religious privileges, or any means of consecrating water for
devotional purposes, they use the well as 'holy water', and will cross themselves
with it as they go by, and carry it in the prow of their boat, as is the pious
custom of the fishermen."*

13

The 'Impossible Place'

"We spend the winter months lonely and dull but I hope summer shall get us relief as we shall be like prisoners during the bad weather. . . I am hoping to leave Mingulay soon."

So wrote Morag Campbell Finlayson, John Finlayson's adoptive daughter, in April 1905; two months later she was in Kentangaval, Barra[1]. No doubt her sentiments were shared by others, as Roderick MacNeil said there had been talk of evacuation long before it started[2]. The community was already in decline by this time: at least two roofless houses can be seen in Robert Adam's photographs taken in June 1905, and the corn mill had been abandoned. Only a year and a half later, in 1907, the emigration to Vatersay began. This process was well documented, as government departments were involved, so we know a good deal about some aspects of the Mingulay community's last years.

This was not the first time people had considered leaving; a few moved to Barra in or before 1883, and others had applied for holdings there. Thereafter, the islanders seem to have been confident of their future in Mingulay, and were even prosperous, for they built improved houses and a mill, and acquired two large herring fishing boats; and a chapel and landing derrick were provided.

Despite these positive signs, conditions in Mingulay were deteriorating. Neil MacPhee (Niall Dhòmhnaill Dhòmhnaill), interviewed in Vatersay in 1907, complained of the problem of access, the lack of land for a house and croft of his own, and the lack of seaweed for fertiliser; instead of seaweed, he had to get fish guts from Castlebay and spread them on the land, all during the fishing season when time was most precious[3]. The difficulty of access – getting to and from Mingulay, landing and loading people and goods, landing and launching boats – was the principal cause of hardship for the islanders. It prevented their taking full advantage of the fishing potential, and made landing of supplies difficult; getting a doctor or priest in an emergency was often impossible. The provision of the derrick in 1901 seems to have done little to ease the problem. The people had been shaken by the loss of the Pabbay fishing boat with all hands in 1897. Living conditions had become crowded and insanitary as the population grew, and there were epidemics of disease. The only remunerative employment was fishing, but, as dependence on cash to buy food and other necessities grew, it was not enough. Some of the men were forced to work away during the winter; in November 1899 it was reported that "most of the men are absent at present in Glasgow"[4], where they worked in the shipyards and gas works[5]. There was nothing new about this, though more men were doing it; a visitor to the school in 1868 had reported that some of the children were able to write letters to friends absent for work in the south and east. The community, which had once been largely self-sufficient and had even exported various commodities, had become increasingly dependent on the outside world.

The inhabitants of Mingulay were not alone in the Barra Isles in suffering overcrowding and land hunger; the townships around Castlebay were amongst the most congested in the Hebrides. Cottars from these townships had been trying for some time to get land on Vatersay, and no doubt the Mingulay people followed these attempts with interest. Vatersay was then run as a single farm, occupied by the tenant farmer and his workers; it had been crofted before 1850, when the people were evicted[6], and had been designated as suitable for crofting by a government commission in 1894[7]. It is easy to understand the attraction of Vatersay to cottars living in squalor – some of them in wooden huts, as they were not allowed to build houses – around Castlebay: there was ample land for house building, grazing for animals, cultivation, and a good harbour and many landing places. Its northern coast is only 2.5 kilometres (1½ miles) from Castlebay. Some of the cottars from Barra were descended from the former inhabitants, and had continued to bury their dead in the graveyard at the south end of Vatersay[8].

In 1883, forty-five Barra cottars, living in wretched conditions and eking out a meagre existence by fishing, applied for holdings on Vatersay, but were turned down by the landowner, Lady Gordon Cathcart. Her reasons were that, based on her experience of Mingulay, there was no guarantee that tenants in Vatersay would pay rent; there would be huge expense in settling crofters there, the water supply was inadequate, and she had recently improved Castlebay pier for fishermen[9]. Further appeals failed, including one from Barra Parish Council, and the men grew desperate. Then, in September 1900, emboldened by the success of cottars raiding (illegally squatting on) the farms at Northbay and Eoligarry in Barra (later bought by the Congested Districts Board for crofting), the men raided Vatersay, though they subsequently withdrew. In 1902 the Board bought some land on Vatersay for potato growing, but this turned out to be unsuitable for the purpose[10].

The cottars again appealed for holdings in 1905 when the tenant farmer's lease of Vatersay expired, but they were again ignored and the farmer's lease was renewed[11]. In July 1906 forty cottars, including three from Mingulay – John Sinclair (Iagan Iain Dhunnchaidh), Hugh MacLean (Eòghann Chaluim Iain) and Donald MacPhee (Dòmhnall Iain Dhòmhnaill) – raided Vatersay to select sites for wooden huts, which some of the Barra men proceeded to build[12]. The Mingulay people hesitated, but in January 1907 the emigration began. The first to leave were Michael Campbell (Teac), who had built a hut the previous month, his sister Catherine Sinclair (Catrìona Nèill Eachainn), and her son Duncan (Dunnchadh Anndra Dhunnchaidh), closely followed by the brothers Hector, Michael and Neil MacPhee (mic Dhòmhnaill Dhòmhnaill), Donald MacNeil, Hugh MacLean and John Sinclair[13]. At first they all crowded into Michael Campbell's hut, but later they built others, mostly near the farm buildings (where Vatersay Village now is); they brought their cattle over and proceeded to cultivate ground for potatoes[14]. Despite appeals and warnings from the estate factor and the farmer, Donald MacDonald, the raiders refused to leave; they knew they were breaking the law but were desperate. In April 1907, therefore, Lady Gordon Cathcart brought an interdict against eleven raiders, ordering them to leave; five were from Mingulay – Michael Campbell, the cousins Duncan and John Sinclair, and Hector and Neil MacPhee – and six from Barra – Donald MacIntyre, John Campbell, William Boyd, Roderick MacNeil, John MacDougall – including their overall leader, Duncan Campbell[15]. They ignored the interdict, and the stream of settlers continued. Although the first raiders from Mingulay were all cottars, they were soon joined by crofters; as we have seen, the land issue was only one of many causes of the evacuation. The Barra settlers, on the other hand, were all cottars.

The government was alarmed, and in May 1907 sent a judge, Sheriff John Wilson, to investigate and persuade the men to leave. He was unsuccessful, but his report was sympathetic to the raiders. He described them as "respectable men, and except in their views as to their right to get land and to take it if need be, they appeared to me to be both intelligent and reasonable. They were not only courteous, but kindly". He found that there was a "considerable body of local opinion to the effect that Lady Gordon Cathcart had not fully appreciated her duty as landowner, and that long indifference to the necessities of the cottars had gone far to drive them to exasperation." He quoted Neil MacPhee as saying that he had "grown sick of waiting and would prefer imprisonment rather than go back to Mingulay to starve or be driven to the US." Having been convinced by the seriousness of the raiders' case, Wilson recommended that the government buy all or part of Vatersay for crofting use[16]. It was most unusual for a judge to support law-breakers in this way, and this must have been a great boost to the raiders.

Vatersay was not the only destination of raiders: in November 1907 six Mingulay men went to Sandray to select sites for houses, and by January they had built two houses of stone and thatch at Sheader[17]. Sandray was then part of the grazing of Vatersay farm and inhabited only by a shepherd. The raiders brought their cattle and cultivated ground; they carried on lobster fishing, which was easier there than from Mingulay, as there was a sheltered beach for landing on, they got better bait there, and Castlebay was much nearer[18]. In October 1908 five of the six raiders wrote to the Board applying for holdings on Sandray:

> *"We are satisfied that it is a most suitable place for us as lobster fishing to make a fairly decent living and we will be very thankful if we are given holdings here instead of the impossible place of Mingulay where hitherto we have been trying to make a living among such dangerous surroundings."*[19]

The Sandray raiders were John Gillies (Iain Nèill Eòghainn), John MacNeil (Iain Sheumais Iain), and Donald MacNeil (Dòmhnall Iain Mhìcheil), John MacKinnon the joiner and his brother Alexander (of whom it was earlier said "There is no woman in the house, they act as if they were steamboat stewards"); and Michael MacNeil (an Rìgh) and his aunt Flora MacNeil. The first three of these had children, and there were twenty-seven people altogether in November, 1908, each family in a separate house[20].

Meanwhile, the Vatersay raiders were conducting a lively correspondence with various politicians who were concerned in the case or whose support might be enlisted. The letters were written by Neil MacPhee (Niall Chaluim Dhòmhnaill) of Mingulay, a man of remarkable ability. The following extract from a letter to Lord Pentland, Chairman of the Congested Districts Board, shows MacPhee's abilities and the feelings of the Mingulay settlers about their former home. It was written in 1909, after the Board had bought Vatersay, and concerns their belief that the ballot for crofts in Vatersay had been rigged, excluding some of the original raiders.

> *"We know it, My Lord, it is the Board's dastardly attempt to compel us to go back to the barren island of Mingulay. It shall never never be, My Lord, it is better a thousand times to die here than to go through the same hardships which were our lot on that island."*[21]

The Vatersay affair, highlighting as it did a widespread problem throughout the crofting areas of Scotland, was debated in both Houses of Parliament. It illustrated a major failing of the Crofters Act, the passing of which more than twenty years before had been intended to solve the land question once and for all: it had made no provision for the creation of new crofts. "The Scotch Office and the Government", commented the *Glasgow Herald*, "have been landed by Vatersay in a bog."[22] The Congested Districts Board had repeatedly declined Lady Gordon Cathcart's offers to sell Vatersay, on the grounds that such a purchase would be against government policy and that the issue of compensation to the tenant farmer was not their concern.

In the absence of an agreement, Lady Gordon Cathcart pressed on with her legal action against the raiders. In January 1908 she had served a complaint for breach of interdict against them, and an order to serve answers; the answers made it clear that they would not leave Vatersay[23]. The raiders, therefore (now ten, the case against Neil MacPhee having been dropped) were summonsed to appear in person before the Court of Session in Edinburgh on the 2nd of June 1908. Mr. Dewar, defending the raiders, stressed that they were not wilfully disobeying the order of the court by refusing to leave Vatersay. But the court regarded the background as irrelevant, and sentenced the men to two months in prison. Before beginning their sentences, they posed for press photographers outside the court. They sit or stand, impassive but dignified, in their Sunday suits and caps, not betraying the incongruity of their circumstances[24].

The case aroused enormous public interest and sympathy; people were intrigued by such goings-on in a remote and little known area. Petitions for the men's release were sent from all over Scotland, including Barra (written by Neil MacPhee)[25], and a relief fund for the raiders' families was launched by the *Edinburgh Evening News*. Memories were revived of previous (mostly pre-Crofters' Act) land raids in the Hebrides, when there were pitched battles between raiders and police sent to clear them off land they had occupied. The *Glasgow Herald* clarified the situation:

> *"An impression has got abroad that the Barra raider is a fiercely rebellious fellow. As a matter of fact, he is rather phlegmatic. He is surely the mildest mannered person who ever set a country's laws at defiance. . . the raiders of Barra have not in them the stuff of the true rebel. . . The talk of gunboats in these waters or a force of Glasgow policemen on the islands to protect the interests of landlordism may be dismissed as the idlest of rhetoric. . . And yet one wonders why anybody should choose to live on Vatersay or Sandray, still less on Mingulay. The raiders in Edinburgh doubtless find the barriers of the Calton Jail irksome enough, yet they choose to return to islands often veritably imprisoned by the sea."[26]*

The publicity surrounding the case and the desire of both the Congested Districts Board and Lady Gordon Cathcart not to lose face must have given negotiations a renewed urgency, for on the 18th of July the Board announced that agreement had been reached on creating crofts in Vatersay, and the men were immediately released. This being two weeks early, *"the public were unaware of what was transpiring, and consequently a probable public demonstration was avoided"*, reported the *Glasgow Herald*. *"The men emerged from the prison gates headed by Councillor Leishman and Mr Shaw [their solicitor], and were directed to the Regent Hotel, Waterloo Place, where a meal was provided. The procession of the men in that blue garb effected by fishermen attracted some attention, and those in the vicinity were quick to divine that the raiders had been set at liberty. Although the hotel is only a few hundred yards from the prison gates, the men eagerly lit their pipes."*[27]

The *Oban Times* said of their return to Barra:

"At Castlebay they were met by large crowds of the inhabitants. . . flags and bunting and stirring pipe music gave the occasion a gala aspect. The general feeling is one of relief and thankfulness that the hope that the government and Lady Gordon Cathcart would come to terms has not been disappointed."[28]

By August 1908 there were thirty-four families in Vatersay, of which fourteen were from Mingulay[29]. Six families, totalling about twenty-six people, remained in Mingulay, and all were planning to leave[30]. John MacLean (Barnaidh), had already been to Vatersay and started building a hut but had stopped when asked to. John Sinclair, one of the original raiders, had also been asked to stop building a hut; he had been staying with other raiders, and his family remained in Mingulay. John MacLean wrote a letter of application for a croft in Vatersay at this time, in which he said: "I am in possession of a holding in Mingulay but as the people have deserted this island I cannot remain there."[31] The others were adults living with parents, brothers or sisters. A seventh family was that of the teacher, Sarah MacShane; they must have been very uncertain of their future. By November there were thirty-seven families in Vatersay, eighteen of which were from Mingulay, and the five in Sandray.[32]

Vatersay was finally purchased by the Congested Districts Board in March 1909 for the sum of £6,250, and fifty-eight crofts were created[33]. The Board invited applications for these crofts, for which a ballot was held; but the Board apparently rigged the ballot to exclude some of the raiders, who were regarded as troublemakers. This impelled them to write the letter quoted above. It would have been ironic and grossly unjust if those who had led the battle for land, and had gone to prison for it, were now, at the last minute, about to be deprived of it. However, as some crofts were not taken up by the people to whom they had been allotted, nearly everyone who wanted a croft got one in the end. About a third of the crofts were taken by Mingulay people, including three of the Sandray raiders: John Gillies, Donald MacNeil and John MacNeil. These three were still in Sandray in March 1909 when the Congested Districts Board ordered them to leave[34]; the island was not considered suitable for settlement, and was to be used as grazing by the southern townships of Vatersay[35]. Despite the order, John Gillies remained there until early 1911[36].

Even after the 'official' settling of Vatersay a handful of people hung on in Mingulay. Fishing continued; twelve fishermen and boys were recorded in 1909, 1910 and 1911[37]. A few families with children, such as John MacLean's, may have stayed because of the school; there was no school in Vatersay until June 1910, two months after the closure of its predecessor in Mingulay. But eleven people were still there in April 1911 when the Congested Districts Board heard of a *"rumour that Lady Cathcart has let, as from Whitsunday, the Islands of Pabbay, Berneray, and Mingulay to one grazing tenant, and that notice has been served on the people resident on these islands that they are to leave, and that their stock if not cleared off will be seized."*[38]

The tenant referred to was Jonathan MacLean, a Castlebay hotelkeeper and merchant, who was known by the Board to be interested in the islands for grazing as early as 1908[39]. He had gained a foothold on the islands in 1910, when he took over a croft on Berneray; by the following year he was the tenant of most of the crofts on all three islands, and by 1915 he was sole occupier. Five years later he completed his empire when he became owner of the three islands[40].

The Board detailed the inhabitants of Mingulay at this time (April 1911)[41]: eleven adults, in six families. Four families were the same as in August 1908; in addition there were the MacKinnon brothers, and Michael MacNeil, all of whom were last heard of in Sandray. Five people, in two families, remained in Pabbay, but none in Berneray. All the islanders were said to be anxious to leave (as they had been three years before!). The Board seems to have taken the rumours seriously, for, keen to avoid those islanders who had nowhere else to go being forced to squat on Vatersay, it found them holdings there. The rumour was kept a secret, for in August (1911) Neil MacPhee wrote to the estate asking for a holding on Mingulay, having been refused one on Berneray[42]. He said he did not intend to live on the holding, so probably wanted it for grazing purposes; he had tried to get another holding on Vatersay for grazing, and in 1908, when most people had left, he was said to have "fenced off a large part of Mingulay, where he has a large stock."[43] The estate must have been keeping all the land in reserve for Jonathan MacLean, a policy the Congested Districts Board would have approved of. It is doubtful whether anybody was, in fact, given notice to quit, for this would have been retained in the collective memory of the people of Barra and Vatersay to this day.

By August 1911 only four of the above eight families remained. The Board's "policy of fetching the Mingulay islanders nearer civilisation" was not completed until the following summer, 1912, when Michael MacNeil (an Rìgh) was finally accommodated in Vatersay[44]. One of the ten fishermen based in Mingulay during the summer of 1912[45] may have been John MacLean who moved to Vatersay in 1910[46], but who was said by Robert Adam to have left in 1912[47]. 1912 was, therefore, the year that Mingulay was finally deserted by its native human population.

It was ironic in the end that, having escaped the notorious 'clearances' of other parts of the Barra Isles the previous century, and after most of the inhabitants had left of their own accord, the remainder were threatened with eviction in favour of sheep. But this was merely the 'last straw'; the people wanted to go, the Congested Districts Board wanted them to go, and Lady Gordon Cathcart would not have further risked her reputation by being involved in evicting tenants (could this have been done legally anyway?) without knowing there was somewhere for them to go.

There are few details of the physical processes of the desertion, as it happened over a number of years. Large items of furniture which could not be transported, such as looms (which were made largely redundant anyway, because imported woollen cloth was now available) were left behind[48], and many things which would have been of no use to their owners in their new lives were probably abandoned. Getting full-grown cattle and ponies into boats must have been quite a problem: perhaps the derrick really was useful here, if the animals could have reached the platform.

What was it like leaving Mingulay? A relief in many ways, no doubt, although the first few years, before people got their crofts and could build proper houses, must have been hard. Although most of the islanders moved to Vatersay, the move spelled the end of the community as an entity, as they were scattered between different townships. There was no longer a need for many of their traditional communal activities, such as waulking cloth, cutting peat, hauling in boats, and holding church services on their own; ceilidhing practically ceased. There was certainly no Home Rule here. Because of their former isolation, the Mingulay people didn't find it easy to fit in with the Barra settlers, and kept themselves to themselves. At least one family opted for Glasgow in preference to Vatersay. Mary Campbell always preferred

Mingulay to Vatersay: it was wild in the winter, but people were friendlier and more content; they changed a lot when they moved to Vatersay[49].

This leads on to another question: how unanimous had the cry for evacuation been? Not everyone wanted to go; John MacLean (Barnaidh), for instance, was doing well with his fishing, but he would have known that he could stay only if several other fishermen did too. A certain minimum number of people would have been needed to make life possible in Mingulay, if only to launch and land boats. MacLean may also have been concerned about his children's education, for he left Mingulay at the time the school closed. Mary Campbell (Màiri Dhòmhnaill Eachainn), who, with her sister Elizabeth, was one of the last to go, is also said to have been reluctant to do so. There were probably a good many people who didn't actually want to go, but knew they had to.

Another consideration is the role of the Castlebay priest, Donald Martin. Despite the recent building of the chapel in Mingulay, he is thought to have encouraged the people to leave (he was said to be "not dissuading" the raiders from Barra in 1907[50]), perhaps for their own good, or, it has been suggested, because he didn't like going there and didn't get much in the collecting box. He is also known to have been friendly with Jonathan MacLean, the new tenant, though whether there is any significance in this is impossible to say.

The process of evacuation had lasted five years, starting with the islanders joining illegal land-grabbing, and ending with the government giving them all they wanted and actively settling the last 'stragglers' in Vatersay. It happened this way only because the sheer numbers of people from Barra and Mingulay raiding Vatersay in search of better conditions forced the land owner and the government to act; the land issue was on the political agenda anyway, with the election in 1906 of a Liberal government under Sir Hugh Campbell-Bannerman of Glasgow, after twenty years of Conservative government[51]; and the public outcry at the sentences had ensured high-level attention. Just as the Vatersay raiders had been spurred on by the success of previous land raiding in Barra, so people in other crofting areas were encouraged by the Vatersay raiders; and government policy was irreversibly changed. The case illustrates the change of attitude to the problems of the islands; not many decades before, emigration was seen as the solution, but now it was recognised that these issues should be faced and solved at home.

The Scottish Office and the Congested Districts Board seem to have encouraged the evacuation of the small islands in the end, because they were keen to avoid the risk of anyone remaining there squatting on Vatersay at a later date. Having made a commitment to the majority by giving them

Vatersay, they may have felt a responsibility for the remainder. Having a few people scattered about in remote islands who might have needed services such as health and education would have been inconvenient and expensive. The state was taking an increasing role in island life, but there were limits to the size of communities on small islands it was considered economic to support. Hence the decision not to settle any crofters on Sandray, largely because providing a school would have been expensive. Such considerations were also behind the willingness to fund the evacuation of St Kilda in 1930, for example.

Depopulation has been a feature of Scotland's islands for two centuries. In the Barra Isles, 27% of the population lived on seven of the smaller islands in 1764. By 1841 the percentage was nineteen (on eight islands), in 1901, eight (on six islands). In Scotland as a whole, over a hundred of the islands described by Monro in 1549, or inhabited since, have since been deserted. Over half of these had fewer than twenty people at the time of their desertion, showing that small numbers were the least viable, and only nine, including Mingulay, had over a hundred[52]. Some of the smaller islands were settled only temporarily by people evicted from elsewhere; and some, like Mingulay, had their populations swelled by such people. Apart from those communities which were evicted, the reasons for their desertion were in most cases similar: the values and living standards of the outside world were rapidly catching up on the islands, and were becoming known to the people through education and travel to the mainland for work. Life on small islands had become an unacceptable struggle. What was unusual about Mingulay was the manner of the desertion.

Those smaller islands which have retained their people to this day have done so for three main reasons: they have employment opportunities, which in most cases means fishing (or members of the family working away, such as at sea); they have a large enough population for provision of services such as schools, and social and shopping facilities; and they have good transport links with their nearest main island in the form of car ferries. Vatersay, for instance, for which the Mingulay people abandoned their island, was itself in danger of being deserted by the 1980s, largely because of the inadequate ferry service to Barra and lack of facilities on the island. It was saved by the building of a causeway from Barra. The island of Scalpay, off the sheltered east coast of Harris, thrives because it has a good harbour for fishing boats, and a car ferry to Harris. In contrast, Scarp, off the Atlantic west coast, was finally abandoned in 1971 because it had no harbour, only a small pier, and no pier was provided on the Harris side of the treacherous sound until most of the people had left. Only three of the small islands of the Outer Hebrides which remain true islands are still inhabited: Scalpay off Harris, Berneray off North Uist, and Eriskay off South Uist. Bridges or causeways are planned to all of them. In 1841 about thirty of the small islands were inhabited.

The eventual desertion of Mingulay was inevitable because of remoteness and the lack of a landing place; its exposure to the Atlantic and the nature of its coast meant that it would never have been possible to create an adequate landing place. The First World War would have been disastrous to Mingulay, as the fishing industry collapsed completely, most of the men being away in the merchant navy if not in the services.

What if. . . the population had not been swelled by evictees from other islands in the 19th century?. . adequate landing facilities had been provided?. . there had not been an empty island to raid? . . the raiders had not been allowed to stay?. . One can speculate endlessly along these lines. Possibly a dwindling number would have struggled on, but the basic fact remains: Mingulay had become an 'impossible place', as the Sandray raiders described it, in the changing social and economic climate around the turn of the century.

14

The Deserted Island

Since the abandonment of Mingulay by its native human inhabitants, it, along with the neighbouring islands, has been used for grazing. Small uninhabited islands are very suitable for this purpose, even if the quality of the grazing is not high, because, since they have natural boundaries, investment in fencing etc is minimal.

The departure of the last inhabitants from Mingulay in the summer of 1912 gave Jonathan MacLean, the new tenant, a free hand. To guard against anyone returning, he dismantled the derrick, using some of its wooden parts as corner posts for fencing (so *he* must have thought it had been useful, even if the islanders didn't, though not useful enough for him to keep). He is reputed to have cut up the rafters of the houses as fence posts, and burnt the thatch. The houses would have been in a sorry state by then. In April 1911, five houses were still occupied and another seven were said to have been 'uninhabited'[1]. If this meant empty though habitable, all the rest were presumably deteriorating; thatched roofs have to be maintained regularly. Certainly, by 1922, when Robert Adam returned to take photographs, only walls remained.

MacLean stocked Mingulay, Pabbay and Berneray with sheep, and the first two with calves as well. He and his successor, John Russell, built small sheep pens, for a milking ewe and lamb, wherever stone – usually the remains of earlier structures – was available. He made the school buildings the centre of his activities, accommodating his shepherds who were to live on the island during the spring and summer in the schoolhouse, and using the school-room as a store. He built a sheep dip next to the schoolhouse and made use of the school enclosure when rounding up the sheep. The school buildings were much more convenient than the Chapel House, being near the landing place and having a view of the route followed by the approaching boat from Castlebay. Because of the problems of landing and launching boats, the shepherds did not keep a boat at Mingulay; the successive owners of the island kept their boat at Castlebay. Their main lifeline, however, was the lighthouse boat which came down weekly in summer, fortnightly in winter calling in with supplies and mail.

MacLean rented the islands until 1919, when he bought them from Lady Gordon Cathcart[2]. In 1930 he sold them to John Russell, who had been sheep farming in Montana and before that in Australia[3]. Russell actually lived on Mingulay all year round, alone except in the spring and summer when he was joined by his two shepherds. The folklorist Margaret Fay Shaw, then living in South Uist, described a visit she made to Russell in the early 1930s:

> *"The coal stove had an oven, which was sometimes hot enough for baking. A whisky bottle was the rolling pin for my oatcakes and there was plenty of milk from the two nanny goats. The eggs were from the cliffs – from gulls, guillemots and razorbills – good for custards and omelettes but never to be boiled, when the taste would be of foul fish. Spam was made interesting in many ways and then we had rabbits which were caught by a pair of ferrets, the treasured friends of Mr. Russell who could pet and handle their wild jumping play as though they were harmless pussies. I was with the shepherds in not daring to touch them".*

Russell also kept 'harmless pussies' – five of them.

Russell sold the islands in 1937 to Mrs Peggy Greer, an Essex farmer[4]. She paid only occasional visits to the islands, leaving them in the care of shepherds from Barra. She fenced off a length of Mingulay's south west coastline to prevent sheep clambering along the cliff ledges in search of grass, getting stuck, and falling off. In 1948 she imported a small motor plough to plough the potato field, previously used by Russell, next to the road alongside the village. Potatoes were stored in the Chapel House. This building had remained church property until Mrs Greer bought it, but the church furnishings were removed earlier in the 1930s, during the time of Father Donald Campbell of Castlebay. The altar, made by John MacKinnon, was taken to the church in Castlebay, where it became the side altar; the altar rail and other fittings were taken to the church in Vatersay, where they were used until recent years. In about 1946 the schoolroom was gutted by fire, when a large lump of beeswax found washed ashore and stored in the room, was ignited by a smouldering fire in the grate.

Mrs Greer tried to sell the three islands in 1951, but couldn't find a buyer she considered suitable for several years; in the meantime she let them to two graziers from Harris. In 1955 the islands were bought by the Barra Head Isles Sheepstock Company, a syndicate of Barra crofters, and they remain in the company's possession. With motor boats being by then in common use, making the islands more accessible, it was no longer necessary for shepherds to live there for long periods; shearing, dipping, taking off lambs can usually be done in a day. However, the schoolhouse continues to be used for overnight stays and as a store, and in 1986 it was re-roofed in corrugated iron.

The Chapel House, sadly, is in a very poor state of repair and its future is bleak. In 1960 a visiting architect reported it to be in excellent condition[5], but only five years later it was described as semi-ruinous[6]. By this time groups of campers had begun to stay on the island, and it was also used for a survival course by the British army, during which the schoolhouse was broken into. (Dun Mingulay was also used by the US navy for a training exercise at some point, during which metal supports for a high wire, one on each side of the neck of the peninsula, were put up.) Campers continued to rob the woodwork of the house for firewood, and a hole in the roof may have been made deliberately.

In 1975 Colin Archer, a teacher of English working overseas, bought the building as a holiday home following a visit to Mingulay. He had doors and windows put in, and had the roof repaired temporarily, pending more permanent work. This was arranged, but the contractor never carried out the work. Another attempt failed, and the building is now beyond repair. Archer tried, unsuccessfully, to interest organisations who might make use of the building, for example as a hostel for small groups. It is a sad story; the building, made to last for ever, served as a church for hardly more than ten years, after which it stood empty and useless for more than sixty years. The work done on it subsequently gave it only a temporary reprieve from eventual dereliction.

Mingulay remained in the hearts of the islanders after they left, despite the hardships they had suffered there, and the strong words some, such as Neil MacPhee, had had for it. MacPhee was able to look back with longing and romance many years later, as his song (Appendix 2) shows. There used to be annual pilgrimages to Mingulay from Vatersay, but these had become irregular by the 1970s. In 1975 some descendants of islanders held a final service in the chapel before it was sold.

Since the desertion, Mingulay and its neighbours have continued to attract ornithologists and botanists. In recent decades the emphasis has been on the conservation of the natural heritage of such remote uninhabited islands, and the importance of Mingulay and Berneray was recognised by their being created a Site of Special Scientific Interest in 1983, and a Special Protection Area, as regards the seabirds, in 1994.

The growth of leisure and the interest of individuals and groups in such areas for recreation or study has meant an increasing number of people visiting Mingulay in recent decades. Unfortunately not all the visitors treat the island with respect, and the village has suffered from people knocking stones off walls, even heaving massive lintels off doorways; crosses in the graveyard have been broken, as have quern stones. Attempts appear to have been made to remove ancient objects such as quern stones. Sheep clambering on walls eating grass, and burrowing rabbits (originally introduced as a source of food by the shepherds after the desertion), have also contributed to the deterioration of the village.

The importance of the human heritage of the island should be recognised and protected, as the natural heritage has been. This applies to the village in particular, which is unique in the Outer Hebrides. This could be done by scheduling sites under the Ancient Monuments Act, which provides legal protection. In recent years Historic Scotland, the agency responsible, has extended scheduling from major archaeological and historic sites in the Hebrides to more recent domestic sites. The small and poorly-preserved settlement on Pabbay has been included in an extended scheduled area which originally applied only to the Pictish symbol stone[7]. Practical protection is another matter, and it is difficult to suggest how the physical deterioration of the village and other sites could be stemmed.

What of the future? Given Mingulay's suitability as grazing, its isolation and inaccessibility, and the restrictions on its use imposed by its designation in conservation terms, it is unlikely that its use will change significantly. Mingulay and its neighbours have not so far been found to have strategic value in the defence of the nation, and have been spared the fate of St Kilda, where the British army built a base as part of the missile testing station on South Uist in 1957. It is to be hoped that human activity on the island will remain at a low level and will not conflict with the conservation of the natural and human heritage.

15

Berneray

Berneray is the most southerly of the Outer Hebrides, and is also known as Barra Head, the name of its southernmost point (see maps 1 and 4). It is the smallest of the four islands, being 3 kilometres (1¾ miles) long, and 1.3 kilometres (¾ mile) across. It resembles a tilted wedge in form, the land rising from the east and north coasts to a central ridge, Mullach a' Lusgan, the southern and western flanks of which plunge down to the sea, in cliffs up to 190 metres (625 feet) high. The cliffs reach to within three metres of the summit of the island at Sotan, and the lighthouse perches on the cliff edge near this point. The power of the sea and wind during times of storm is here so great that the lighthouse compound is deluged with salt spray, and small fish have even found their way up. As on Mingulay, the cliffs are the breeding ground of seabirds which were caught for food by the islanders.

A visitor to Berneray in 1868, Captain Elwes, wrote:

"It was the grandest sight I ever experienced, to look out of the window of the lighthouse on a very stormy day, and see oneself hanging, as it were, over the ocean, surrounded on three sides by a fearful chasm in which the air was so thickly crowded with birds as to produce the appearance of a heavy snowstorm, whilst the cries of these myriads, mingled with the roar of the ocean and the howling of the tremendous gusts of wind coming up from below as if forced through a blast pipe, made it almost impossible to hear a person speak."

Apart from its cliffs, Berneray is less varied and interesting than the other islands; there is no glen, bay, or beach, and the few streams are very small. The only relatively flat area is around the north east coast, where settlement was concentrated.

Berneray was thoroughly surveyed archaeologically for the first time in 1992, by a team of archaeologists from Sheffield University and from Prague[1]. As in the other islands, a large number of sites was located. The earliest identifiable sites were possible burial monuments, both Neolithic chambered tombs and Bronze Age cairns, in the settlement area and on the south side of the central ridge. Hut circles of possible Iron Age date were also found. A Bronze Age stone circle was identified by Thom near the north coast, and Muir mentioned a "cairn or dolmen" near the lighthouse.

The Iron Age is represented by the most prominent ancient site – the dun, Dùn Sròn an Dùin, dramatically situated on the cliff-bound promontory near the lighthouse. It attracted attention as early as 1695, when Martin Martin wrote: "There is an old Fort in this Island, having a Vacuity round the Walls, divided in little Apartments." It was also mentioned in 1768, 1794 and 1828[2], and was described by late 19th century antiquarians. Until recently, the outer wall of the dun was thought to have survived as a curved wall crossing the neck of the promontory[3]. Some of the lintels of the gallery between it and the inner wall, which has disappeared, survive. This wall forms the western wall of a compound associated with the lighthouse. The Sheffield survey, however, cast doubt on this interpretation. Most of the wall is built of massive blocks, but there is an abrupt change to much smaller stones at its northern end, which includes a lintelled doorway, and is much less ruined than the rest. Some features of the doorway are very uncharacteristic of duns, though earlier observers identified features similar to other dun entrances. Furthermore, the presence of a gallery suggests that the dun formed a complete enclosure, but no trace of the rest remains, and the lighthouse builders quarried stone from the area it would have covered. MacQueen's 1794 description of the dun as being "more entire" than any of the duns in the Barra Isles, for which, he believed, it had served "as a pharos or watch tower", supports this theory. If this is the case, some deterioration had occurred by 1828, when the dun was described as a "segment of a circle" by thirteen-year-old David Stevenson, on a visit to Berneray with his father Robert, who was to build the lighthouse. So it seems very likely that the

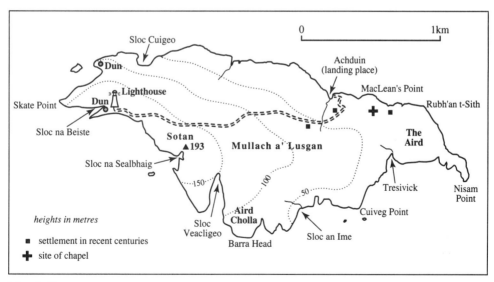

Map 4. Berneray

A romanticised view of the dun and Barra Head lighthouse, Berneray (from Bird, 1866). The depiction of the dun is fanciful, but the lighthouse was like this before its top was remodelled.

lighthouse builders built the northern section of the dun wall, but it is difficult to explain why they gave it the appearance of being ancient, thereby deluding generations of observers. The doorway, which gave access to the compound from the quarry, is also curious; it is rather small, and apparently incorporates some elements of the original dun entrance. Further investigation is needed before anything more definite can be said about this intriguing site. According to a local tradition, the dun was used as a refuge by an outlawed laird of Barra[4].

North of the lighthouse, another promontory was defended by a single massive wall stretching across it. It is known as Dùn Briste, and is also assumed to be Iron Age in date, but being so near the other dun it is unlikely to be contemporary with it[5].

The recent survey revealed a number of boat-shaped stone settings resembling Norse boat graves. They were located on the south side of the central ridge and in the settlement area. Definite evidence of Norse presence is in the form of many of the island's place names; the name Berneray itself (Gaelic *Beàrnaraigh*) comes from the Old Norse *Bjarnaray*, 'Bjorn's Isle'.

In medieval times a chapel was built, its traditional site being in the graveyard in the settlement, near MacLean's Point[6]. No trace of the building has ever been found, and its dedication is unknown. There may have been a chapel in Early Christian times, for a stone slab with a simple incised cross has been found here, possibly dating to between the sixth and ninth centuries[7]. Another stone in the graveyard has a hollow in it, thought to have been used for grinding up shellfish for bait. The graveyard is a complex site. Its earliest structure is a low mound, over part of which buildings or enclosures were later built. The graveyard was in use up to the time of the desertion of the island. The area seems to have been a focus of settlement at one time, and there are traces of a field system earlier than the present one[8]. The houses of the last inhabitants are scattered about over a wider area, some near the road to the lighthouse, with no particular focus.

Berneray was inhabited in Monro's time, 1549, and it was one of the islands where Cornelius Ward, the Irish Franciscan, worked in 1636. In 1794 it was referred to as the Bishop's Isle (*Beàrnaraigh an Easbaig*)[9], a memory of the former connection of all five southern islands with the Bishop of the Isles; it is interesting that the name became associated only with Berneray, but that could simply be to distinguish it from other Bernerays in the Outer Hebrides. In 1764 its population was twenty (paying £6 rent)[10] and thirty years later there were three families[11]. These figures remained similar right up until the last people left. In 1841 there were twenty-one people in four families, the highest figure of twenty-eight being reached in 1851. In subsequent census years up to 1891 figures varied between seventeen and twenty-one, in two or three families. These figures exclude the lighthouse keepers and, from 1871, fishermen stayed temporarily on the island. The 1901 figure for the whole island was seventeen, suggesting a drop in the number of native islanders, the last of whom left about 1910.

This stability of population contrasts with Mingulay and shows that the figures were about right for the island to support. The main family names in the 19th century included MacNeil, MacLean, Campbell, MacIntyre, and Sinclair. The MacLeans are believed to have come from Mull originally; and Ranald Carmichael, recorded in the 1841 census as having been born outside Inverness-shire, may have come from Argyll, as the name suggests. John MacNeill (Iain Mhìcheil Iain, 1880-1958) became a Canon in the Catholic Church at Morar; his father Michael, crofter and fish-curer, had attended the Ladies' School in Mingulay[12]. It is likely that Michael's brother Allan (born 1846) also went to the school, for he became an assistant keeper at the lighthouse[13], which was most unusual as most of the keepers were from other parts of Scotland. He later moved to Tangusdale in Barra. The Sinclairs were the family of Duncan, originally from Argyll, who settled in Berneray in the 1840s. Most of his children settled in other islands, but one of his sons, Peter, remained in Berneray. He was a huge man, known as Pàdraig Mòr, 'Big Peter', or the 'Barra Giant'. The antiquary T S Muir put his tape measure to unusual use on his visit in 1866; Peter, then seventeen, was 6 feet 8 inches

(2.06 metres) tall. He joined a travelling show for a time, but disliked the publicity and returned to the islands. He used to bring his cattle to Castlebay in the summer months and run a dairy, returning to his distant home in the winter[14].

The people lived, like their neighbours in Mingulay, by crofting, fishing and fowling. There were four crofts in 1840 (paying £20 rent)[15], and there remained four right up until the end, but one of these was held by the Lighthouse Commissioners for much of that time, presumably for grazing. The people grew barley, oats, potatoes, turnips and cabbages when Muir visited in 1866; and kept cattle, sheep and ponies. What the ponies were kept for is not clear, for there was no peat for them to carry; perhaps they were hired out for lighthouse work. Miss Bird recorded goats in 1863. In 1856 there were six ponies, twelve cattle and twenty-eight sheep[16]; in 1883 there were no ponies, forty cattle – a huge increase, almost all of them calves which would have been sold – and twenty-one sheep[17]. Berneray's common grazing included the islet of Geirum Mor, in the sound between Berneray and Mingulay. Although not high like Mingulay's stacks, it was accessible only in exceptional weather. It was still being used as late as 1907, when Robert Adam accompanied five men and five dogs in rounding up just seven sheep, the survivors of twelve which had been landed the year before[18]. Agriculture on Berneray was limited, as there is little naturally fertile land, and lazy-beds, which can be seen around the settlement area, had to be made. Berneray had no peat, so the islanders had to cross to Mingulay for it. This must have been an enormous undertaking, and was one reason why, Muir said in 1866, Duncan Sinclair reckoned the Mingulay people to be much better off than he and his neighbours were.

Berneray was an easier place to fish from than Mingulay, on account of its superior landing place. This was a sheltered creek on the north coast, Achduin[19], where there is a small 'beach' of boulders, and a pier was built here for the use of the lighthouse. Boats were dragged onto the rocks. In the late 19th century the islanders had only one boat, which was used mainly for catching white fish such as ling and cod[20]. In 1903 this was owned by Peter Sinclair, and called *The Three Brothers*[21]. In the late 19th century, Berneray was used as a base by fishermen from Mingulay, Pabbay and Barra exploiting the rich stocks of white fish around Barra Head. The censuses, taken in early April when the season had begun, show these fishermen in Berneray. By 1871 the practice was beginning, perhaps because of the recent development of Castlebay as a fishing port, and seven fishermen were   lodging with crofters; in 1881 twenty fishermen were living in four temporary huts, and ten years later, there were eleven in two huts. The fishermen cured fish there, perhaps for their own consumption, as they sold most of their catches in Castlebay.

The seabirds nesting on the cliffs provided the islanders with an important item of food, and feathers for sale; in 1868 the islanders were supplying birds to the crews of fishing boats from Islay. A fowler was recorded as having caught 600 birds in six to eight hours, using the pole method, in 1868[22]; nooses must have been used also, but they are not recorded. An early visitor to Berneray mentions the use of birds and their eggs. William MacGillivray, professor of Natural History at Aberdeen University, and a landowner in Harris, wrote in 1818:

> *"On reaching Berneray we landed and soon after betook ourselves to a hut which we found cleared for our reception. We dined on roasted mutton, wild fowls' eggs, bread, butter and whisky. The goodman [head] of the house came home with a basketful of eggs from the rocks, and some birds which he had caught."*

In 1829 Berneray was chosen as the site for a lighthouse, and a number of descriptions of the island by visitors to the lighthouse are known. David Stevenson described one of the houses in 1828:

> *"We found several women and a number of children all squatting on the ground round a fire of peats on the floor and without any chimney and except for a few cooking materials we saw no other articles of furniture whatever. In the other apartment there was a large box-bed and a rude weaving loom. There 4 or 5 children of the family made their bed of straw on the floor, with only a single plaid to cover them. They had no school nor did they seem to make the least provision for acquiring the simplest rudiments of education. The women and children had a tolerably clean appearance. The men were more rough. They had neither shoes on their feet nor covering of any kind on their head nor coats on their backs."*[23]

Another visitor was Isabella Bird, who travelled the world and wrote prolifically about her adventures. She landed in 1863 from the *Shamrock*, under the charge of Captain Otter, who was engaged in mapping the islands for the Admiralty. At that time there was no pier, only a *"shelving table of rock at the foot of a rent in the cliff, and this is only available in calm weather and in certain winds. As it was, we had to watch our opportunity when the boat went in on the top of a wave, and spring ashore. The shelving rock was steep to climb, and so slippery with fish scales and fish oil that one of the officers fell on his face. At the top of this inhospitable pier there were several trays full of dog fish and skate lying in brine. . . Long poles, with which the natives kill the sea-fowl, were lying about. Above the ledge of rock on which we landed, the whole island population was congregated. We received an outrageous welcome; everybody shook hands with somebody, all the people poured out torrents of words in the vernacular, and a few made the most of some very lame sentences in English, resorting to patting and stroking to make them more emphatic. There was something only half civilised about the whole affair, and I doubt not that strings of beads, and looking-glasses, would have been as gleefully received as in Central Africa. Yet these people were all well-dressed, cleanly, and healthy looking, and most anxious to take us to their abodes. We spent some time in one of them, and were regaled with delicious cream, in large, clean, wooden bowls.*

This was the lightest, cleanest, best appointed Highland hut I ever entered. Its inmates seemed entirely dependent on their own resources; tobacco and tea, and the last used not as a beverage, but as a luxury, appeared the only exotic articles. The garments were all made of homespun wool, and the striped winceys of the women, woven by themselves, would not have disgraced Aberdeen. Crinoline had penetrated even to Bernera, but it too was home-manufactured, out of hoops of barrels thrown up from a wreck. Two buxom girls had never seen 'ladies' before, and occupied themselves with a minute but surreptitious scrutiny of the garments of those of our party. The hut was furnished with tables, benches, boxes, beds and stools of driftwood. The guidman [Duncan Sinclair] was the only native Protestant on the island, and as if in proof of a fact no doubt of considerable importance in this little insular world, he bought a Bible, paying for it in the currency of Bernera – dried skate. His son, a fine boy of ten years [Duncan], has the distinction of being the scholar of the island, and, after diving from the top of a rock and swimming out to see the 'Shamrock', he returned, ruddy and dripping, to read a lesson in English, a tongue of which he evidently comprehended not one word.

After receiving us thus hospitably, the whole population set off in their great boat to the 'Shamrock', where curiosity and bargaining kept them for three hours chaffering with the cook and sailors, paying for their purchases in fish. To their credit be it recorded that they seemed more disposed to give than to take. . . It seemed they were never weary of the sight of the black cook, whom at first they had taken for the devil!

Far out in the Atlantic, exposed to its fullest fury, and generally inaccessible, [Bernera] yet has nursed a population before, rather than behind, those of the other Hebrides. Without any advantages or other religious ordinances than are supplied by the annual visit of a priest from Barra, these very interesting people thirst for education, and would make considerable sacrifices to obtain it."

Another visitor who was moved to write about Berneray was William Chambers, a Commissioner of Northern Lighthouses, after a tour of lighthouses in 1866:

"The road slanted across the open hillside, which was devoted chiefly to the

pasturage of a few cattle and sheep. Here and there were small patches of barley and oats, enclosed with fences of turf; but so meagre were the crops and so plentifully interspersed with tall dock weeds, that there was promise of but an insignificant harvest." Where the road crossed the stream which enters the sea at the landing place, Chambers noticed "*a low building which appeared to be a mill of some kind, with a wheel at one end... The mill is entirely the handiwork of an ingenious assistant lighthouse keeper (a Fife man), who diverted his leisure hours in its construction. He erected the building, covered it with a tarpaulin roof, and fabricated the whole of the grinding apparatus. The most difficult part of the undertaking was accomplished by adapting an old cart-wheel. The idea of erecting a mill was suggested by the absence from the island of all means of grinding except for a primitive species of hand-querns. Glad of the opportunity of so easily transforming their corn into meal, the crofters besought the privilege of using it, which was of course allowed; and the multure was arranged on the convenient footing of giving a lamb for a grist, be the quantity much or little... The interior of the mill... [is] about eight feet square; adjoining is a kiln, equally diminutive, made from a piece of old sheet-iron, for drying the grain.*

I afterwards visited two thatched dwellings, poor lowly biggings with no attempt at neatness or cleanliness in their miserable surroundings... A leading feature consists in a twisted orifice in the roof to let out the smoke from the peat fire in the middle of the clay floor... I had learned, from various knowing hints and looks of a Commissioner, that it was not advisable to enter any of the dwellings... In the first hut there was an old woman barefooted, who could speak only a few words of English, but seemed anxious to be hospitable, and set a chair for me beside the peat fire. The cottage contained a loom in one corner, in which was a web of dark woollen cloth, for the clothing of the family. In the other hut was an old woman carding wool, and her daughter neatly dressed in tartan, who spoke English tolerably. Here also was a loom... The husband and sons connected with these families occupy their time partly as fishermen, and take cargoes of cured fish to Portrush on the northern coast of Ireland, or sell them to Glasgow traders."

It seems from this account that the mill was built partly with the crofters in mind, and partly for fun. The lighthouse keepers would not have needed it, as they must have imported their own flour, though they grew vegetables in plots near the lighthouse. The mill was built on the vertical principle, and can only have worked after heavy rain swelled the tiny stream which powered it. It was one of only two mills marked on maps of the Barra Isles in 1861-3 and 1878[24], and without Chambers's account it would be hard to explain, the native population being so small. The builder was very probably

James Oswald, from St Monans, Fife, who served an exceptionally long time at the lighthouse: he was recorded in the censuses of 1851 (as 'occasional lightkeeper'), 1861 and 1871, and at Muir's visit in 1866. He had gone by 1881, and the mill eventually fell into disuse. John MacKinnon of Mingulay copied this mill, and may even have used some of its parts.

Isabella Bird mentioned the people's 'thirst for education'. This was not the first time the people had tried to get a teacher; they nearly got one in 1859, but the teacher went to Mingulay instead. Earlier, in 1851, several of Duncan Sinclair's children were described as 'scholars at home'. Some Berneray children attended the Mingulay school, and eventually, Barra School Board established a school in Berneray, as a 'sub school' of the Mingulay school. It was mentioned briefly in the log book of its parent between 1884 and 1887, when it closed. It cannot have had many pupils, for there were under ten children on the island in 1881 and in 1891. The children were examined with their Mingulay neighbours, and the inspectors' comments were complimentary. On the school's closure, some of these children, and presumably others before and after, attended the Board school in Mingulay, perhaps as weekly boarders. The children of Michael MacNeil did so, lodging with relatives, the family of Angus MacNeil (Aonghas Dhòmhnaill Ruairidh). Eight 'scholars', including a daughter of a lighthouse keeper, were recorded in the 1891 census, but only one of these appears in the admission register of Mingulay school, so in what sense the others were scholars is unclear.

There is a story about one of the teachers at Berneray, a woman from London who applied for the advertised job without any idea where the school was. She was appointed, and on arrival at Oban asked for a cab to take her to the school. She was informed that she would have to take a steamer to Castlebay; on arrival there she again asked for a cab, only to be told that she would have to take a boat. She was taken over in August, but had to wait until May of the following year before she could return to Barra, whereupon she boarded the steamer back to Oban and no more was ever heard of her[25]. One can imagine what the experience would have been like for a Londoner unaware of what she was letting herself in for.

Berneray was deserted in about 1910, after many years of dwindling numbers. It was even more remote than Mingulay, though it did not have the congestion of Mingulay or such severe landing problems. Donald Campbell (Dòmhnall Dhòmhnaill) built a shed in Vatersay in spring 1908[26], and Michael Campbell and his mother were there by October 1908[27]; Peter Sinclair was still in Berneray in October 1909[28], but by April 1911 nobody was left[29]. The grazier, Jonathan MacLean, had taken over one of the crofts in

146

1910, and by 1914 he had the whole island. Berneray has since been used for grazing, and has had the same owners as Mingulay.

Berneray's most prominent monument is the lighthouse, known as the Barra Head Lighthouse, situated on the very top of the island. It was built by the Commissioners of Northern Lighthouses (later the Northern Lighthouse Board) as part of a programme to improve navigation and safety for shipping on the west coast of Scotland, resulting from reports by Robert Stevenson of the engineering family in 1828 and 1829. Barra Head was chosen because it is the southern point of the Outer Hebrides, and at the entrance to the Minch, and, being visible from almost every direction, would assist coastal shipping as well as shipping heading for, or approaching from, the Atlantic. It was the second lighthouse to be erected in the Outer Hebrides, the first having been built at Eilean Glas, Scalpay, Harris, in 1789[30].

Robert Stevenson designed the lighthouse, and the building contractor was James Smith of Inverness. Construction began in 1830, and the following year forty-eight workers were employed at the site[31]. Robert Stevenson wrote of the conditions at this time:

> *"Such is the violence of the wind in this station that the temporary buildings occupied by the artificers were repeatedly unroofed. On the face of the precipitous cliffs the winds and seas acquire a force which the reporter has never experienced elsewhere. It is not indeed uncommon to be actually struck down by the more violent and sudden gusts of wind, while the seas remove incredible masses of rock. The artificers are often reduced to the necessity of passing the most exposed places on their knees clinging with their hands to the ground. . . In one of these storms the lighthouse cart and horse overturned by the force of the wind. Both shafts were broken and the body of the cart was carried into the air. . . It is remarkable that the horse sustained no injury."*[32]

The lighthouse and the three keepers' cottages, all within a paved courtyard, together with storehouses and enclosure walls, were built from stone quarried from the nearby promontory. Everything else, however, had to be imported, and landed laboriously at the landing place at the other end of the island. It is curious that no attempt was made to build a landing slip at this time; this had to wait about forty years, and a derrick similar to Mingulay's was later provided. A macadamised road was constructed up to the lighthouse, and a team of horses was brought in to drag up the materials and equipment. A house was built for the hauliers, and a storehouse was built near the landing place. A well, with pump provided, was sunk near the road at its eastern end, and a cemetery, enclosed by a massive circular wall, was made near the cliff top for the use of the keepers. It contains a number of children's graves.

The lighthouse itself was built of bolted and clamped blocks of stone, with a roof of sheet lead. It is not high, only 18 metres (60 feet), being already 190 metres (625 feet) above the sea. Indeed, it was criticised at an early stage for its lofty situation, as the light was often obscured by cloud. In clear weather, the light could be seen from a distance of 53 kilometres (33 miles). The light, first lit on 15 October 1833, was fired by oil and used reflectors, and was fitted with an ingenious mechanism to obscure it intermittently. The total building costs were £12,000 – amongst the highest of any lighthouse built at the time, on account of its remoteness.

There were always three lighthouse keepers at Barra Head, each living in his own cottage, and their families lived with them. The keepers worked four-hour shifts, with two always on duty. At the end of a shift the relief keeper was summoned by means of a speaking tube to the cottages. They usually stayed for four or five years at a time, though there were notable exceptions, as related. One of them, George MacLachlan, was interested in the bird life, and became very knowledgeable during his stay in the 1860s[33]. He was presumably the 'Mac' who accompanied the Walker brothers on cliff-scaling excursions on their visit in about 1869, and who collected seabirds' eggs for his own consumption. For most of the men, however, it must have been a somewhat grim existence, particularly in winter, idling away their shifts in the lightroom with little to do but make sure the machinery kept going. It must have been hard for the families too. Some of the families were large: their total population in 1851 was sixteen. They

A comically romanticised view of Berneray (from Bird, 1866)

came from all over the coastal parts of Scotland, including Orkney and Shetland. There was probably not much contact between the keepers and the crofters, although Duncan Sinclair, being from the mainland, would have had more in common with the keepers. The initial invasion of the technology of the outside world, and of dozens of strangers, must have been bewildering, if not traumatic, for the islanders.

The keepers kept in regular touch with Castlebay by means of the mail/relief boat which was based there. In the later 19th century the boat came once a week in summer, once a fortnight in winter, though conditions often made the intervals much longer. In 1866 the boatman was Rory MacPhee[34;] later it was Malcolm MacAulay from Castlebay, who had a croft on the island for some years[35], and he was succeeded by his son Donald. The boatmen had a 'refuge' on the island for use if they were stranded by bad weather. In the early years a boat was employed to take mail to and from Tobermory, Mull, rather than using the much longer route via Dunvegan, Skye.

While Berneray was still inhabited, the keepers could make use of the islanders' boat in case of emergency; afterwards a system of visual signals was devised between the lighthouse and Barra, but this was unreliable because of weather conditions. A radio telephone link was established in 1925, and a wireless beacon was installed in 1936.

During the Second World War a plane crashed into the cliffs near the lighthouse, but it must have crashed during a storm, for no one heard it. Its remains were discovered many years later by a climber on the cliffs.

The lighthouse was finally automated in October 1980[36]. The light is electric, powered by batteries which are charged by two generators operated by remote control from Edinburgh. The light completes one revolution every thirty seconds. The equipment is automatically started and shut down by a sunvalve. The lighthouse is visited regularly by maintenance crews, who nowadays stay in fibreglass accommodation units rather than the old cottages. A tractor is used to take goods up the tarmac road to the lighthouse, and helicopters bring in anything too large to be landed by boat. Berneray is the only one of the islands south of Vatersay to keep up-to-date with the technology of the outside world.

16
Pabbay

Pabbay lies roughly midway between Mingulay and Sandray. It is smaller than both, the main body of the island being a rough rectangle about 2 kilometres (1¼ miles) long, and 1½ kilometres (1 mile) wide. A long finger-like peninsula, Rosinish, springs from the north east corner of the island in a south easterly direction, enclosing a sheltered bay. Rosinish (Gaelic *Roisinis*, from the Norse for 'Horse Headland') is now a tidal island, being separated from the main island by a channel covered by the sea at high tide; this channel appears to have originated from the collapse of the natural arch marked on the early Ordnance Survey maps.

Like its southern neighbours, Pabbay slopes up from the east to the west. Its highest point is The Hoe, 171 metres (564 feet) high, the southern and western slopes of which descend steeply to the sea. In places there are cliffs up to about 120 metres (400 feet) high, but they are not extensive and are not used by breeding seabirds as in the other islands. This is thought to be because of the wide shelf separating their base from the sea[1].

There is a curious depression in the middle of the island formed where several igneous dykes intersect and have been eroded away. Its sides are steep, occupied in places by eared willow growing up to 1.2 metres (4 feet) high[2], and its floor is a marshy peat bog, fed by small streams and draining out to the east. It is a rather sinister place, contrasting with the pleasant green slopes of the small, intimate glen occupied by the settlement area, between it and the bay.

Bàgh Bàn ('White Bay') on the east of the island is more sheltered than Mingulay's bay, and is backed by a beach of dazzling white sand. Behind the beach is a rampart of dunes which has developed since earlier this century; these are now stabilised by marram grass, but the sand continues for a long way inland. The sand is rich in lime from sea-shells, and in places it has solidified into a form of impure limestone. As on Mingulay, drifting sand has been a feature for thousands of years, and no doubt has overwhelmed formerly fertile land; "this island is greatly spoiled by the Sand Drift," said Walker in 1764.

Pabbay was almost certainly occupied in Neolithic or Bronze Age times, for Alexander Carmichael found worked flint flakes in what he called an "immense subterranean natural cave" in 1872[3]. Neolithic chambered tombs have been identified in the settlement area, and there are other possible burial cairns on the main island and Rosinish. A possible standing stone of Bronze Age date, and hut circles and round houses, also prehistoric, have been identified[4].

In the Iron Age a dun, Dùnan Ruadh, the 'Red Dun', was built on a low rocky promontory on the north coast near the neck of Rosinish. It was a galleried dun, consisting of a stretch of double walling, with a gallery between, on the landward side of the promontory[5]. Much of it has fallen victim to the sea, and its original form is uncertain. The dun could have been used as a permanent habitation, being near a landing place, a well, and cultivable land.

The most interesting ancient site in Pabbay, and perhaps in all the islands, is the mound occupied by the graveyard on the east side of the recent settlement. This is a prominent steep-sided hillock between 4.5 and 7.5 metres (15-25 feet) above the surrounding ground; it is exceptional in the islands, and certainly looks artificial. It is now grass-grown, but when Wedderspoon examined it early this century there was "very little grass on the mound except on the graves, which are neatly covered with turf. . . the interior consists principally of sand, bones, and shells of the edible mollusc varieties. . . there can be no doubt that the mound occupies the site of a

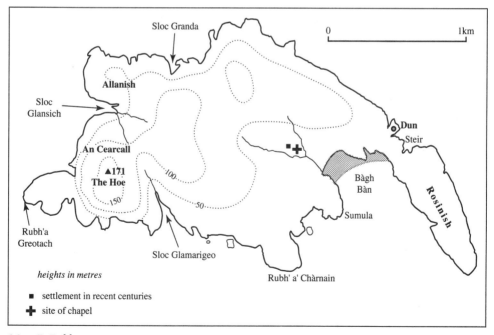

Map 5. Pabbay

prehistoric midden." The mound was "covered with graves, each marked at head and foot with an upright slab of native rock, from three to six feet in height." Quantities of human bones are said to have been found[6].

The most important feature of the mound is the Pictish symbol stone, one of only two known in the Outer Hebrides. It is an unshaped stone slab 1.1 metres (3 feet 6 inches) long, bearing incised symbols of Pictish type: a crescent and V-rod, and a lily, and these date the stone to sometime between the sixth and eighth centuries AD, probably before the Picts adopted Christianity. A cross was subsequently added to the stone, perhaps to represent the Christianising of the inhabitants, or simply to turn it into a grave stone[7]. The symbol stone was found in 1889 by Father Allan McDonald of South Uist where it was lying on the southern flank of the mound, exposed by shifting sand. He notified Joseph Anderson, Keeper of the National Museum of Antiquities in Edinburgh, but it was seven years before an antiquary, Erskine Beveridge, could get to the island to examine the stone[8].

There are, in addition, three cross-incised slabs, two of them standing near the summit of the mound, and likely to be grave markers. They probably date from between the sixth and ninth centuries, though their simple style is not closely datable[9]. The importance of the mound and its monuments has

The Pictish symbol stone, Pabbay
(from Anderson, 1897)

been recognised by its being scheduled under the Ancient Monuments Act, the protected area including the adjacent recent settlement.

Wedderspoon described other signs of early occupation between the mound and the beach, revealed a few years before when the inhabitants stripped off turf to burn as fuel, and a depth of 6 feet (2 metres) of sand was blown away. These included "small detached middens, each with a broken down ring of stones bearing marks of fire", and human and animal bone, teeth, hammerstones, and pottery. He was told that "many old things had been got and sold to Jew pedlars at Castlebay." Beveridge donated an enamelled bronze pin of the late seventh century AD to the Museum in Edinburgh[10], and Wedderspoon said one of the inhabitants had a similar pin.

The mound is also the traditional site of a medieval chapel, of unknown dedication[11]. The remains of the chapel were identified by the Royal Commissioners in 1915 on the mound, measuring 31 x 14 feet (9.4 x 4.2 metres)[12]. Although there are traces of what may be walling on the mound, it is not clear what they saw, and no building of these dimensions could fit anywhere near the summit; the casual nature of some of their work in the islands casts doubt on its reliability. However, it is possible that the mound has changed over the centuries and was once larger. The cross slabs on its southern flank, however, seem to be in their original position.

Another clue to Pabbay's early inhabitants is provided by its name. Its Gaelic name, *Pabaigh*, derives from the Old Norse *Papa-ey*, 'Hermit's Isle', a reference to the inhabitants of the island at the time of the Norse settlement of the Hebrides, which began in the ninth century[13]. It is one of several Pabbays in the Hebrides. Hermitages on small islands were common in Early Christian times, often associated with a 'mother' church, which in Pabbay's case may have been Cille Bharra in Barra. The hermitage, with chapel, if any, may have been on the mound. As on Mingulay, many of the place names of Pabbay are Norse in origin, and indicate an intimate knowledge of the island by Norse speakers, who almost certainly inhabited it.

Pabbay was inhabited, and had a chapel, in Monro's time, 1549. There are few subsequent accounts, and no 19th-century visitors' accounts are known. Martin Martin's comment of 1695 is hardly worth repeating: "The Natives observe, that if six Sheep are put a-grazing in the little Island Pabbay, five of them still appear fat, but the sixth a poor Skeleton." This is more likely to refer to one of the small islands or stacks off Mingulay. In 1764 Pabbay had sixteen inhabitants (paying £5 rent)[14], and in 1794, three families[15]. These figures remained similar right up until the island's desertion in 1911 or 1912, although the families did not remain constant. In 1851 there were twenty-five people, the maximum recorded, in three families, those of Neil

MacNeil, fisherman, Hector MacPhee, tailor, and John MacPhee, crofter. Tailors were often itinerant, but Hector MacPhee seems to have been resident as his family was with him. In 1851 only Neil MacNeil, tenant, remained, now joined by the family of his daughter Flora, married to John MacLean of Mingulay. By the time of the 1861 census the population had completely changed – the island had been taken over by people from South Uist, the families of Donald Morison, his son Alexander and his daughter Marion, married to John MacCormick.

No one knows exactly why this happened. The Uist families had crofts at the south end of South Uist, but how they ended up in Pabbay, of all places, is not known. It is hard to believe that they would have actually chosen to settle there, so far from home, where they would have had to depend on boats and fishing which they were not used to. The single holding remained a croft, Donald Morison being the tenant, and the small increase in rent, from £16 to £18, was not necessarily related to the change in tenants. £16 was a very high rent for one croft in the islands at the time, so perhaps Neil MacNeil left for that reason. Whatever happened, the MacNeils and MacLeans left, the MacLeans settling in Mingulay. What is more certain is the date of the change. MacNeil was still tenant in 1856, and in April 1858 Flora MacLean gave birth to a daughter, Margaret, there. Alexander Morison's family had arrived by May 1859, when his son Ronald was born there, and a year later Donald MacCormick, whose parents had married in South Uist in 1858, was born. The foreigners, as they would have been regarded, and felt themselves to be, were subsequently joined by cottar families from Berneray and Mingulay; three of the Uist women married Mingulay men and stayed in Pabbay. The Morisons remained in Pabbay but John MacCormick's family left for Barra in the 1880s.

The incomers are known today for their activities as illicit whisky distillers. They set up their still in Sloc Glansich, a steep-sided inlet on the north west coast, which the customs and excise men knew about but never found. Could this be a reason why they came to Pabbay? The whisky found a ready market in neighbouring islands. This was not the first still there, for tradition has it that an Irishman named Glancy, after whom the inlet was named, was engaged in similar business; the officers of the Ordnance Survey may not have got the whole story when they were told that Glancy had fallen over a cliff and drowned[16].

The people, natives and incomers alike, lived by crofting and fishing. There was good land on the east of the island, and the central valley was also cultivated. There were ten acres of arable in 1891[17], a surprisingly large area, perhaps big enough to produce a surplus. In 1840 there were two crofts, rented at £20; in 1845, three crofts[18], and from 1850, one croft. This meant that the single tenant had the whole of the island as grazing except for the cultivated area. Considering this, it is surprising that the grazing included the small island of Outer Heisker, 2 kilometres (1¼ miles) into the Atlantic[19]. The tenant, before and after 1859, seems to have sublet some of his land and received income for it[20]. In 1856 the island had one pony, one cow, and six sheep[21]. In 1883 it had one pony, forty-six cattle – mostly calves, bred for sale - and thirty-seven sheep[22], a huge increase in cattle and sheep, perhaps explained by the fact that there were now four families rather than one as in 1856. In 1820 tallow was being produced and sold, as on the other islands[23].

Pabbay provided peat until the later years when the islanders got it from the small island of Lingay to the north. At one time a pony was kept there all year round to carry the peat cut inland to the landing place. The islanders also stripped turf for fuel near their own houses, with, as seen above, devastating results.

Fishing was an important part of the economy of Pabbay, though landing conditions were only marginally better than on Mingulay. The landing place was at Steir, an inlet on the north side of the narrow neck joining Rosinish to the main island, and it is also possible to land on the rocks at the south side of the bay; boats were beached. In 1888 the islanders had a large herring fishing boat, presumably kept at Castlebay, and three smaller boats used for lobster fishing and line fishing[24]. The herring boat is not recorded again, and numbers of the smaller boats vary between one and three until 1897. On May Day of that year disaster struck the community; their only boat was lost in a storm and its crew of five drowned.

Donald MacPhee of Mingulay (Dòmhnall Bàn, later, in Barra, known as Dòmhnall Mòr Eileanach) told the story of the disaster which had been foreseen by a Mingulay girl long before, to Seton Gordon fifty-three years later. He and the Pabbay men were lifting their fishing lines in the area known as Cuan a' Bhòcain, 'Sea of the Ghosts', about 8 kilometres (5 miles) south of Barra Head, when a south easterly gale blew up, turning the sea wild. The boats made for home, but the Pabbay boat was never seen again.

"When they had fought their way to the neighbourhood of Barra Head they reached, said Donald Mor, the abode of two great and terrible giants. These giants lived in the air currents which the gale for a time imprisoned in two high ravines, Sloc na Beiste (Ravine of the Monster), Berneray, and Sloc Dubh an Dùin (Black Ravine of the Fort), Mingulay. The wind currents, which for a time were held prisoner in the ravines, burst out from them with extraordinary violence, and contended with each other with extreme ferocity above the sound between Barra Head and Mingulay. . . by this time the wind had veered to the south-south-west,

155

bringing in the full might of the Atlantic waves and making the task of the
Pabbay boat still more formidable. . . their one chance was to have sailed across
the Minch to Skye; Donald Mor Eileanach believes that the boat filled when
attempting to reach Pabbay" [25].

Four of the five crew were from Pabbay: the brothers Ranald and Alexander
Morison (mic Alasdair Dhòmhnaill), Donald MacNeil (Dòmhnall Choinnich
Mhìcheil, originally from Mingulay), and Ronald Campbell (Raghnall Iain
Dhòmhnaill). The fifth was a visiting Barra man, John Gillies, whose sister,
Margaret, was married to Ranald Morison. Gillies is said to have been
against going out that day. The loss of the boat and of four breadwinners was
a disaster for the community from which it never recovered fully. But it was
not defeated; the people remained and, although Pabbay disappears from the
fishing records, they must have had a boat and carried on fishing, as life
would have been impossible otherwise. It is said that the disaster was seen
by some as an act of God, a punishment for the islanders' whisky distilling
activities. Some of the bodies were washed ashore on the coast of Ireland.

Some curing of fish was done on the island. Near the south western corner
of the bay a large concrete 'box' sits on the rocks. This was used for storing
salt used in the curing process, and the flat rocks in the area were used for
laying out the fish.

Pabbay's cliffs are not inhabited by seabirds in the breeding season, and so
that resource was not available to the islanders. However, in 1820 Pabbay
men were selling feathers, which they presumably got from Mingulay or
Berneray. One huge consignment of 109 pounds (49 kilos) of feathers was
sold in Greenock[26]. Later, in the 1880s, Pabbay men sailed to the stack of
Lianamul, off Mingulay, and could take 2,000 guillemots in a day, at a time
when few Mingulay men were still fowling[27].

The islanders' houses were huddled together in a sheltered spot near the
stream which runs into the bay. The surviving buildings, of the traditional
thatched type, were joined together in a single complex. They are poorly
preserved, largely because they were turned into a sheep pen and dip after
the people left. Nearby is the shell of a fine gabled house of modern type,
built of dressed stone and mortar with chimneys and windows. It was built
for one of the Uist families by Donald MacAulay of Castlebay, probably in
the 1890s[28].

The lack of educational opportunities was a drawback to living in Pabbay,
at least in the later decades when education became compulsory, and had
been available in Mingulay since 1859. One of the families, that of Alexander
Morison, had a tutor living with them in 1871, a lad of fourteen from Barra.

The children of John Campbell (Iain Dhòmhnaill) later attended the school in Mingulay, where they lived with his brother Roderick.

Visits from the priest were probably even less frequent than in Mingulay's case; in 1820 Lachlan MacNeil was paying an annual amount for seats in the church at Craigstone in Barra[29].

The disaster of 1897 sounded the death-knell for the community, although some of the people stayed for another fourteen years. In 1901 the population was eleven, only two fewer than ten years previously, in three families; but the islanders must have known there was no future there, and when their neighbours in Mingulay began to leave, they joined them. In July 1907 John and Matilda Campbell, their son Donald and daughter Anne abandoned their home for Vatersay[30]. In 1910 nineteen year-old Kenneth MacNeil, left fatherless in 1897, applied (through the Castlebay priest, Hugh Cameron) for a croft in Vatersay[31]. The following April (1911) he and his sister were still in Pabbay, as was the family of Margaret Morison, the tenant, widowed in 1897[32]. These two families, seven people, probably left later in the year, and certainly by the summer of the next, 1912[33.] Johnathan MacLean, the grazier, became tenant of some of Pabbay in 1911, and the following year rented the whole island.

Pabbay has been used for grazing since it was deserted. Its flora and ornithology have been the subject of studies along with its two southern neighbours, but these have not been designated in the same way as Mingulay's and Berneray's.

17

Sandray

Sandray, the most northerly of the four islands, lies only 1 kilometre (half a mile) south of Vatersay. It is roughly circular in shape, and up to about 3 kilometres (1¾ miles) in diameter. There is symmetry also in its profile: the land rises in a sort of double cone to the centre of the island, where the highest point is Cairn Galtar, 207 metres (678 feet) high. There are no high cliffs, and there are several beaches and other places where landing and settlement were possible. The rocky interior is varied, with various glens and streams, and pleasant grassy areas near the coast; there is even a freshwater loch, Loch na Cuilce ('Reed Loch') on the west side, and another loch, entirely reed-choked, nearby.

The name Sandray (Gaelic *Sanndraigh*) is probably derived from Old Norse *Sandr-ay*, 'Sand Isle', and this is an appropriate description[1]. As on Mingulay and Pabbay, sand has been blown to a considerable height on the east coast. The sandscape is, however, quite different - it has been sculpted into high hills and deep depressions, and large areas are constantly shifting. In the past the sand seems to have been even more prominent than now – in 1816 MacCulloch said that "at a distance the island appears as if covered with a coating of snow."

Sandray's archaeology was investigated by Sheffield University in 1991, and evidence of human settlement going back to Neolithic times was found in midden deposits at Sheader on the north west coast. Elsewhere Neolithic chambered tombs and Bronze Age cairns and standing stones were identified[2]. Sandray's most prominent ancient monument is its Iron Age dun, atop a steep ridge high up on the western slopes of Cairn Galtar. It was originally a roughly circular galleried dun, the walls of which survive to a height of nearly two metres in places[3]. There are a number of possibly Iron Age round house sites elsewhere in the island.

Sandray has the only definite Norse settlement name in the four islands – *Siadar*, Anglicised as *Sheader*, where there is a sheltered beach and fertile ground. The name probably derives from Old Norse *setr*, 'dwelling place'. There are many other Norse names or Norse elements in names, as in the other islands. Like them, Sandray had its medieval chapel; dedicated to St Bride or Bridget, its traditional site, as pointed out to the officers of the

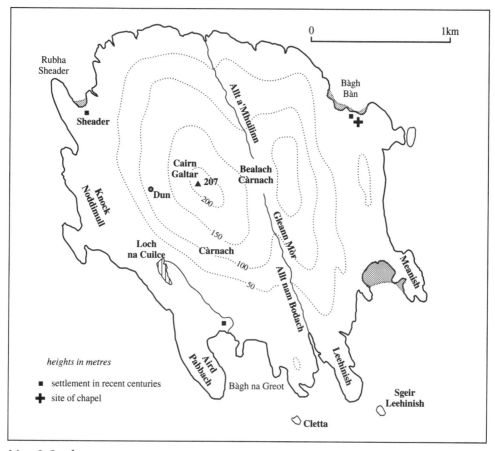

Map 6. Sandray

Ordnance Survey in 1878, was in the graveyard above Bàgh Bàn ('White Bay') on the north east coast. The graveyard was by then disused, and being covered by drifting sand[4], under which it has since disappeared entirely. The Royal Commissioners identified the remains of the chapel in 1915 as being partly occupied by a sheep dip, but this is uncertain[5].

Sandray was inhabited in Monro's day (1549), and it was "fruitful in Corn and Grass" in Martin Martin's day, 1695. In 1764 the population was forty (paying £12 rent)[6], and in 1794 there were nine families[7]. In the 18th century Sandray was leased by tacksmen, relatives of the chief who received the rents from the tenants. Two of these are known: Archibald MacNeil, who was alleged to have amassed a fortune by selling off the cargo of a wreck off the east coast of Barra, and left £200 for the poor of Barra[8]; and Roderick MacNeil, who died about 1783[9].

The later history of Sandray is quite different from that of the other islands. The native tenant population was evicted in about 1835, when

159

Sandray was turned over to grazing for sheep, and shepherds were installed to tend them. These stayed until about 1908, when 'raiders' from Mingulay arrived, remaining until 1911. These latest inhabitants are the only ones about whom much is known, but there are some stories from Sandray recorded from Mingulay people, some of whose ancestors had come from Sandray.

In the early 19th century there were several families of MacNeils, also MacLeans, MacInneses and MacSweens[10]. The population was substantial, similar to Mingulay's, judging by the 1794 figure and the fact that thirty-two people attended a school in 1822, as we will see. Around 1820 the people were much more in the Barra sphere of influence than the other islands, being much nearer; they also paid an annual amount for seats in the church. Tallow was produced, as on the other islands[11].

The islanders had three boats in 1819: the *Margaret*, the *Mary*, and the *Flora*[12]. The fishermen incurred the displeasure of the chief, General Roderick MacNeil, in 1825. He had accused the Barra fishermen of laziness and therefore not earning enough money, a share of which he wanted. In a letter to the priest of Barra, Angus MacDonald, he said:

> *"You will do well to advise your friends at Sandra, and all the Leaders as they are termed, to mind well what they are about, if they wish to remain at Barra. They are of little or no importance to me, whatever may be their value to you and if I don't on my arrival find them heart and hand engaged in fishing, I pledge you my honour they shall tramp, and the Land shall this ensuing spring be occupied by strangers."*[13]

The fishermen's grievances could be the result of a tax levied by MacNeil on each boat, mentioned by MacCulloch as happening in one of the Barra Isles in 1816[14]. Or it could be that the conditions of the tenancy of their crofts included fishing, and that this was resented; but it is not known if crofting had been introduced to Sandray at this time. Whether or not MacNeil carried out his threat in Sandray (which he did in Barra), several families were there for at least another ten years. This pre-eviction population has left abundant traces on the island, in the form of field walls, lazy-beds, buildings (and other structures, some of which may be much earlier, and some may be associated with the shepherds), and place names.

There were three main settlement sites around the coast. Sheader on the north west was the most attractive. Near the houses of the raiders from Mingulay, foundations of earlier buildings can be seen, and the Ordnance Survey noted in 1878 that the area was formerly cultivated, a reference perhaps to the large rectangular enclosure behind the houses there[15].

Lazy-beds can be seen south from here towards another area of settlement, at the head of Bàgh na Greòt ('Bay of the Groat') on the south coast. Here there are the remains of buildings, and there are lazy-beds in the surrounding area. This was the place from which a family, or perhaps more than one, emigrated to Nova Scotia in 1802, and a descendant returned some years ago to see the place. The third area of settlement was at Bàgh Bàn on the north east coast. This was clearly a focus of settlement in medieval times, and the shepherds subsequently lived there. There are lazy-beds in the area, and as their use only became widespread in the later 18th century, their presence is an indicator of settlement from that time onwards. It is notable that there are few field walls on Sandray, suggesting that agriculture was still being practised on the pre-crofting runrig system. Place names are another indicator of past inhabitants - the stream draining the northern slopes is Allt a' Mhuillinn, 'Stream of the Mill', while its southern counterpart is Allt nam Bodach, 'Stream of the Old Men'. On the north coast of the island is a grassy area known as Goirtein MhicPhàil, 'MacPhail's Meadow'.

In 1822 the Sandray people had the privilege of being sent a teacher by the Gaelic Schools Society. This society had been set up in 1811 with the aim of providing teachers for short periods – up to two years – in remote areas to teach people to read the Bible in Gaelic. Barra had various schools between 1818 and 1825. The minister of Barra, Alexander Nicolson, wrote in June 1822:

> *"I have likewise to request the attention of the Society to the destitute situation of the island of Sandra* in this parish. It is inhabited by several families, who have never as yet had the opportunity of acquiring the least degree of knowledge. They are all Roman Catholics, and as far as I know have not a single Bible amongst them. I have spoke to the people about the prospect they had of a School from your Society, and they seemed highly delighted at the idea of their children being soon able to read. The promised to have a comfortable house provided for the Teacher's reception, and that the number of scholars would amount to from twenty-five to thirty. One man said he would send eight of his own family to school.*
>
> ** A Gaelic teacher has been appointed to Sandra; the school was opened in November last, and was then attended by twenty-two males, and ten females."*
(added the ?following year).[16]

A bizarre story is told about Sandray, relating to the time when it was inhabited by tenants. A family living at Sheader was in the habit of sending their little girl to another settlement somewhere else on the island for milk, before their own cows were in milk. One day the girl disappeared on her way home. She was never found, but the pail was found, broken[17]. Years later, men from somewhere in western Scotland were in a cafe in the West Indies, when a white woman approached them and asked where they were from. It was the Sandray girl; she had been abducted and sold into slavery by the crew of a boat lurking off the coast. The story is not as far-fetched as may appear. There is a well-documented case of the abduction of over a hundred people from Finsbay, Harris, in 1739. A vessel from Ireland arrived at night, and people were dragged or tricked on board, to be sold into slavery on the sugar plantations in the West Indies. The vessel got no further than Ireland, where the captives escaped; it was discovered that the plot had been master-minded at the highest levels of clan society, involving an officer on the ship, from Berneray, Harris, and two clan chiefs in Skye – MacDonald of Sleat and MacLeod of Dunvegan[18].

Various emigrations from Sandray are known about. These occurred between 1799 and 1821, and there may have been earlier and later ones[19]. Emigrants from Sandray and Barra settled on a peninsula in the Bras d'Or Lake in Cape Breton, Nova Scotia, which they named Sandray, but which was later renamed Iona.

These were voluntary departures, but the final exodus was almost certainly not. Children were being born and baptised in Sandray regularly, at least one almost every year, until 1835. The following year Flora MacNeil, whose parents John and Mary MacNeil were previously in Sandray, was born in Mingulay, so that it was probably in that interval that the people were evicted or 'cleared' in favour of sheep, which were more profitable than tenants. Presumably this happened when Sandray became part of the grazing of Vatersay farm[20], and about fifteen years later all the crofting tenants of that island were in turn evicted.

By 1841 the first of several families of shepherds was in residence at Bàgh Bàn. This was the family of John MacKinnon, and the family of an agricultural labourer, Donald Cameron, was also there, fourteen people altogether. Subsequently there was only one shepherd and his family, successively Murdoch Cameron, born in Skye, Hector MacKinnon, born in Barra parish, and Donald MacMillan, born in South Uist.

Donald MacMillan died in 1904, and his successor, John MacKinnon, had only a short stay, for he would probably have left in 1908 or 1909 when Vatersay and Sandray were bought by the Congested Districts Board. Although Sandray had been designated as suitable for crofters' holdings in 1894[21], it was not thought fertile enough for many crofts, and education was now an issue – the population would not have been large enough to justify the expense of providing a school. It was therefore decided not to create crofts there, but to use the island as the common grazing of the southern townships of Vatersay[22].

Sandray's last inhabitants were 'raiders' from Mingulay who settled at Sheader in 1908. There were originally five families there, and the ruins of five houses built end-to-end in traditional style still stand. However, the people were not allowed to stay; two families left after about a year, leaving three by March 1909: John Gillies in an easterly house, John MacNeil in the middle, and Donald MacNeil on the west. In 1908 or 1909 Dom Odo Blundell visited the people with Father Hugh Cameron of Castlebay, who had been summoned by a sick call from an old lady. According to Blundell, the old lady, who had no family, had recently returned to the place where she had lived as a child, and from where the family had been evicted; her nephew had built a house on the site of the old family home. This could be the Flora MacNeil mentioned above, except that she was born in Mingulay; and she did go to Sandray with her nephew Michael MacNeil (an Rìgh). Some of Blundell's details conflict with this, but his account cannot be regarded as fully accurate, and was clearly written long after the visit. But there is no reason to doubt that the children there "were the nearest approach to angels in human form that Father Cameron or I had ever seen. . . the happiness and joy of life were a real pleasure to behold." These must have been John Gillies's children, and Blundell took photographs of them and the other inhabitants, a total of fourteen people, in front of their houses.

John Gillies was the last to leave Sandray for Vatersay, in early 1911, and the island has not been inhabited since. Like Vatersay, it remains in the ownership of the Department of Agriculture, the successor of the Congested Districts Board.

Sandray has been the scene of various wrecks. Two vessels, the names and origins of which were unknown, were found wrecked there in 1866, one carrying timber, another carrying paraffin. It was reported that the people made use of the latter's cargo "in all kinds of vessels extemporised for the occasion, one having it in a teapot, the wick through the spout"[23]. The *Maple Branch* was wrecked on Sgeir Leehinish off the south coast around the turn of the century. During the Second World War, two ships came to grief on the south coast: the *Empire Homer*, on her maiden voyage from Greenock to New York was driven ashore by storms, being empty and light[24]; and the *Baron Ardrossan*, carrying linseed.

Each of these four Barra isles has its own story to tell, but together they are representative of the group as a whole, and in a wider sense they illustrate many themes in the archaeology, history, economy, culture and society of the Highlands and Islands. They were inhabited over a period of around 5,000 years; but their physical nature, and the social and economic changes which led to their desertion, make it certain that they will never again be inhabited – by people living largely off their natural resources, at any rate.

Notes and References

Abbreviations

CEBB	Comunn Eachdraidh Bharraigh agus Bhatarsaigh (Barra and Vatersay Historical Society)
GROS	General Register Office for Scotland
MNE	Museum nan Eilean, Stornoway
NLS	National Library of Scotland
NMRS	National Monuments Record of Scotland
PP	*Parliamentary Papers*
RCAHMS	Royal Commission on the Ancient and Historical Monuments of Scotland
RMS	Royal Museum of Scotland
SAU	St Andrews University
SCR	Scots' College, Rome
SPL	Stornoway Public Library
SRO	Scottish Record Office
SEARCH	Sheffield Environment and Research Campaign in the Hebrides
SSS	School of Scottish Studies

Chapter 1: 'The Nearer St. Kilda'

1. *PP* XXXIII, 1847-8, 65
2. Nicolson in J L Campbell (ed) 1936, 191
3. SRO RHP 44187. Harvie-Brown said that white-tailed eagles bred there until c.1850
4. SRO RH4/23/106
5. Carmichael 1884, 456
6. Scottish Natural Heritage 1993
7. Harvie-Brown and Buckley 1888, lxxvii, 165
8. Boyd and Boyd 1990, 208
9. SRO HH62/14
10. Geirum Mor was also known as Horse Island (SRO RHP 44187) and Sinclair's Rock (T Walker 1870). Wave incident was recorded by Elwes (1869) and T Walker. Rock incident: Geikie 1865
11. geology: Jehu and Craig 1925; Robertson 1964
12. botany: Ball 1976; NE Buxton 1987; Cheke and Reed 1987; Clark 1938;
13. Pankhurst and Mullin 1991, 170
14. Ratcliffe 1977, I, 64; II, 43; Boyd and Boyd 1990, 208, 374-6
15. Few detailed island histories have been written; an example is D MacDonald 1978
16. Steel 1975
17. Aspects of the history and culture of Barra itself have been well documented, notably by J L Campbell; for the background to his *The Book of Barra*, see J L Campbell 1975
18. MacGregor 1967, 161-2
19. RMS: Scottish Ethnological Archive. Adam photographs: SAU. Norrie also took 'Life on Mingulay', which has not survived (RMS: Norrie letter)
20. J L Campbell and Hall 1968
21. B Buxton 1991

Chapter 2: Early Times

1.   SEARCH; Branigan and Foster (forthcoming)
2.   General works on Outer Hebridean archaeology and history include: Barber and
     Magee 1984, Historic Scotland 1994, RCAHMS 1928; for specific periods see Armit
     1992 and Crawford 1987
3.   B Buxton 1981
4.   Branigan and Foster (forthcoming)
5.   SEARCH 1991, 1992, 1993
6.   Ball 1976
7.   B Buxton (forthcoming)
8.   Patrick Foster, personal information
9.   SEARCH 1993
10. B Buxton 1981
11. *ibid*
12. RCAHMS 1928, 134
13. SEARCH 1993
14. NMRS: NMRS database; SEARCH 1993; Patrick Foster, personal information
15. RCAHMS 1928, 137; Wedderspoon 1912, 331-2
16. Macquarrie 1989, 8
17. SRO RH4/23/106. Monro may not be entirely reliable as he said that the tiny islands
     of Flodday, Lingay, and Greanamul had chapels; but no traces or traditions of them
     survive
18. B Buxton 1981
19. Muir 1867, 5; NMRS: field notebook 1915
20. SRO RH4/23/106
21. RCAHMS 1928, 137
22. Macquarrie 1989, 12
23. SEARCH 1992
24. Borgström 1936; Macquarrie 1989; Ian Fraser and Ian MacDonald, personal information;
     (names in general in Crawford 1987)
25. Anon 1620 in J L Campbell (ed) 1936, 44
26. Other sources: A MacDonald 1903, and unpublished notebook (270 names); RMS:
     John Finlayson letter 9.3.1892; SSS PN 1976/9; SRO RHP 44187; local knowledge.
     Information on derivation of place names from Ian Fraser and Ian MacDonald.
27. Borgstrom (1936) believed the suffix *sdale* in Barra to be derived from Old Norse
     stödhull, 'milking place', which is a likely use of Skipisdale
28. A McDonald 1903, 433
29. Information on details from Patrick Foster
30. *ibid*
31. *ibid*; SEARCH 1993

Chapter 3: The People and their Culture

1.   J L Campbell and Eastwick 1966, 90
2.   SRO AF56/225
3.   GROS: 1851 census and Cuithir register; other details from SRO RH21/50
4.   *Carmina Gadelica* III, 4
5.   McKay 1980, 85
6.   MacQueen in J L Campbell (ed) 1936, 69

7. Jolly 1883; Murray 1888; the petition of 1896 (SRO AF56/225), which may have been deliberately exaggerated
8. SRO: AF56/225, AF42/1580
9. GROS: 1891 census
10. C MacNeil 1988, 40
11. SSS SA 1960/100 A2
12. SSS SA 1960/95 B7
13. SSS SA 1960/95 B4
14. SSS SA 1960/94 B1
15. SSS SA 1960/95 B6
16. SSS SA 1960/100 A5
17. Johnson 1775 (1924 edition, 115)
18. *PP* XXV 1867, 43
19. SSS SA 1960/95 B3
20. J F Campbell 1862, I, iv
21, NLS Adv. MS 50 2 1, f 226-7
22. NLS Adv. MS 50 4 6, f 120
23. *Carmina Gadelica* II, 352
24. *Carmina Gadelica* I, xxiv
25. NLS Adv. MS 50 4 6, f 120
26. GROS: 1871 census
27. MacGregor 1934, 79-81 (fairy music given)
28. SSS SA 1960/100 A11
20. MacGregor 1929, 235-6
30. SSS SA 1960/96 A6
31. SSS SA 1960/100 A5
32. J L Campbell and Collinson 1981, 5
33. SCR: N MacDonald letter 12.1.1830
34. A McDonald 1958, 9
35. Christine Johnson, personal information
36. Roberton Publications, personal information; Cooper 1985, 2, 211

Chapter 4: Chiefs, Landlords, Tenants

1. *Tocher* 38, 1983, 5
2. Goodrich-Freer 1902, 398
3. Ladies' Highland Association 1868
4. *Collectanea de Rebus Albanicis* 1839, 4
5. J L Campbell 1954, 37
6. J L Campbell (ed) 1936, 43
7. Carmichael 1884, 456
8. McKay 1980, 85
9. Hunter 1976
10. J L Campbell (ed) 1936, 151-188
11. McKay 1980, 87
12. MacCulloch in J L Campbell (ed) 1936, 108; J L Campbell (ed) 1936, 152-3, 167 Carmichael (1884) describes runrig in Barra
13. J L Campbell 1990, 72
14. Barron 1903, II, 245, 291
15. MacQueen in J L Campbell (ed) 1936, 69

16. McKay 1980, 85
17. SRO RH21/50/1-3
18. *Carmina Gadelica* III, 111. This quote has been erroneously interpreted as evidence of eviction *from* Mingulay; see J Prebble, *The Highland Clearances*, 1963
19. CEBB: estate document
20. J L Campbell 1990, 73 (SCR: N MacDonald letter 4.3.1831)
21. *ibid*, 72 (SCR: N MacDonald letter 13.7.1828)
22. MacKenzie 1983; S R MacNeil 1979
23. SSS SA 1960/89
24. *PP* 1895 XXXIX(i), 931
25. *ibid*
26. MacCulloch in J L Campbell (ed) 1936, 128
27. *PP* 1847 LIII, 190-2
28. J L Campbell (ed) 1936, 219-226; Richards 1982, 402-418
29. PP 1847 LIII, 297
30. SRO RHP 44187
31. see chapter 13, note 6
32. *PP* 1895 XXXIX(i), 931
33. J L Campbell (ed) 1936, 231; PP 1884 XXXIII, 655
34. RMS: letter 4.10.1888
35. *PP* 1884 XXXIII, 695
36. *PP* 1895 XXXIX(i), 927 (Glen and quote); Storrie 1962 (Garrygall)
37. SRO AF50/7/5, VR103
38. SRO LC15/2/13
39. RMS: letter 27.2.1897
40. *ibid*
41. *PP* 1906 CIV, xvii
42. RMS: letter 26.7.1889

Chapter 5: A Living from the Land

1. SRO LC15/528, partially reproduced in *PP* 1892 LXIV; conflicts with less detailed figures in SRO AF50/7/5 and LC15/2/13. No map of individual crofts has been located
2. SRO VR103; croft division in Barra: *PP* 1844 XXI, 363
3. both *PP* 1895 XXXIX, 931
4. CEBB: estate document
5. SRO AF50/7/5
6. SRO LC15/2/13
7. Hunter 1976
8. SSS SA 1960/99 A1
9. *PP* 1908 LXXXVIII, 34
10. SSS SA 1960/92 A3
11. J L Campbell (forthcoming); see also I F Grant 1961
12. SSS SA 1960/99 A6
13. SSS SA 1960/99 A1
14. details of crops, planting, harvesting, in SSS SA 1960/92, /95, /99, /100; see also I F Grant 1961
15. many refs, eg C MacNeil 1992, MacGregor 1929
16. E Sinclair said 'everyone or every other household' (SSS SA 1960/97 A2) had one, M Campbell said every crofter (SA 1960/99 A2). Only three crofters mentioned having barns

in 1887 (SRO LC15/2/13)

17. details of winnowing and drying in SSS SA 1960/95, /99. C MacNeil said husks were loosened with a spade before winnowing (SA 1960/95 A4)
18. Mitchell 1880
19. *PP* 1884, XXXIII, 663
20. SSS SA 1960/99 A2
21. Nan MacKinnon, personal information
22. I F Grant 1961, 65
23. details in SRO LC15/2/13; stock numbers in SRO AF50/7/5
24. Anon in J L Campbell (ed) 1936, 44
25. SRO RH21/50/4
26. F Shaw 1980
27. MacQueen in J L Campbell (ed) 1936, 80
28. CEBB: estate document
29. SRO AF50/7/5
30. SSS SA 1960/95 A1
31. SPL: school log book, eg 1905
32. CEBB: estate document
33. SRO AF50/7/5
34. SSS SA 1960/95, 99
35. SSS SA 1960/99 A1
36. CEBB: estate document
37. SRO AF50/7/5
38. SRO LC15/2/13
39. Steel 1975
40. Report on ponies in Highlands and Islands SRO AF42/3213; J M MacDonald 1937, 45- 9
41. RMS: letter 24.8.1899
42. peat cutting: SSS SA 1960/97 A1, /99 A5, A8; creels, SA 1960/92 A2, A4

Chapter 6: Fishing and the Sea

1. These and other statistical details from SRO AF17/156, /157; other details from SSS SA 1960/92, /95, /96, /99
2. SRO AF56/225
3. *PP* 1884 XXXIII, 673
4. F Shaw 1980
5. *PP* 1847 LIII, 190
6. RMS: letter 24.8.1899
7. *Tocher* 20, 159
8. dogfish oil: John Finlayson letter, undated (RMS)
9. *PP* 1884 XXXIII, 673
10. *Scottish Fishermens' Nautical Almanack* 1903
11. SRO HH62/19 (1900)
12. *Scottish Fishermens' Nautical Almanack* 1903
13. MacGregor 1971, 144
14. SRO RH21/50/4
15. *Tocher* 20, 157
16. GROS: register of deaths
17. Carmichael 1884, 458
18. SRO AF17/157

19. Hunter 1976, 171
20. description of beach landings and launchings in Lewis in D MacDonald 1978, 94
21. MacGregor 1967, 163
22. B Buxton 1981
23. de l'Hoste Ranking, 1904
24. GROS: register of births 6.8.1907 (informant); SRO AF67/137 (police report 14.7.1908)
25. SSS SA 1960/95 A2
26. SRO HH62/14 (1897)
27. _PP_ 1890 XXVII, 14
28. details of derrick in SRO AF42/146, /833, /1580
29. SRO AF42/5369 (report on Mingulay)
30. _PP_ 1906 CVII

Chapter 7: Catching the 'Feathered Tribes'

1. Ladies' Highland Association 1868
2. SRO RH21/50/4
3. Nicolson in J L Campbell (ed) 1936, 195
4. RMS: letter 27.4.1903
5. Baldwin 1974
6. from SSS SA 1960/99 B8, and personally from Lisa Storey, unless otherwise indicated
7. Harvie-Brown and Buckley 1888, 162
8. RMS: letter 27.2.1897
9. _Carmina Gadelica_ II, 364
10. Gordon 1937, 127
11. names also in Elwes 1869
12. descriptions in Harvie-Brown and Buckley 1888, 163; Bird 1866; Elwes 1869; Walker 1870; SSS SA 1960/96 A5, /99 B6
13. Baldwin 1974
14. Harvie-Brown and Buckley 1888, lxxxiii
15. _ibid_, 162
16. SSS SA 1960/92 A1
17. Elwes 1869
18. Harvie-Brown and Buckley 1888, 163
19. Steel 1975
20. SSS SA 1960/99 B8
21. SSS SA 1960/96/B4
22. Gordon 1937, 127
23. RMS: letter 24.8.1899
24. RMS: Harvie-Brown's journal 16.7.1887
25. RMS: letter 27.2.1897
26. Baldwin 1974
27. MacGregor 1967, 162

Chapter 8: The Village: Walls and Work

1. details of the village in B Buxton 1981
2. SRO RHP 44187
3. respectively J MacDonald 1811, 793; PP 1867 XXV, 43; Nicolson 1840; descriptions of Barra

housing in SRO HH62/19 (1900), /21 (1901); MacLellan 1961, 207-8
4.   roofing details in SSS SA 1960/97 A2
5.   CEBB 1994
6.   Historic Scotland 1994, 59
7.   SRO HH62; Sanitary Department of Inverness; Day 1918
8.   in 1891: SRO LC15/2/13
9.   Goodrich-Freer 1902, 400; SSS SA 1960/99 A7
10. SRO HH62/21 (1901), /33 (1907)
11. details of interior in SSS SA 1960/97
12. SSS SA 1960/97 A7
13. SSS SA 1960/99 A7 (workshop), /95 A5 (clothing)
14. details of food in SSS SA 1960/95, /97
15. MacGregor 1967, 162
16. *Tocher* 38, 19, 21
17. RMS: letter 27.2.1897
18. Weir 1984, quoting Nan MacKinnon
19. SSS SA 1960/97 A9
20. SSS SA 1960/92 B1
21. Buchanan 1942, 156
22. SSS SA 1960/98 A7
23. *Tocher* 38, 7
24. *Carmina Gadelica* IV, 89
25. SSS SA 1960/97 A8
26. Cheape 1989

Chapter 9: Sickness and Death

1.   SRO HH62/4 (1892)
2.   SRO HH62/14 (1897)
3.   Sanitary Department of Inverness 1893; Day 1918
4.   SRO HH62/19 (1900)
5.   SRO HH62/8 (1894)
6.   this and next paragraph: SRO HH58/6
7.   SRO HH62/14 (1897)
8.   GROS: entered in register of births
9.   *PP* 1906 CIV, xix
10. SRO HH62/19 (1900), 21 (1901)
11. C MacNeil 1992
12. SRO HH62/14 (1897)
13. description in B Buxton 1981
14. *Tocher* 38, 43-5
15. *ibid*, 45

Chapter 10: The Ladies' School

1.   for early education in Barra see D Buchanan 1942, J L Campbell (ed) 1936, J L Campbell
     and Eastwick 1966
2.   *PP* 1867 XXV, 46
3.   *PP* 1867 XXV, 90; N Walker 1895

4. on which much of this chapter is based; dates refer to the reports of those years
5. the most north-easterly building. Muir's sketch (Muir 1867, 14) shows it to have been on the same site as the Board school in 1878 (OS map), but the map of 1861-3 (SRO RHP 44187), of uncertain accuracy, shows it as the northernmost building; however, no change of schoolroom is recorded after 1859
6. GROS: 1861 census
7. *Celtic Monthly* 1898
8. he and his brother Alexander were among students requesting a book of lectures by Rev J McLachlan; the certificate issued him for the Board school indicates that he was a non-graduate
9. 'uncle' John Finlayson letter 27.4.1875. Letters of 'uncle' John, who emigrated to Canada in 1832, to Mingulay John's brother Alexander, survive (in private hands)
10. Ladies' Highland Association 1871, 32
11. N Walker 1895
12. *Celtic Monthly* 1898
13. *PP* 1884 XXXII, 103

Chapter 11: Mingulay Public School

1. *PP* 1884 XXXII; Day 1918
2. *PP* 1884 XXXII, 67ff, 96ff; XXXIII, 697; J L Campbell in Rea 1964, xivff
3. the source of most of the information and quotes (excluding Jolly's, which are in Jolly 1883) in this chapter (SPL); also used is the Minute Book of Barra School Board (MNE)
4. *PP* 1884 XXXIII, 697
5. Withers 1984
6. *PP* 1884 XXVI, 284
7. RMS: letter 27.4.1903
8. A McDonald's diary, quoted in J L Campbell (forthcoming)
9. RMS: letter 24.8.1899
10. RMS: various letters
11. RMS: letter 13.8.1904
12. Chaimbeul 1982, 46; translation by Roderick MacNeil
13. J L Campbell (ed) 1960
14. information on Sarah MacShane from Eleanor Hunter
15. SSS SA 1960/98 A5
16. SRO AF42 8181
17. SSS SA 1960/100 A10
18. J L Campbell (ed) 1936, 97

Chapter 12: A 'most devout group of Catholics'

1. Giblin 1964, 172-4
2. J L Campbell (ed) 1936, 10
3. *ibid*
4. Blundell 1917, 10
5. *ibid*, 18; Macquarrie 1989, 25
6. SRO RH21/50, various dates in registers of baptisms
7. SRO RH21/50/2
8. SRO RH21/50/4

9. *Catholic Directory*
10. Blundell 1917, 21
11. SSS SA 1960/95 B2
12. SSS SA 1960/98 A6
13. Buchanan 1942, 99
14. RMS: John Finlayson letter 24.8.1899
15. R MacDonald 1978
16. A McDonald's diary, quoted in J L Campbell (forthcoming)
17. *ibid*
18. these stories are not in McDonald's collection
19. *Catholic Directory* 1909, 1910

Chapter 13: The 'Impossible Place'

1. RMS: letter 7.4.1905
2. SSS SA 1960/96 B3
3. *PP* 1908 LXXXVIII, 34
4. SRO AF42/146 (Fr J Chisholm letter)
5. *Tocher* 38, 6
6. NLS: N MacPhee letter 26.6.1909; *PP* 1908 LXXXVIII, 35; *PP* 1895 XXXIX, 920-2; crofters evicted by April 1851 (census)
7. *PP* 1895 XXXVIII, 28; XXXIX(ii), map 58
8. *PP* 1908 LXXXVIII, 35
9. *PP* 1895 XXXIX 932
10. Hunter 1976, 188; Day 1918, 215
11. *Glasgow Herald* 19.2.1908
12. SRO AF67/134 (police report 30.6.1906)
13. SSS SA 1960/92 B1; SRO AF67/134
14. SRO AF67/134 (police report 26.2.1907)
15. *Glasgow Herald* 21.1.1908
16. *PP* 1908 LXXXVIII, 34
17. SRO AF67/137 (police reports 2.1.1908 and later); AF67/135
18. *Glasgow Herald* 18.7.1908
19. SRO AF42/5380
20. SRO AF42/5369 (list of August 1908): AF42/5494 (list of November 1908)
21. NLS: letter 19.6.1909; see also petition in J L Campbell (ed) 1936, 274
22. 1.4.1908
23. *Glasgow Herald* 19.2.1908
24. report and photo in *Edinburgh Evening News* 2.6.1908 (according to which they had been dressed in their "fishermens' garb" in court)
25. SRO AF67/136
26. 19.7.1908
27. 20.7.1908
28. 25.7.1908
29. SRO AF42/5369
30. *ibid* (report on Mingulay)
31. *ibid*; see also letter from John Sinclair AF42/5269
32. SRO AF42/5494
33. Day 1918, 218
34. SRO AF42/5990

35. SRO AF42/5369 (report on Vatersay farm, 1908)
36. SRO AF42/8287; gone by April (census)
37. SRO AF17/156
38. SRO AF42/8425
39. SRO AF42/5369 (report on Vatersay farm, 1908)
40. SRO VR103
41. SRO AF42/8425; the April 1911 census (published statistics) recorded five families, each in a separate house
42. NLS: letter 14.8.1911
43. SRO AF42/5494 (list of November 1908)
44. SRO AF42/8425
45. SRO AF17/156
46. SRO AF42/7198
47. SAU: note on negative 1181, 1922
48. SSS SA 1960/92 B1
49. SSS SA 1960/99 B7
50. SRO AF67/134 (police report 24.5.1907)
51. Hunter 1976, 190
52. Moisley 1966

Chapter 14: The Deserted Island

1. GROS: 1911 census (published statistics)
2. SRO VR103
3. SRO VR103; Sutherland 1940; M Shaw 1993
4. SRO VR103; account of Greer's tenure in MacGregor 1971; Pochin-Mould 1953
5. notes on the Chapel House by D E Baird (in private hands)
6. NMRS: database
7. Noel Fojut, personal information

Chapter 15: Berneray

1. Foster and Krivanek 1993; SEARCH 1992
2. MacPherson 1768, 321; MacQueen in J L Campbell (ed) 1936, 76; diary of David Stevenson, 1828 (in private hands)
3. described by Bird in 1866, 650, and RCAHMS 1928, 132-3; and at second hand by Anderson 1893 (quoting F W Thomas's 1890 paper) and Armit 1992, 94
4. SRO RH4/23/106
5. Foster and Krivanek 1993; RCAHMS 1928, 133. SRO RHP 44187 calls it an 'ancient burial ground'
6. Foster and Krivanek 1993; RCAHMS 1928, 137; SRO RH4/23/106
7. RCAHMS 1928, 137
8. Foster and Krivanek 1993
9. MacQueen in J L Campbell (ed) 1936, 69
10. McKay 1980, 85
11. MacQueen in J L Campbell (ed) 1936, 69
12. J L Campbell (forthcoming)
13. GROS: marriage register, 1877
14. C MacNeil 1988, 32

15. *PP* 1895 XXXIX(i), 931
16. CEBB: estate document
17. SRO AF50/7/5
18. MacGregor 1967, 163
19. RMS: John Finlayson letter 9.3.1892
20. SRO AF17/155
21. *Scottish Fishermens' Nautical Almanack* 1903
22. Elwes 1869
23. David Stevenson's diary, quoted in Mair 1978, 129
24. SRO RHP 44187, Ordnance Survey 1880
25. Rea 1964, 24
26. SRO AF67/137 (police report 18.7.1908)
27. SRO AF42/5367
28. SRO AF42/6592
29. SRO AF42/8425; GROS: 1911 census (published statistics)
30. this and most of following from Munro 1979; Bird 1866
31. GROS: note in 1831 census for Barra parish
32. Mair 1978, 5
33. Harvie-Brown and Buckley 1888, lxxxiii; T Walker 1870
34. *PP* 1867 LXIV, 68
35. SRO VR103
36. *West Highland Free Press* 21.11.1980

Chapter 16: Pabbay

1. Cheke and Reed 1987, 74
2. *ibid*, 71
3. Carmichael 1874
4. Patrick Foster, personal information
5. RCAHMS 1928, 130
6. *ibid*, 126
7. *ibid*
8. Anderson 1897
9. Edwards 1981; RCAHMS 1928, 126
10. *Proceedings of the Society of Antiquaries of Scotland* XXXV, 278
11. SRO RH4/23/106
12. RCAHMS 1928, 126
13. Macquarrie 1989, 8
14. McKay 1980, 85
15. MacQueen in J L Campbell (ed) 1936, 69
16. SRO RH4/23/106
17. SRO LC15/528
18. *PP* 1895 XXXIX(i), 931
19. SRO LC15/528
20. CEBB: estate document; SRO AF50/7/5
21. CEBB: estate document
22. SRO AF50/7/5
23. SRO RH21/50/4
24. SRO AF17/155
25. Gordon 1950

26. SRO RH21/50/4
27. Harvie-Brown and Buckley 1888, 163
28. by the time of the 1901 Ordnance Survey map; MacAulay was born in 1864
29. SRO RH21/50/4
30. SRO AF67/137 (police report 18.7.1908); AF42/5369
31. SRO AF42/7688
32. SRO AF42/8425
33. *ibid*

Chapter 17: Sandray

1. Borgström 1936; 290
2. SEARCH
3. RCAHMS 1928,130
4. SRO RH4/23/106
5. RCAHMS 1928, 137
6. McKay 1980, 85
7. MacQueen in J L Campbell (ed) 1936, 69
8. J L Campbell (ed) 1960, 128
9. J M MacDonald 1937, 49
10. SRO RH21/50/1
11. SRO RH21/50/4
12. *ibid*
13. J L Campbell (ed) 1936, 187
14. *ibid*, 127
15. SRO RH4/23/106
16. J L Campbell (ed) 1936, 96
17. this part of the story in SSS SA 1960/101 B8, /97 A11
18. Finsbay story: J S Grant 1987, 152-5
19. MacKenzie 1983; S R MacNeil 1979; J L Campbell (ed) 1936, 167
20. It remained so until 1883, when Dr Macgillivray, tenant of Eoligarry farm, was given it and Flodday in exchange for the grazing at Garrygall (*PP* 1895 XXXIX(i), 933), but it was returned to Vatersay before 1908
21. *PP* 1895 XXXVIII, 28; XXXIX(ii), map 58. The small islands of Flodday and Lingay were also so designated (!)
22. SRO AF42/5369
23. *PP* 1867 LXIV, 44, 72. This anecdote presumably refers to Vatersay; the report is confused
24. C MacNeil 1988, 65

Bibliography

Published sources and theses

Anderson, Joseph, 1893: 'Notice of Dun Stron Duin, Bernera, Barra Head', *Proceedings of the Society of Antiquaries of Scotland* XXVII, 1892-3, 341-6
- 1897: 'Notices of some recently discovered inscribed and sculptured stones' *Proceedings of the Society of Antiquaries of Scotland* XXXI 1896-7, 293-308

Anon, c.1620: description of Barra in A Mitchell (ed), 1907: *Walter MacFarlane's Geographical Collections Relating to Scotland*, (reproduced in J L Campbell (ed) 1936)

Armit, Ian, 1992: *The Later Prehistory of the Western Isles of Scotland*, British Archaeological Reports, British Series 221, Oxford

Baldwin, John, 1974: 'Seabird fowling in Scotland and Faroe', *Folklife* 12, 1974, 60-103

Ball, Timothy R, 1976: 'An investigation of the soils and vegetation, including fungi, of Mingulay, Outer Hebrides', unpublished BSc dissertation, University of Aberystwyth

Barber, John, and Magee, D, 1984: *Innsegall: The Western Isles*, Edinburgh

Barron, James, 1903: *The Northern Highlands in the Nineteenth Century*, Edinburgh (3 vols) (an index to the *Inverness Courier*)

Bird, Miss, 1866: 'Pen and pencil sketches among the Outer Hebrides', *Leisure Hour* XV, 1866, 646-50, 668-9 (Berneray)

Blundell, Odo, 1917: *The Catholic Highlands of Scotland*, London

Borgström, C H, 1936: 'The Norse place-names of Barra' in J L Campbell (ed) 1936

Boyd, J M and Boyd, I L, 1990: *The Hebrides, a Natural History*, London

Branigan, Keith, and Foster, P (forthcoming): *Barra: Archaeological Research on Ben Tangaval*, Sheffield

Buchanan, Donald, 1942: *Reflections of the Isle of Barra*, London

Buchanan, G, (1582): 'History of Scotland', in P Hume Brown, 1893: *Scotland Before* 1700, 232-5

Buxton, Ben, 1975: 'Blackhouses' (Mingulay), Schools Hebridean Society *Annual Report*, 1975
- 1981: 'The Archaeology of Mingulay Bay, Mingulay, Outer Hebrides', unpublished BA dissertation, Department of Archaeology, University of Durham
- 1991: 'Museum Provision in Barra, Western Isles', unpublished MA dissertation, Department of Museum Studies, University of Leicester
- (forthcoming): 'A stone object from Mingulay, Outer Hebrides', *Oxford Journal of Archaeology*

Buxton, N E, 1987: 'Report on the Vegetation of Mingulay' *Royal Air Force Ornithological Society Journal* 17, 1987, 64-77

Campbell, J F, 1862: *Popular Tales of the West Highlands*, Edinburgh (4 vols)

Campbell, J L, 1954: 'The MacNeils of Barra and the Irish Franciscans' *Innes Review* V, 1954, 33-38
- 1975: 'Our Barra Years', *Scots Magazine* 1975, 494-503, 613-623
- 1990: *Songs Remembered in Exile*, Aberdeen (includes historical background to 19th century emigrations from Barra)
- (forthcoming) *Echoes from the Hebrides*, Edinburgh
- (ed) 1936: *The Book of Barra*, London (compilation of contemporary accounts, letters etc, with editorials, and chapters on various subjects)
- (ed) 1960: *Tales from Barra Told by The Coddy*, Edinburgh
- and Collinson, F, 1981: *Hebridean Folksongs* vol III, Oxford
- and Eastwick, C, 1966: 'The MacNeils of Barra in the Forty-five', *Innes Review* XVII 1966, 82-90

- and Hall, T H, 1968: *Strange Things*, London

Carmichael, Alexander, 1874: 'On a Hypogeum at Valaquie, Island of Uist' *Journal of the Anthropological Institute* III, 1874
- 1884: 'Grazing and Agrestic Customs of the Outer Hebrides', *PP* 1884 XXXII, 451-473 (Barra sections partially reproduced in JL Campbell (ed) 1936)

Carmina Gadelica, edited by Alexander Carmichael and others, 1900-1971, Edinburgh (6 vols)

Catholic Directory, dates indicated in references

Celtic Monthly VI, 1898, 225: 'Dr Alexander Finlayson, Munlochy'

Chaimbeul, Ealasaid, 1982: *Air Mo Chuairt*, Stornoway

Chambers, William, 1866: 'My Holiday', *Chambers's Journal* 1866, 632-3 (Berneray)

Cheape, Hugh, 1989: 'Shawls and plaids in the Outer Hebrides', *Costume* 23, 1989, 114-9

Cheke, A S, and Reed, T M, 1987: 'The flora of Berneray, Mingulay and Pabbay, Outer Hebrides, in 1964', *Scottish Naturalist* 99, 1987, 63-106

Clark, W A, 1938: 'The flora of the islands of Mingulay and Berneray', *Proceedings of the University of Durham Philosophical Society* X, 1938, 56-70

Collectanea de Rebus Albanicis, Iona Club 1839

Comunn Eachdraidh Bharraigh agus Bhatarsaigh (CEBB) (Barra and Vatersay Historical Society) 1994: *Mingulay, an Island Guide*, Castlebay
- 1993: *Tales, Songs, Tradition, from Barra and Vatersay* (recorded from Nan MacKinnon), Castlebay

Congested Districts Board *Annual Reports* 1899-1912 (published in *Parliamentary Papers*)

Cooper, Derek, 1985: *The Road to Mingulay: a View of the Western Isles,* London

County Medical Officers *Annual Reports* for Inverness-shire, 1892-, Inverness (see SRO)

Crawford, Barbara E, 1987: *Scandinavian Scotland*, Leicester

Day J P, 1918: *Public Administration in the Highlands and Islands of Scotland*, London

de l'Hoste Ranking, DF, 1904: 'The Island of Barra, past and present', *Celtic Monthly* 12, 1904, 175-7, 202-4

Diamond, A W, 1965: 'Notes on the birds of Berneray, Mingulay and Pabbay', *Scottish Birds* 3, 1965, 397-404

Edinburgh Evening News: 'The Vatersay Squatters in Court Today', 2.6.1908

Edwards, Marion, 1981: 'An Archaeological Survey of Pabbay, Barra', unpublished BA dissertation, Department of Archaeology, University of Durham

Elwes, H J, 1869: 'The bird stations of the Outer Hebrides', *The Ibis* 1869, 20-37 (Mingulay and Berneray)

Foster, Patrick, and Krivanek, R, 1993: 'The Anglo-Czech survey of the island of Berneray in the Outer Hebrides, Scotland', *Archeologicke rozhledy* XLV, 1993, 418-27

Gaelic Schools Society: *Annual Reports* 1811-1845, Edinburgh (Barra sections reproduced in J L Campbell (ed) 1936)

Geikie, Archibald, 1865: *The Scenery of Scotland*, Edinburgh

Giblin, C, 1964: *The Irish Franciscan Mission to Scotland*, Dublin

Glasgow Herald: 'The crofters' raid on Vatersay', 21.1.1908
- 'The Vatersay land seizure', 19.2.1908
- 'Opinion', 1.4.1908
- 'Vatersay land seizure', 3.6.1908
- 'The Barra raiders', 18.7.1908

- 'The Vatersay raiders released', 20.7.1908
- 'The Barra raiders', 20.7.1908

Goodrich-Freer, A, 1902: *Outer Isles*, London (Mingulay pp 394-404)

Gordon, Seton, 1937: *Afoot in Wild Places*, Edinburgh
-1950: 'A half-forgotten tragedy of the sea' *Country Life*, 30 June 1950 (Pabbay)

Grant, I F, 1961: *Highland Folk Ways*, London

Grant, James S, 1987: *Discovering Lewis and Harris*, Edinburgh

Hall, James, 1807: *Travels in Scotland*, London

Harvie-Brown, J A, and Buckley, T E, 1888: *A Vertebrate Fauna of the Outer Hebrides*, Edinburgh (Mingulay and Berneray lxxvii-lxxxiii, and under individual species)

Historic Scotland, 1994: *The Ancient Monuments of the Western Isles*, Edinburgh

Hunter, James, 1976: *The Making of the Crofting Community*, Edinburgh

Jehu, T J and Craig, R M, 1925: 'Geology of the Outer Hebrides part 1: the Barra Isles', *Transactions of the Royal Society of Edinburgh* 53, 1925, 419-441

Johnson, Samuel, 1775: *A Journey to the Western Islands of Scotland, London* (1924 edition Oxford)

Jolly, William, 1883: 'The Nearer St Kilda: Impressions of the Island of Minglay', *Good Words* 1883, 716-720

Ladies' Highland Association: *Annual Reports* 1850-, Edinburgh (held by Church of Scotland, Edinburgh)

MacCulloch, John, 1824: *The Highlands and Western Isles of Scotland*, London (4 vols) (Barra sections reproduced in J L Campbell (ed) 1936)

McDonald, Allan, 1903: 'The Norsemen in Uist Folklore', *Saga Book of the Viking Club*, III, 1901-1903, 413-433 (includes Mingulay place names)
- 1958: *Gaelic Words and Expressions from South Uist and Eriskay*, Dublin (edited by J L Campbell)

MacDonald, Donald, 1978: *Lewis: a History of the Island*, Edinburgh

MacDonald, James, 1811: *General View of the Agriculture of the Hebrides*, Edinburgh

MacDonald, J M, 1937: *Highland Ponies and some Reminiscences of Highland Men*, Stirling

MacDonald, R, 1978: 'The Catholic Gaidhealtachd' in D MacRoberts, 1978: *Modern Scottish Catholicism*, Edinburgh

MacGillivray, William, 1830: 'On the birds of the Outer Hebrides', *Edinburgh Journal of Natural and Geographical Science*, 1830 II

MacGregor, Alasdair A, 1929: *Summer Days among the Western Isles*, Edinburgh
- 1934: *The Haunted Isles*, Edinburgh
- 1967: *The Enchanted Isles*, London
- 1971: *Islands by the Score*, London (Mingulay pp 126-153; illustrations)

McKay, Margaret M (ed), 1980: *The Rev. Dr. John Walker's Report on the Hebrides of 1764 and 1771*, Edinburgh

MacKenzie, Archibald, 1983: *The MacKenzies' History of Christmas Island*, Ontario

MacLellan, Angus, 1961: *Stories from South Uist*, London (translated and edited by J L Campbell)
MacNeil, Catriona, 1988: *Only the Sunny Days: Memories of a Barra Childhood*, Glasgow
- 1992: *Mo Bhrògan Ura*, Glasgow

MacNeil, S R, 1979: *All Call Iona Home*, Antigonish, Nova Scotia

MacPherson, John, 1768: *Critical Dissertations on the Origin, Antiquities,. . . of the Ancient Caledonians*, London

Macquarrie, Alan, 1989: *Cille Bharra, The Church of St Finbarr*, Droitwich (covers Early Christian, Norse, and later medieval periods in Barra)

MacQueen, Edward, 1794: 'Parish of Barray', *Statistical Account of Scotland*, vol XIII, 326-342 (reproduced in J L Campbell (ed) 1936)

Mair, Craig, 1978: *A Star for Seamen: the Stevenson Family of Engineers*, London

Martin, Martin, 1703: *A Description of the Western Islands of Scotland*, London (Barra section reproduced in J L Campbell (ed) 1936)

Mitchell, Arthur, 1880: *The Past in the Present*, Edinburgh

Moisley, H A, 1966: 'The Deserted Hebrides', *Scottish Studies* 10, 1966

Monro, Donald, 1774: *A Description of the Western Isles of Scotland called Hybrides* (c.1549), Edinburgh (Barra section reproduced in J L Campbell (ed) 1936)

Munro, R W, 1979: *Scottish Lighthouses*, Stornoway

Muir, T S, 1867: *Barra Head, a Sketch*, Leith (Mingulay and Berneray; drawings in the 15 copies printed were by hand and details are not consistent)
  - 1885: *Ecclesiological Notes on some of the Islands of Scotland etc*, Edinburgh (reproduces text but not drawings of above)

Murray, Mrs, 1888: 'Yachting in the Hebrides', reprinted from *Helensburgh and Gareloch Times*, November 1888 (Mingulay)

Nicolson, Alexander, 1845: 'Parish of Barray', *New Statistical Account of Scotland*, Edinburgh (reproduced in J L Campbell (ed) 1936)

Oban Times: 'The Vatersay men's release', 25.7.1908

O Lochlainn, Colm, 1948: *Deoch-Slàinte nan Gillean*, Dublin

Ordnance Survey: 1:10,560 map sheets LXVI (Sandray), LXIX (Pabbay), LXX (Mingulay and Berneray); 1st edition 1880 (surveyed 1878), 2nd edition 1904 (surveyed 1901)

Pankhurst, R J, and Mullin, J M, 1991: *The Flora of the Outer Hebrides*, London

Parliamentary Papers (PP); 1844 XXI: 'Minutes of Evidence Taken Before the Poor Law Inquiry Commission for Scotland'
  - 1847 LIII: 'Correspondence... related to measures adopted for the relief of the distress in Scotland'
  - 1847-8 XXXIII: 'Second Annual Report of the Board of Supervision for Relief of the Poor (Scotland)' (Appendix B)
  - 1851 XXVI: 'Report to the Board of Supervision by Sir John McNeill on the Western Highlands and Islands'
  - 1867 XXV: 'Report on the State of Education in the Hebrides'
  - 1867 XXVI: 'Statistics Relative to Schools in Scotland'
  - 1867 LXIV: 'Wrecking in the Hebrides'
  - 1884 XXVI: 'Report of the Committee of Council on Education in Scotland 1883-4'
  - 1884 XXXII-XXXVI: 'Report of Her Majesty's Commissioners of Inquiry into the Condition of the Crofters and Cottars in the Highlands and Islands of Scotland'
  - 1890 XXVII: 'Report of the Commission Appointed to Inquire into Certain Matters Affecting the Interests of the Population of the Western Highlands and Islands of Scotland'
  - 1892 LXIV: 'Report of the Crofters Commission for 1891'
  - 1895 XXXVII, XXXIX: 'Royal Commission (Highlands and Islands, 1892)'
  - 1906 CIV: 'Reports... on the Burden of the Existing Rates and the General Financial Position of the Outer Hebrides'
  - 1906 CVII: 'Eighth Annual Report of the Congested Districts Board'
  - 1908 LXXXVIII: 'Return of Correspondence... with Reference to the Seizure and Occupation of the Island of Vatersay'

- 1908 LXXXVIII: 'Report... of the County Council of Inverness upon Applications for Allotments in North Uist and Barra in 1897'

Pochin-Mould, D D, 1953: *West-Over-Sea*, Edinburgh

Proceedings of the Society of Antiquaries of Scotland XXXV, 1900-1901: 'Proceedings of the Society, May 13, 1901', 276-280

Ratcliffe, D A, 1977: *A Nature Conservation Review*, Cambridge (2 vols)

Rea, F G, 1964: *A School in South Uist: Reminiscences of a Hebridean Schoolmaster 1890-1913*, London (edited by J L Campbell)

Richards, Eric, 1982: *A History of the Highland Clearances*, London

Robertson, J F, 1964: 'The Glasgow University Exploration Society Expedition to Mingulay', *Nature* 4953, 1964, 25

RCAHMS 1928: *Inventory of Monuments and Constructions in the Outer Hebrides, Skye, and the Small Isles*, Edinburgh

Sanitary Department of the County of Inverness: *Annual Reports* 1891-, Inverness (held by Inverness Public Library)

Scottish Fishermens' Nautical Almanack 1903

Scottish Natural Heritage, 1993: *Information sheet, Mingulay and Berneray*

SEARCH: *Interim Reports* 1988-1993 (Department of Archaeology and Prehistory, Sheffield University)

Sergeant, D E, and Whidbourne, R F, 1951: 'Birds on Mingulay in the summer of 1949', *Scottish Naturalist* 63, 1951, 18-25

Shaw, Frances, 1980: *The Northern and Western Isles of Scotland: their Economy and Society in the 17th Century*, Edinburgh

Shaw, Margaret Fay, 1993: *From the Alleghenies to the Hebrides: an Autobiography*, Edinburgh (Mingulay pp 100-103, illustrations)

Steel, Tom, 1975: *The Life and Death of St Kilda*, London

Storrie, Margaret C, 1962: 'Two early resettlement schemes in Barra', *Scottish Studies* VI, 1962, 71-84

Sutherland, Halliday, 1940: *Hebridean Journey*, London

Thom, Alexander, 1967: *Megalithic Sites in Britain*, Oxford

Thompson, Francis, 1974: *The Uists and Barra*, Newton Abbot

Tocher 20, 1975: 'Hook, line, and sickle', 146-164
- 38, 1983: 'Nan MacKinnon', 1-48

Walker, John, 1764: see McKay 1980

Walker, N, 1895: *Chapters from the History of the Free Church of Scotland*, Edinburgh

Walker, Theodore, 1870: 'Bird-haunts of the Outer Hebrides', *The Zoologist* V, 1870, 2073-7, 2113-9, 2163-71; VI, 1871, 2423-9 (Mingulay and Berneray)

Warwick, T, 1939: 'Animal Life on Mingulay', *Scottish Naturalist* 1939, 127

Wedderspoon, J, 1912: 'The shell middens of the Outer Hebrides', *Transactions of the Inverness Scientific Society and Field Club,* VII, 1906-1912, 326-335 (Mingulay and Pabbay)

Weir, Tom, 1984: 'The Curse of St Kilda', *Scots Magazine* 1984, 630-635

West Highland Free Press 21.11.1980: 'Berneray, depopulated but not forgotten'

Withers, C W J, 1984: *Gaelic in Scotland 1698-1981*, Edinburgh

Unpublished sources (listed under institution in which they are housed)

Comunn Eachdraidh Bharraigh agus Bhatarsaigh (CEBB) (Barra and Vatersay Historical Society):
estate document, 1856, giving details of crofters and their stock
photograph of Mingulay men in Vatersay, R M R Milne, August 1909

General Register Office for Scotland (GROS):
census enumerators' returns, 1841-91; published statistics only thereafter
registers of births, marriages and deaths, 1855 onwards
Church of Scotland register of baptisms, Barra Parish, 1836-54

Museum nan Eilean (MNE), Stornoway:
admissions register of Mingulay Public School, 1889-94
minute book of Barra School Board, 1888-1918

National Library of Scotland (NLS):
J F Campbell collection:
    letter H MacLean to J F Campbell, 30.9.1860 (Adv.MS.50.2.1, ff 226-7);
    Rory Rum portrait (Adv.MS.50.4.6, f.119v)
letterbook of Neil MacPhee of Vatersay, 1909-12 (microfilm copy, Acc. 10688; access restricted)

National Monuments Record of Scotland (NMRS):
NMRS database of sites (formerly Ordnance Survey cards)
RCAHMS field notebook, Barra Parish, 1915

Royal Museum of Scotland (RMS)
Harvie-Brown Collection:
    letters of John Finlayson to Harvie-Brown: 4.10.1888, 26.7.1889, 9.3.1892, 17.10.1892,
        27.2.1897, 24.8.1899, 27.4.1903, one undated
    letters of Morag Campbell Finlayson to Harvie-Brown, 13.8.1904, 7.4.1905 (both box 20,
        file 329)
    letter of William Norrie to Harvie-Brown, 25.2.1889 (box 37, file 628)
    Harvie-Brown's journal, 16.7.1887.
Scottish Ethnological Archive:
    photograph of houses in Mingulay village, R M R Milne, August 1909 (C19406)
    Alasdair A MacGregor collection of photographs: Mingulay, 1948-9 (C15083-15104)

St Andrews University (SAU)
Robert M Adam collection of photographs: Mingulay, June 1905, July 1922

School of Scottish Studies (SSS)
tape recordings of Mingulay people made in 1960: SA 1960/89, /92, /93, /94, /95, /96, /97, /98, /99,
    /100, /101
place name tape PN 1976/9
Robert Atkinson collection of photographs: Mingulay 1950

Scots College, Rome (SCR)
letters of Fr Neil MacDonald to Fr Angus MacDonald, 13.7.1828, 12.1.1830, 4.3.1831 (reproduced
in part in J L Campbell 1990)

Bibliography

Scottish Record Office (SRO):

AF 17: Fishery Board records. AF17/156, /157, Stornoway Fisheries Office records, from 1888

AF 42: Congested Districts Board records, relating to the derrick (AF42/146, /833, /1580), and to the settlement of Vatersay (numerous files, given in references)

AF 50: Royal Commission on the Highlands and Islands, 1883. AF50/7/5, details of crofts and stock

AF 56: Scottish Office Fishery Files; AF56/225, petition for landing facilities in Mingulay, 1896

AF 67: Scottish Office Crofting Files. AF67/134, /135, /136, /137, relating to raiding and settlement of Vatersay

HH 58: Scottish Home and Health Department, infectious diseases. HH58/6 includes typhoid on Mingulay, 1894

HH 62: Scottish Home and Health Department, County Medical Officers reports from 1892

LC 15: Scottish Land Court records. LC15/2/13, applications for rent reductions, details of croft improvements, 1887

LC15/528, details of crofts and arrears, 1891

RH4/23/106: Ordnance Survey Object Name Book, Barra Parish, 1878

RH 21: Roman Catholic Diocese of Argyll and the Isles records. RH21/50/1, /2, /3, registers of baptisms, marriages and deaths (Craigstone), 1805 onwards

RH21/50/4, account book of Fr Angus MacDonald, Craigstone, 1818-22

RHP 44187: plan of Barra Parish, 1861-3, by Otter and Edye, scale approx. 1:15,000 (Admiralty Chart)

VR 103: valuation rolls, Inverness-shire, 1855 onwards

Stornoway Public Library *(SPL)*

logbook of Mingulay Public School, 1875-1910

In private hands:

school library lending register 1907 onwards

letters of 'uncle' John Finlayson to Mingulay John's brother, Alexander

notes on the Chapel House, D E Baird, 28.8.1960

diary of David Stevenson, 1828

Appendix 1

Population table for the southern islands and Barra

	Mingulay	Berneray*	Pabbay	Sandray	Vatersay	Barra**
1764	52	20	16	40	104	1,097
1794	8	3	3	9	–	–
(families)						
1841	113	21 (30)	25	14	84	1,977
1851	114	28 (44)	10	10	64	1,624
1861	145	20 (33)	14	9	32	1,569
1871	144	20 (38)	24	7	23	1,751
1881	150	21 (56)	16	10	19	1,854
1891	141	17 (36)	13	4	32	2,125
1901	135	– (17)	11	3	13	2,417
1911	11	0 (5)	5	0	288	2,311

– not recorded (1794) or not yet available (1901)

Figures include persons recorded as 'temporarily absent', and exclude those 'temporarily present' between 1861 and 1901; but see * below (applies to Mingulay and Barra only). Numbers present on census night in Mingulay, if different, were: 1861: 139;   1871: 144;   1891: 142.

* Figures in the first column are residents; those in brackets are totals including lighthouse keepers, and fishermen staying temporarily (the latter not regarded as 'temporarily present' there, or 'temporarily absent', in the case of Mingulay men, from Mingulay). 1911 figure is lighthouse keepers only.

** Figures for Barra Parish as a whole between 1801 and 1831:
1801: 1,925;   1811: 2,114;   1821: 2,303;   1831: 2,097

Appendix 2

This song was composed by Neil MacPhee of Mingulay (Niall Chaluim Dhòmhnaill, 1874-1929) many years after the desertion of the island. The emotions contrast starkly with those he expressed in his letters at the time of the desertion, though of course the circumstances and purpose of these were quite different. Still, one feels that time has healed the wounds of the suffering the people endured in Mingulay in their last years there.

Song to the Isle of Mingulay

My mind takes a trip,
Travelling on the wings of my thoughts,
Conveying esteem from the bottom of my heart
To a stormy lonely rock
Where my beloved mother
Brought me into the circle of humankind
And where I would desire the tranquillity of death,
If it were my fate to receive it there.

I have seen the fishing fleet
Proceeding with sails spread,
Piercing the blue shell of the sky –
No lie that though it may seem so:
My eyesight then was not faint,
And no deceiving bewitched sight was it
But something that was and shall be,
And the children shall always see it.

Often have I listened to the roar of the waves
On the bare shores of the sounds,
And my thoughts so attuned to its note,
And my heart heavy thinking of it –
How many turns the tidal stream has made
Since the world was created,
backwards and forward to this day,
And the sound of its voice never changing.

Often on a calm evening in May,
Alone but for a flock of seagulls,
Have I sat without any thoughts
On the peak of the moorland ridge;
At the time of the sun dipping into the ocean,
Beautiful was the appearance of her face to me,
And despite her thousands of rounds,
She does not appear aged.

Great my desire to look afar;
On a cold January morning
Noting the power of the waves,
So forbidding, gloomy and white-tipped,
Rolling one after the other
With their white crests in great groups,
Washing the base of the grey rocks
And shaking off the shellfish.

Oran do Dh'eilean Mhiulaidh

Bidh m' aigne fhèin a' gabhail reug
Air siubhail sgèith mo smaointinnean,
Ag aiseag spèis o ghrunnd mo chlèibh
Gu sgeireag èidich aonaraich
Far an tug mo mhàthair ghràidh
A dh' àireamh chlann nan daoine mi,
Is far an iarrainn fois a' bhàis
Nam biodh e ' n dàn dhomh fhaotainn ann.

Chunnaic mise 'n càbhlach èisg
A' falbh 's am brèidean sgaoilt' orra,
A' tolladh slige ghorm nan speur -
Cha bhreug tha sin ged shaoilear e:
Cha robh san àm mo fhradharc fann,
'S cha sealladh meallta draoidheachd e
Ach rud a bh' ann 's a bhitheas ann,
Is chì a' chlann dhiubh daonnan e.

'S tric a dh'èisd mi gàir nan tonn
Ri cladach lom nan caolasan,
Is m' aigne fhèin cho rèidh ri phong
'S mo chridhe trom a' smaointinn air
A liuthad car a chaidh den t-sruth
On chruthaicheadh an saoghal seo
Air ais 's air aghaidh gus an-diugh,
Is fuaim a ghuth gun chaochladh air.

'S tric air feasgar Chèitein chiùin,
'S gun leam ach speil de dh'fhaoileagan,
A shuidh mi greis gun mòran suim
Air binneag druim na h-aoineige;
An àm don ghrèin bhith dol sa chuan,
Bu mhaiseach snuadh a h-aodainn leam,
'S ged rinn i mìle mìle cuairt,
Cha tàinig tuar na h-aois' oirre.

Leam bu mhiann bhith 'g amharc uam
Air madainn fhuaraidh Fhaoilleachail,
A' gabhail beachd air neart nan stuadh
Bu ghreannach, gruamach, caoir-ghealach,
A' cur nan car dhiubh, tè mu seach,
Len cìrein geal 'nan laomannan,
A' nighe cas nan creagan glas
'S a' froiseadh as a' mhaoraiche,

The open ocean with raging waves,
Divided, fearsome, wide-open waves,
Flowing up from the sea bottom,
Streaming, peaked, spouting;
Stormy, fierce, dark-grey and dark blue,
Bellied, pressing out, white at opening,
With the intense movement of thousands of aeons
Since the early centuries of this earth.

There the fierce challenge of the elements
Without chain, bridle or halter on it,
Conveying strength and riding the elements
On the cold wings of the winds;
The sudden bending shiver of the lightning
Setting the skies aglow in belts
And the thunder following,
Bringing the Majesty of God to my thoughts.

Of the joyful family who sat each night
Round the hearth – there were nine of them –
There are not today alive
But I alone lamenting;
The green grass is about their fireplaces cold,
With sheep alone alive around them,
And my beloved folk in their chamber of slumber,
The eternal fetters of death on them.

Its rocks unstable and with clefts dark grey,
The grey garment of age on them,
Rise up like a protecting wall
Against the elements of winter.
Though storm has wrought bareness and surly scowl
On the peaks and brows,
There are sheltered meadows within the arms of
  the bens
With the bloom of summer even on them.

In the heat of summer the crops
Would be growing in the fields
In green clumps with high strands
And veins full to overflowing;
Barley and oats of the early sowing
Eared, grained, spreading,
With green leaf on the potato
And the white flower spreading on it.

Bhiodh druim a' chuain bu cholgach stuadh
Gu sgolbach duaichnidh braois-thonnach,
A' sròlachadh suas on aigeal chruaidh
Gu colbhach, cruachach, craobh-steallach;
Gu molach, borb, dubh-ghlas is gorm,
Gu bronnach, bolgach, craos-ghealach,
Le luasgadh dian nam mìltean sian
O linntean cian an t-saoghail seo.

An siud bidh dùbhlan borb na h-iarmailt
Gun chuibhreach, srian no taod oirre,
Ag iomairt neart 's a' marcrachd sian
Air sgiathan fuar nan gaothannan;
An dealan lùb-chlischritheach geur
A' lasadh speur nan craoslaichean,
'S an tàrneanach a' tighinn 'na dhèidh,
Toirt Mòrachd Dhè gum smaointinnean.

Den teachlach ghreadhnach shuidh gach oidch'
Mun chagailt cruinn – bha naoinear ann –
Chan eil an-diugh air lom an tuinn
Ach mise caoidh ' nam aonaran.
Tha 'n tràthach gorm mun teinntean fuar,
Gun beò mun cuairt ach caoraich air,
Is luchd mo ghràidh 'nan seòmar suain
Is glasan buan an aoig orra.

Tha chreagan corrach, sgorach, ciar,
Is trusgan liath na h-aois orra,
Ag èirigh suas mar bhalla-dìon
An aghaidh sian nam Faoillichean.
Ged thug gailleann gart is greann
Air barr nam meall 's nam maolaidhean,
Tha cluaintean fasgach 'n achlais
  bheann
Is dreach an t-samhraidh daonnan orr'.

San Iuchar Shamhraidh bhiodh am bàrr
Le cinneas fàs air raonaidhean,
'Na bhanndail uaine dualach àrd
Le cuisle làn gu laomadh air;
Bhiodh eòrna 's coirc' na curachd thràth
Gudiasach, grànach, craobhagach,
Is duilleag ghorm air a' bhuntàt'
'S am flùr bàn air sgaoileadh air.

Translation by Roderick MacNeil

Appendix 3

Neil's trip to Mingulay (*Turas Nèill a Mhiùghlaigh*)

This song concerns the adventure of Niall Mòr Mac Nèill 'Ic Iain Bhàin ('Big Neil son of Neil son of Fair John') of Mingulay. He was in Castlebay while on his way home after working at the barley harvest in the Lowlands. He had been drinking with some other Mingulay people with whom he was to return to the island, but he left early in the morning without them, and in no state to control a boat. The boat drifted south and, luckily for Neil, landed on Sgeir Leehinish, a rocky islet off the south coast of Sandray. By a further stroke of fortune, he was spotted by some fishermen working out of Castlebay, who rescued him and put him ashore at Sandray. The boat drifted away, with "Hector's jacket that he had only worn for part of a Sunday", and Neil was concerned about earning the money to repay the boat's owner, ?Donald Campbell. None of the characters in the song are definitely identified.

The song was composed by Father Allan MacLean, known locally as *Sagart Beag na Spàinne*, 'the Curate of Spain', as he had been at the Scots College at Valladolid. He was priest or curate at Craigstone, Barra, from 1837 to 1840, and known to be a composer of songs. He may have composed it at this period, but there are clues suggesting it may have been later. MacLean was subsequently a curate in South Uist until 1850, and later emigrated to Cape Breton, Nova Scotia, where he died in 1872.

The song was put in the mouth of the person involved in the event, a common practice in Gaelic, and the tune is a well-known one. This version was recorded from Ealasaid Sinclair of Mingulay (SSS SA 1960/97 B4; the song, with the title used here, was also recorded from John Johnston and published by Colm Ó Lochlainn in 1948). The song is still known in Barra today.

Is och mar tha mi, is mi nam ao - nar, Dol
throimh na cao - lais far robh mi eò-lach: Cho
moch's a dh'fha-lbh mi gun bhiadh gun ùr-naigh -'S e
thug mo thùr a-sam sùgh an eòr - na.

187

Neil's Trip to Mingulay

Alas for my state, my solitary state,
Sailing through the narrows I knew so well:
I left so early without breakfast or prayers –
And what deprived me of my wits was
  John Barleycorn[1].

Across by Sandray the wind was against us:
The mast leapt out of its place in the step.
But for Sgeir Lìthinnis I would have been destroyed;
Though I got ashore there my mind was full of misery.

Hugh Stewart himself got agitated,
Because he took me for an evil spirit,
While I was so devoutly on my knees
Saying my prayers, as well I might.

John Campbell was a mighty man:
He had no fear, it was hardly his way.
What he said was: "Steer her over towards it:
What's there is someone whisky has made a fool of."

When they brought me across to Sandray,
I was so weak I was scarcely alive:
The fine people there gave me food –
May God never see them in pain or sorrow.

The Campbells are angry with me:
This is not something that surprises me.
They had done great deeds in her [the boat]:
By the time I pay her ransom what good will my
  barley [money] do?

When summer comes I'll go to the Lowlands
To pay the damages due on every rope [of her];
Even if I have to earn my money in Germany,
I won't let my sheep be taken away by Donald.

Iain Mhìcheil's son is a well-behaved lad:
I'm glad he has been so loyal to me.
We'll find a serviceable boat in her place:
You'll never have to pay me a farthing.

Turas Nèill a Mhiùghlaigh

(Is) Och mar tha mì, is mi nam aonar,
Dol throimh na caolais far robh mi eòlach:
Cho moch 's a dh'fhalbh mi gun bhiadh
  gun ùrnaigh –
'S e thug mo thùr asam sùgh an eòrna.

A-null aig Sanntraigh bha 'ghaoth an ceann oirnn:
Gun do leum an crann a-mach a broinn na bròige.
Mur a biodh Sgeir Lìthinnis gu robh mi millte;
Ged a fhuair mi innte bha m'inntinn brònach.

Bha Eòghain Stiùbhart e fhèin fo chùram. . .
Gu robh e 'n dùil gur e bh'unnam bòcan,
'S mi cho dùrachdach air mo ghlùinean
'S mi gabhail m'ùnaigh, 's ann dhomh bu chòir e.

Bha Iain Caimbeul na dhuine làidir:
Cha robh e sgràthail [sgàthail], bu bheag a chòir ris.
'S e thuirt e: "Stiùiribh i null ga h-ionnsaigh,
'S e th'ann ball-bùrta rinn Mac an Tòisich."

Nuair a thug iad mi null a Shanntraigh,
Bha mi cho fann 's gum bu ghann bu bheò mi:
Na daoine ciatach a bh'ann thug biadh dhomh –
Nar fhaiceadh Dia iad am pian no 'n dòrainn.

Tha na Caimbeulaich orm-sa 'n diombadh:
Chan eil sin leam-sa na ghnothach neònach.
Móran euchdan ac' innt' le chèile:
Mam pàidh mi 'n éirig gu dè nì m'eòrna?

Nuair a thig a' samhradh théid mi gu Galldachd
A thoirt na calldachd a ceann gach ròpa:
Ged a b'ann sa Ghearmailt a gheibhinn-s' airgead,
Cha lig mi 'm meanbh-chrodh air falbh le Dòmhnall.

Tha mac Iain Mhìcheil na ghille sìobhalt':
'S math cho dìleas 's a bha e dhòmh-sa.
'S ann a gheibh sinn bàta nì feum na h-àite:
A chaoidh cha phàigh thu bonn fàrdainn dhòmh-sa.

1. Literally 'the juice of the barley.'

Transcribed and translated by Alan Bruford and Donald Archie MacDonald.

Appendix 4

Tape-recording informants

The following are those Mingulay people recorded on tape by the School of Scottish Studies in 1960, who are referred to in the text:

Mary Campbell (maiden surname MacNeil; Màiri Aonghais Nèill Bhig), born 1887, family moved to Castlebay sometime after her mother's death in 1898, and to Vatersay about 1908 (SSS SA 1960/89, /98, /99, /100). (Her father appears in plate 4.)

Catherine MacNeil (maiden surname MacLean; Catrìona Iain Chaluim; plate 18), born 1892, moved to Vatersay in 1910 (SSS SA 1960/94, /95).

Roderick MacNeil (Ruairidh Iain Sheumais), born 1882, moved to Sandray in 1908, then to Vatersay in 1909 (SSS SA 1960/94, /96).

Michael MacPhee (Mìcheal Dhòmhnaill Dhòmhnaill), born 1885, moved to Vatersay in 1907 (SSS SA 1960/92, /96).

Ealasaid Sinclair (Ealasaid Iain Dhunnchaidh), born 1885, moved to Vatersay in 1907-8 (SSS SA 1960/93, /97, /98, /101).

Appendix 5

Glossary of some Gaelic personal names quoted

Genitive forms are given if different from nominative.

Alasdair: Alexander
Aonghas, Aonghais: Angus
Calum, Chaluim: Malcolm
Coinneach, Choinnich: Kenneth
Dòmhnall, Dhòmhnaill: Donald
Dunnchadh, Dhunnchaidh: Duncan
Eachann, Eachainn: Hector
Eòghann, Eòghainn: Hugh
Fionnlagh, Fhionnlaigh: Finlay
Iain: John
Iagan, Iagain: John (Johnny)
Mìcheal, Mhìcheil: Michael
Niall, Nèill: Neil
Ruairidh: Roderick
Seumas, Sheumais: James

Catrìona: Catherine
Ealasaid: Elizabeth
Flòraidh: Flora
Màiri: Mary
Mòr, Mòrag: Marion

Index

Subject headings in the main index exclude Berneray, Pabbay and Sandray, for which see the separate indexes at the end, but the names of people, organisations and other places mentioned in chapters 15, 16 and 17 are included in the main index.

access, difficulty of 15, 41, 74-8, 123, 133
Adam, James 21
Adam, Robert M, photographer 21-2, 75, 78, 83,89-90, 123, 130, 134, 142
Admiralty, the 143
agriculture 27, 28, 60-65
Ailsa Craig 81
alcohol 91
America 15, 17, 76, 125
Ancient Monuments Act 137
Anderson, Joseph 152
Aneir 67, 75, 77
Appin 39
arable land 52, 53, 60, 61, 62, 63
archaeology 20, 21, 25-26
Archer, Colin 136
Ard nan Capuill 34
Ard, the 11, 68
Argyll 32, 34, 39, 141
Arnamul 13, 14, 33, 67
Arran 80, 89
Australia, emigration to 54

bagpipes 43, 47
Baillie, James, MP 70
Bannish 34
bannocks 89-90
baptisms 39, 116, 118, 119
barley 51, 63, 64, 89, 117
barns 64, 85, 87, 118
Barra: Allasdale 54; Allt Crysal 27; Borve 109; Castlebay 11, 13, 30, 40, 58, 62, 67, 69-72, 75, 76, 91, 95, 109, 112, 113, 121, 123, 124, 128, 134, 135, 142, 149, 153; Cille Bharra 31, 33, 35, 117, 153; Craigstone church 40, 119, 157, 160 (registers of) 21, 38; Cuithir 112; Eoligarry 49, 50, 66, 124; Garrygall 162 (note 20) (Mingulay families in) 58; Glen 54 (Mingulay families in) 58; Greian 46, 54; Kentangaval 39, 123; Loch an Duin 65; Northbay 106, 124; Tangusdale 39, 40, 54, 55, 141
Barra Head *see* Berneray, Barra Head

Barra Head Isles Sheepstock Company 135
Barra Historical Society 23
Barra Isles 9, 11, 25, 33, 34, 41, 45, 47, 52, 57, 65, 67, 69, 70, 85, 90, 116-7, 160, 164 *see also* southern isles
Barra Parish 11, 40
Barra Parish Council 77, 124
Barra School Board 106, 107, 108, 109, 112, 114, 146
Bay Sletta 34, 76
beach 15, 16, 18-19, 27, 74, 75, 78, 84, 87, 105, 120
Benbecula 56, 117
Berneray (North Uist) 133
Beveridge, Erskine, antiquary 152, 153
Bible 102
Bird, Isabella 90, 142, 143-4
birth, last 114
births 97, 99 *see also* childbirth
births, illegitimate 40
births, marriages and deaths, registers of 21, 106, 115
Bishop's Isles 50-1, 116, 141
Biulacraig 11-13, 34
Blaikie, Walter 122
blankets 122
Blundell, Dom Odo 163
boat building 39, 41, 73
boat shelters 75
boats 15, 16, 69-78, 109, 113, 123, 131, 134; landing of 42; names of 72, 73
Brendan, Saint 40
Bronze Age 27, 28, 32
Buchanan, Dr Donald 94, 116
Buchanan, George 14
burial, last 99
burial cairns 26, 28
burial monuments 30
burials 43, 97
butter 51, 66, 90, 117
byres 62, 66, 85, 86, 87

cabbages 43, 63, 89
Caithness 31, 39
Cameron, Fr Hugh 157, 163
Cameron families, Sandray 162
Campbell families 38, 55, 131, 141, 146, 157
Campbell, Fr Donald 135
Campbell, Duncan, leader of the Vatersay raiders 125
Campbell, Jane *see* Finlayson, Jane